Spring MVC Beginner's Guide

Your ultimate guide to building a complete web application using all the capabilities of Spring MVC

Amuthan G

[PACKT] open source *
PUBLISHING
community experience distilled

BIRMINGHAM - MUMBAI

Spring MVC Beginner's Guide

First published: June 2014

Production reference: 1190614

Published by Packt Publishing Ltd.
Livery Place
35 Livery Street
Birmingham B3 2PB, UK.

ISBN 978-1-78328-487-0

www.packtpub.com

Cover image by Aniket Sawant (aniket_sawant_photography@hotmail.com)

Credits

Author
Amuthan G

Reviewers
Rafał Borowiec
Pawan Chopra
Rubén Clemente Serna

Acquisition Editor
Vinay Argekar

Content Development Editor
Azharuddin Sheikh

Technical Editors
Monica John
Neha Mankare
Shiny Poojary

Copy Editors
Gladson Monteiro
Insiya Morbiwala
Aditya Nair
Stuti Srivastava

Project Coordinators
Kinjal Bari
Wendell Palmer

Proofreaders
Simran Bhogal
Stephen Copestake
Maria Gould
Ameesha Green
Paul Hindle

Indexer
Hemangini Bari

Graphics
Disha Haria
Abhinash Sahu

Production Coordinator
Aparna Bhagat

Cover Work
Aparna Bhagat

About the Author

Amuthan G has over six years of experience as a professional software developer. He currently works for a large cloud platform company and has strong product development experience in Java, Spring, JPA, and many other enterprise technologies. In his free time, he enjoys blogging on his site (`http://www.madebycode.in`). He can be contacted at `mr.amuthan@gmail.com`.

I would like to gratefully and sincerely thank Mr. Vincent Kok for his guidance, understanding, patience, and most importantly, his friendship during my first job at Educator Inc. His mentorship has shaped me to become a well-rounded professional. He encouraged me to not only grow as a developer, but also as an independent thinker.

I want to take a moment and express my gratitude to the entire team at Packt Publishing for their patience and cooperation. When I signed up for this book, I really had no idea how things would turn out. I couldn't have pulled this off without their guidance.

I would like to express my gratitude to all my friends and family for providing me with unending encouragement and support. I owe every challenge and accomplishment to all my lovely colleagues who taught me a lot over the years.

A special thanks to Divya and Arun for their encouragement, friendship, and support. They were a strong shoulder to lean on in the most difficult times during the writing of this book.

Finally, and most importantly, I would like to thank my wife Manju who believes me more than myself. Her support, encouragement, quiet patience, and unwavering love were undeniably the bedrock upon which my life has been built.

About the Reviewers

Rafał Borowiec is an IT specialist with about eight years of commercial experience, specializing in software testing and quality assurance, software development, project management, and team leadership.

He currently holds the position of a Team Leader at Goyello, where he is mainly responsible for building and managing teams of professional developers and testers. He is also responsible for maintaining relations with customers and acquiring new ones, mainly through consultancy.

He believes in agile project management and is a big fan of technology, especially technology that is Java related (but not limited to it). He likes sharing knowledge about software development and practices through his blog (`blog.codeleak.pl`) and Twitter account (`@kolorobot`) and also at internal and external events such as conferences or workshops.

Pawan Chopra is an Agile developer with eight years of experience in the software industry. He currently works at Webners (`http://www.webnersolutions.com/`) on some cool JavaScript, Java, HTML5, Node, and AngularJS projects. He is an open source enthusiast. He loves sharing knowledge through training and blogging. He is also very strong on the server side with vast experience in Spring and Hibernate tools. He blogs at `www.itspawan.com`.

Rubén Clemente Serna is a software engineer by profession with over eight years of experience in software development. He recently moved to the UK and is currently working as a Java Developer at Piksel, a company that creates and manages OTT video solutions for some of the world's leading media brands. Prior to Piksel, he has worked at GFI Informática in Spain on many Java development projects, mainly for telecom and government service customers.

More detailed information about his skills and experience can be found at `http://www.linkedin.com/in/rubenclementeserna`. He can be contacted at `rubenclemente@gmail.com`.

www.PacktPub.com

Support files, eBooks, discount offers, and more

You might want to visit www.PacktPub.com for support files and downloads related to your book.

Did you know that Packt offers eBook versions of every book published, with PDF and ePub files available? You can upgrade to the eBook version at www.PacktPub.com and as a print book customer, you are entitled to a discount on the eBook copy. Get in touch with us at service@packtpub.com for more details.

At www.PacktPub.com, you can also read a collection of free technical articles, sign up for a range of free newsletters and receive exclusive discounts and offers on Packt books and eBooks.

http://PacktLib.PacktPub.com

Do you need instant solutions to your IT questions? PacktLib is Packt's online digital book library. Here, you can access, read and search across Packt's entire library of books.

Why subscribe?

- Fully searchable across every book published by Packt
- Copy and paste, print and bookmark content
- On demand and accessible via web browser

Free access for Packt account holders

If you have an account with Packt at www.PacktPub.com, you can use this to access PacktLib today and view nine entirely free books. Simply use your login credentials for immediate access.

Table of Contents

Preface

This book has a very clear aim: to introduce you to the incredible simplicity and power of Spring MVC. I still remember first learning about the Spring framework back in 2009. The best way to test whether or not you really understand a concept is to try to teach it to someone else. In my case, I have taught Spring MVC to MVC; are you confused? I mean that back in 2009, I taught it to my wife Manju Viswambaran Chandrika (MVC). During that course, I was able to understand the kind of doubts that arise in a beginner's mind. I have gathered all my teaching knowledge and put it in this book in an elegant way so that it can be understood without confusion.

This book follows a theme of developing a simple e-commerce site step-by-step. In every successive chapter, you will learn a new concept of Spring MVC. Obviously, the aim is to teach you how you can use Spring MVC effectively. Developing a full-blown, production-ready e-commerce site is not the purpose of this book.

What this book covers

Chapter 1, *Configuring a Spring Development Environment*, will give you a quick overview of Spring MVC and its architecture and guide you through detailed notes and step-by-step instructions to set up your development environment. After installing the required prerequisites, you will try out a quick example of how to develop an application with Spring MVC. Although the chapter doesn't explain all the code in detail, you'll pick up a few things intuitively.

Chapter 2, *Spring MVC Architecture – Architecting Your Web Store*, will lay down the ground work for the sample application that we are going to build along the way, chapter by chapter. This chapter will introduce you to concepts such as request mapping, web application context, Spring MVC request flow, and the layered architecture of a typical web application.

Chapter 3, Control Your Store with Controllers, will take you through the concept of a controller; you will learn more about how to define a controller, and use URI template patterns, matrix variables, and request parameters.

Chapter 4, Working with Spring Tag Libraries, will teach you how to use Spring and Spring form tag libraries in web form handling. You will learn how to bind domain objects with views and how to use message bundles to externalize label caption texts. At the end of this chapter, you will see how to add a login form.

Chapter 5, Working with View Resolver, will present the inner mechanics of how `InternalResourceViewResolver` resolves a view and takes you through how to use various view types, such as redirect view and static view. You will also learn about the multipart resolver and content negotiation view resolver. Finally, you will learn how to use exception handler resolvers.

Chapter 6, Intercept Your Store with Interceptor, will present the concept of an interceptor to you. You will learn how to leverage the interceptor to handle or transform requests and responses flexibly. This chapter will teach you how to make your web page support internalization with the help of `LocaleChangeInterceptor`. This chapter also introduces how to perform audit logging in a log file using the interceptor concept.

Chapter 7, Validate Your Products with a Validator, will give you an overview of the validation concept. You will learn about bean validation, and you will learn how to perform custom validation along with the standard bean validation. You will also learn about the classic Spring validation and how to combine it with bean validation.

Chapter 8, Give REST to Your Application with Ajax, will teach you the basic principles of REST and Ajax. You will learn how to develop an application in RESTful services. The basic concept of HTTP verbs and how they are related to standard CRUD operations will be explained, and you will learn how to fire an Ajax request and handle it from a web page.

Chapter 9, Apache Tiles and Spring Web Flow in Action, will teach you how to use the Spring web flow to develop workflow-based web pages. You will learn more about states and transitions in web flow and how to define a flow definition. This chapter also teaches you how to decompose a page using Apache tiles. You will also learn more about `TileViewResolver` and how to define reusable Apache tiles templates.

Chapter 10, Testing your Application, will teach you how to leverage the Spring testing capability to test your controllers. You will learn how to load the test context and how to mock the service and repository layers. This chapter also introduces you to the Spring MVC test module and teaches you how to use that.

Appendix A, Using the Gradle Build Tool, introduces you to using the Gradle build tool for our sample application. You will learn about the Gradle script that is required to build our project using Gradle build tool.

What you need for this book

To run the examples in the book, the following software will be required:

- Java SE Development Kit 7u45 or newer
- Maven 3.1.0
- Apache Tomcat 7.0
- STS 3.4.0 release (Spring Tool Suite)

Who this book is for

This book is designed to be followed from beginning to end, although those with existing knowledge of Spring MVC will be able to jump in to the later chapters and pick out things that are important to them. You are not expected to be experienced with the Spring framework. Some knowledge of servlet programming and dependency injection will be helpful but not essential. In a nutshell, the book provides clear pictures, illustrations, concepts, and is ideally suited for beginners and intermediate developers.

Conventions

In this book, you will find several headings appearing frequently.

To give clear instructions of how to complete a procedure or task, we use:

Time for action – heading

1. Action 1
2. Action 2
3. Action 3

Instructions often need some extra explanation so that they make sense, so they are followed with:

What just happened?

This heading explains the working of tasks or instructions that you have just completed.

You will also find some other learning aids in the book, including:

Pop quiz – heading

These are short multiple-choice questions intended to help you test your own understanding.

Have a go hero – heading

These practical challenges give you ideas for experimenting with what you have learned.

You will also find a number of styles of text that distinguish between different kinds of information. Here are some examples of these styles and an explanation of their meaning.

Code words in text, database table names, folder names, filenames, file extensions, pathnames, dummy URLs, user input, and Twitter handles are shown as follows: "Once the download is finished, go to the downloaded directory and extract the `.zip` file into a convenient directory of your choice."

A block of code is set as follows:

```
<body>
  <section>
    <div class="jumbotron">
      <div class="container">
        <h1> ${greeting} </h1>
        <p> ${tagline} </p>
      </div>
    </div>
  </section>
</body>
```

When we wish to draw your attention to a particular part of a code block, the relevant lines or items are set in bold:

```
<servlet>
  <servlet-name>DefaultServlet</servlet-name>
  <servlet class> org.springframework.web.servlet.DispatcherServlet
</servlet-class>
</servlet>
```

Any command-line input or output is written as follows:

```
C:\>mvn -version
Apache Maven 3.2.1 (ea8b2b07643dbb1b84b6d16e1f08391b666bc1e9; 2014-02-14T12:37:52-05:00)
Maven home: C:\Program Files\apache-maven-3.2.1
```

```
Java version: 1.7.0_51, vendor: Oracle Corporation
Java home: C:\Program Files\Java\jdk1.7.0_51\jre
Default locale: en_SG, platform encoding: Cp1252
OS name: "windows 7", version: "6.1", arch: "amd64", family: "windows"
```

New terms and **important words** are shown in bold. Words that you see on the screen, in menus or dialog boxes for example, appear in the text like this: "A **System Properties** window will appear; in this window, select the **Advanced** tab and click on the **Environment Variables** button to open the environment variables window."

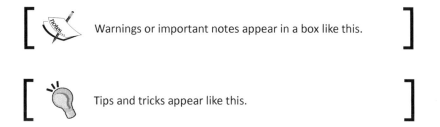

Warnings or important notes appear in a box like this.

Tips and tricks appear like this.

Reader feedback

Feedback from our readers is always welcome. Let us know what you think about this book—what you liked or may have disliked. Reader feedback is important for us to develop titles that you really get the most out of.

To send us general feedback, simply send an e-mail to feedback@packtpub.com, and mention the book title through the subject of your message.

If there is a topic that you have expertise in and you are interested in either writing or contributing to a book, see our author guide on www.packtpub.com/authors.

Customer support

Now that you are the proud owner of a Packt book, we have a number of things to help you to get the most from your purchase.

Downloading the example code

You can download the example code files for all Packt books you have purchased from your account at http://www.packtpub.com. If you purchased this book elsewhere, you can visit http://www.packtpub.com/support and register to have the files e-mailed directly to you.

Errata

Although we have taken every care to ensure the accuracy of our content, mistakes do happen. If you find a mistake in one of our books—maybe a mistake in the text or the code—we would be grateful if you would report this to us. By doing so, you can save other readers from frustration and help us improve subsequent versions of this book. If you find any errata, please report them by visiting http://www.packtpub.com/submit-errata, selecting your book, clicking on the **errata submission form** link, and entering the details of your errata. Once your errata are verified, your submission will be accepted and the errata will be uploaded to our website, or added to any list of existing errata, under the Errata section of that title.

Piracy

Piracy of copyright material on the Internet is an ongoing problem across all media. At Packt, we take the protection of our copyright and licenses very seriously. If you come across any illegal copies of our works, in any form, on the Internet, please provide us with the location address or website name immediately so that we can pursue a remedy.

Please contact us at copyright@packtpub.com with a link to the suspected pirated material.

We appreciate your help in protecting our authors, and our ability to bring you valuable content.

Questions

You can contact us at questions@packtpub.com if you are having a problem with any aspect of the book, and we will do our best to address it.

1

Configuring a Spring Development Environment

In this chapter, we are going take a look at how we can create a basic Spring MVC application. In order to develop a Spring MVC application, we need some prerequisite software and tools. First, we are going to learn how to install all the prerequisites that are required to set up our development environment so that we can start developing the application.

The setup and installation steps given here are for Windows operating systems, but don't worry, as the steps may change only slightly for other operating systems. You can always refer to the respective tools/software vendor's websites to install them in other operating systems. In this chapter, we will learn how to set up Java and configure the Maven build tool, install the Tomcat web server, install and configure the Spring tool suite, and create and run our first Spring MVC project.

Setting up Java

Obviously, the first thing that we need to do is get started with Java. The more technical name for Java is **Java Development Kit (JDK)**. JDK includes a Java compiler (javac), a Java virtual machine, and a variety of other tools to compile and run Java programs.

Time for action – installing JDK

We are going to use Java 7 but Java 6 or any higher version is also sufficient. Let's take a look at how we can install JDK on Windows operating systems:

1. Go to the Java SE download page on the Oracle website by entering the following URL in your browser: `http://www.oracle.com/technetwork/java/javase/downloads/index.html`.

2. Click on the Java platform **JDK 7** download link; this will take you to the license agreement page. Accept the license agreement by selecting that option in radio button.

3. Now, click on the listed download link that corresponds to your Windows operating system architecture; for instance, if your operating system is of type 32 bit, click on the download link that corresponds to Windows x86. Or, if your operating system is of type 64 bit, click on the download link that corresponds to Windows x64.

4. Now, it will start downloading the installer. Once the download is finished, go to the downloaded directory and double-click on the installer. This will open up the following wizard window; just click on the **Next** button in the wizard, leaving the default options alone, and click on the **Close** button at the end of the wizard:

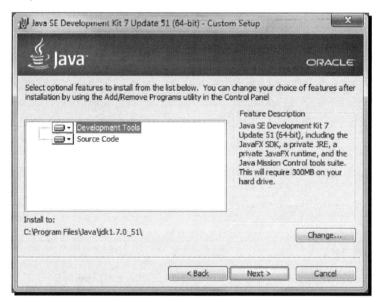

JDK installation wizard

 Additionally, a separate wizard also prompts you to install **Java Runtime Environment (JRE)**. Go through that wizard as well to install JRE in your system.

5. Now you can see the installed JDK directory in the default location; in our case, the default location is `C:\Program Files\Java\jdk1.7.0_25`.

Time for action – setting up environment variables

After installing JDK, we still need to perform some more configurations to use Java conveniently from any directory on our computer. By setting up the environment variables for Java in the Windows operating system, we can make the Java compiler and tools available to the entire operating system:

1. Navigate to **Control Panel | System | Advanced system settings**.

2. A **System Properties** window will appear; in this window, select the **Advanced** tab and click on the **Environment Variables** button to open the environment variables window.

3. Now, click on the **New** button in the **System variables** panel, enter JAVA_HOME as the variable name, and enter the installed JDK directory path as the variable value; in our case, this is `C:\Program Files\Java\jdk1.7.0_51`. In case you do not have proper rights for the operating system, you will not be able to edit **System variables**; in that case, you can create the JAVA_HOME variable under the **User variables** panel.

4. Now, in the same **System variables** panel, double-click on the **PATH** variable entry; an **Edit System Variable** window will appear.

Setting PATH Environment variable

5. Edit **Variable value** of **Path** by appending the `;%JAVA_HOME%\bin` text to its existing value.

 Edit the path variable carefully; you should only append the text at the end of existing value. Don't delete or disturb the existing values; make sure you haven't missed the `;` (semicolon) mark as that is the first letter in the text that you will append.

6. Now click on the **OK** button.

Now we have installed Java in our computer. To verify whether our installation has been carried out correctly, open a new command window and type `java -version` and press *Enter*; you will see the installed version of Java on the screen:

```
C:\>java -version
java version "1.7.0_51"
Java(TM) SE Runtime Environment (build 1.7.0_51-b13)
Java HotSpot(TM) 64-Bit Server VM (build 24.51-b03, mixed mode)
```

Configuring a build tool

Building a software project typically includes some activities such as the following:

- Compiling all the source code
- Generating the documentation from the source code
- Packaging the compiled code into a JAR or WAR archive file
- Installing the packaged archives files on a server

Manually performing all these tasks is time consuming and is prone to errors. Therefore, we take the help of a build tool. A build tool is a tool that automates everything related to building a software project, from compiling to deploying.

Time for action – installing the Maven build tool

Many build tools are available for building a Java project. We are going to use Maven 3.2.1 as our build tool. Let's take a look at how we can install Maven:

1. Go to Maven's download page by entering the following URL on your browser:

`http://maven.apache.org/download.cgi`

2. Click on the **apache-maven-3.2.1-bin.zip** download link, and start the download.

3. Once the download is finished, go to the downloaded directory and extract the .zip file into a convenient directory of your choice.

4. Now we need to create one more environment variable, called M2_HOME, in a way that is similar to the way in which we created JAVA_HOME. Enter the extracted Maven zip directory's path as the value for the M2_HOME environment variable.

5. Create one more environment variable, called M2, with the value %M2_HOME%\bin, as shown in the following screenshot:

Setting the M2 environment variable

6. Finally append the M2 variable to the PATH environment variable as well by simply appending the ;%M2% text to the PATH variable's value.

Now we have installed the Maven build tool in our computer. To verify whether our installation has been carried out correctly, we need to follow steps that are similar to the Java installation verification. Open a new command window, type mvn -version, and press *Enter*; you will see the following details of the Maven version:

```
C:\>mvn -version
Apache Maven 3.2.1 (ea8b2b07643dbb1b84b6d16e1f08391b666bc1e9; 2014-02-
14T12:37:52-05:00)
Maven home: C:\Program Files\apache-maven-3.2.1
Java version: 1.7.0_51, vendor: Oracle Corporation
Java home: C:\Program Files\Java\jdk1.7.0_51\jre
Default locale: en_SG, platform encoding: Cp1252
OS name: "windows 7", version: "6.1", arch: "amd64", family: "windows"
```

Installing a web server

So far, we have learned how to install JDK and Maven. Using these tools, we can compile the Java source code into the .class files and package these .class files into the .jar or .war archives. However, how do we run our packaged archives? To do this, we take the help of a web server; a web server will host our packaged archives as a running application.

Time for action – installing the Tomcat web server

Apache Tomcat is a popular Java web server cum servlet container. We are going use Apache Tomcat Version 7.0. Let's take a look at how we can install the Tomcat web server:

1. Go to the Apache Tomcat home page using the following URL link:

   ```
   http://tomcat.apache.org/
   ```

2. Click on the Tomcat 7.0 download link, and it will take you to the download page.

3. Click on the **32-bit/64-bit Windows Service Installer** link; it will start downloading the installer.

4. Once the download is finished, go to the downloaded directory and double-click on the installer; this will open up a wizard window.

5. Just click through the next buttons in the wizard, leaving the default options alone, and click on the **Finish** button at the end of the wizard. Note that before clicking on the **Finish** button, just ensure that you have unchecked **Run Apache Tomcat** checkbox.

Installing Apache Tomcat with the default option works successfully only if you have installed Java in the default location. Otherwise, you have to correctly provide the JRE path according to the location of your Java installation during the installation of Tomcat, as shown in the following screenshot:

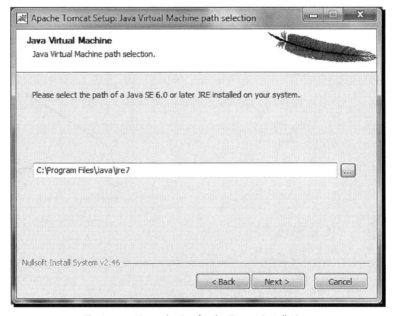

The Java runtime selection for the Tomcat installation

Configuring a development environment

We installed Java and Maven to compile and package Java source code, and we installed Tomcat to deploy and run our application. However, prior to all this, we have to write the Spring MVC code so that we can compile, package, and run the code.

We can use any simple text editor on our computer to write our code, but that won't help us much with features such as finding syntax errors as we type, autosuggesting important key words, syntax highlighting, easy navigation, and so on.

Integrated Development Environment (IDE) can help us with these features to develop the code faster and error free. We are going to use **Spring Tool Suite (STS)** as our IDE.

Time for action – installing Spring Tool Suite

STS is the best Eclipse-powered development environment to build Spring applications. Let's take a look at how we can install STS:

1. Go to the STS download page at `http://spring.io/tools/sts/all`.

2. Click on the STS installer `.exe` link to download the file that corresponds to your windows operating system architecture type (32 bit or 62 bit); this will start the download of the installer. The STS stable release version at the time of writing this book is STS 3.4.0.RELEASE based on Eclipse 4.3.1.

3. Once the download is finished, go to the downloaded directory and double-click on the installer; this will open up a wizard window.

4. Just click through the next buttons in the wizard, leaving the default options alone; if you want to customize the installation directory, you can specify that in the steps you perform in the wizard.

Downloading the example code

You can download the example code files for all Packt books you have purchased from your account at `http://www.packtpub.com`. If you purchased this book elsewhere, you can visit `http://www.packtpub.com/support` and register to have the files e-mailed directly to you.

5. In step 5 of the wizard, you have to provide the JDK path; just enter the JDK path that you configured for the JAVA_HOME environment variable, as shown in the following screenshot:

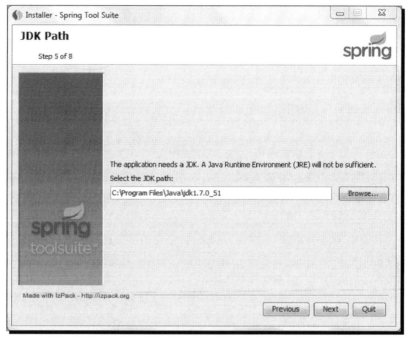

Setting the JDK path during the STS installation

We have almost installed all the tools and software required to develop a Spring MVC application, so now, we can create our Spring MVC project on STS. However, before jumping into creating a project, we need to perform a final configuration for STS.

Time for action – configuring Tomcat on STS

As I already mentioned, we can use the Tomcat web server to deploy our application, but we have to inform STS about the location of the Tomcat container so that we can easily deploy our project from STS to Tomcat. Let's configure Tomcat on STS:

1. Open STS from the start menu option or the desktop icon.

2. STS will ask you to provide a workspace directory location; provide a workspace directory path as you wish and click on the **OK** button.

3. Now, STS will show you a welcome screen. Close the welcome screen and go to the menu bar and navigate to **Window | preferences | Server | Runtime Environments**.

4. You can see the available servers listed on the right-hand side; you may also see **VMware vFabric tc Server** listed under the available servers, which comes along with the STS installation.

5. Now click on the **Add** button to add our Tomcat web server.

6. A wizard window will appear; type `tomcat` in the **Select the type of runtime environment:** text box, and a list of available Tomcat versions will be shown. Just select **Tomcat v7.0** and select the **Create a new local server** checkbox. Finally, click on the **Next** button, as shown in the following screenshot:

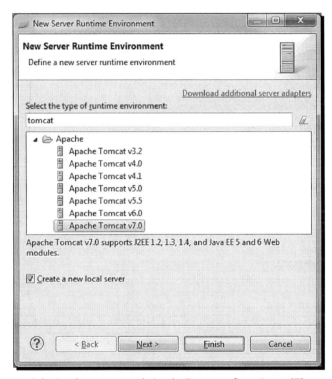

Selecting the server type during the Tomcat configuration on STS

7. In the next window, click on the **Browse** button and locate Tomcat's installed directory, and click on the **OK** button. You can find Tomcat's installed directory under `C:\Program Files\Apache Software Foundation\Tomcat 7.0` if you have installed Tomcat in the default location. Then, click on the **Finish** button, as shown in the following screenshot:

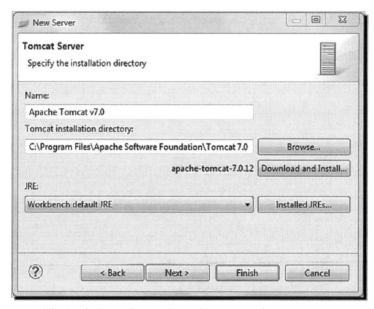

Selecting the Tomcat location during the Tomcat configuration on STS

What just happened?

In step 2, we provided a workspace path for STS. When you open STS for the very first time after installing STS, it will ask you to provide a workspace location. This is because when you create a project on STS, all your project files will be created under this location only.

Once we enter STS, we should inform STS where the Tomcat has been installed. Only then can STS use your Tomcat web server to deploy the project. This is also a one-time configuration; you need not perform this configuration every time you open STS. We did this by creating a new server runtime environment in step 5. Although STS might come with an internal **VMware vFabric tc Server**, we chose to use the Tomcat web server as our server runtime environment.

Time for action – configuring Maven on STS

We learned how to configure Tomcat on STS. Similarly, to build our project, STS will use Maven. But we have to tell STS where Maven has been installed so that it can use the Maven installation to build our projects. Let's take a look at how we can configure Maven on STS:

1. Open STS if it is not already open.
2. Navigate to **Window** | **Preferences** | **Maven** | **Installations**.
3. On the right-hand side, you can see the **Add** button, to locate Maven's installation.
4. Click on the **Add** button and choose Maven's installed directory, as shown in the following screenshot:

Selecting Maven's location during the Maven configuration on STS

5. Now click on the **OK** button in the **Preferences** window and close it.

Creating our first Spring MVC project

So far, we have learned how we can install all the prerequisite tools and software. Now we are going to develop our first Spring MVC application using STS. STS provides an easy-to-use project template. Using these templates, we can quickly create our project directory structures without many problems.

Time for action – creating a Spring MVC project in STS

Let's create our first spring MVC project in STS:

1. In STS, navigate to **File** | **New** | **Project**; a **New Project** wizard window will appear.

2. Select **Maven Project** from the list and click on the **Next** button, as shown in the following screenshot:

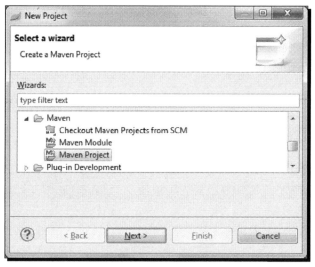

Maven project's template selection

3. Now, a **New Maven Project** dialog window will appear; just select the checkbox that has the **Create a simple project (skip archetype selection)** caption, and click on the **Next** button.

4. The wizard will ask you to specify artifact-related information for your project; just enter **Group Id** as com.packt, **Artifact Id** as webstore. Then, select **Packaging** as war and click on the **Finish** button, as shown in the following screenshot:

What just happened?

We just created the basic project structure. Any Java project follows a certain directory structure to organize its source code and static resources. Instead of manually creating the whole directory hierarchy by ourselves, we just handed over that job to STS. By collecting some basic information about our project, such as **Group Id**, **Artifact Id**, and the **Packaging** style from us, it is clear that STS is smart enough to create the whole project directory structure with the help of the Maven plugin. Actually, what is happening behind the screen is that STS is internally using Maven to create the project structure.

We want our project to be deployable in any servlet container-based web server, such as Tomcat, and that's why we selected the **Packaging** style as `war`. After executing step 4, you will see the project structure in **Package Explorer**, as shown in the following screenshot:

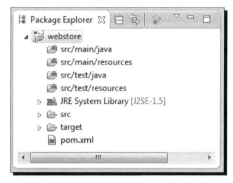

The project structure of the application

Spring MVC dependencies

As we are going to use Spring MVC APIs heavily in our project, we need the Spring jars in our project during the development. As I already mentioned, Maven will take care of managing dependencies and packaging the project.

Time for action – adding Spring jars to the project

Let's take a look at how we can add the spring-related jars via the Maven configuration:

1. Open `pom.xml`; you can find `pom.xml` under the root directory of the project itself.

2. You will see some tabs at the bottom of the `pom.xml` file. If you do not see these tabs, then right-click on `pom.xml` and select the **Open With** option from the context menu and choose **Maven POM editor**. Select the **Dependencies** tab and click on the **Add** button in the **Dependencies** section. Don't get confused with the **Add** button of the **Dependencies Management** section. You should choose the **Add** button in the left-hand side pane.

3. A **Select Dependency** window will appear; enter **Group Id** as `org.springframework`, **Artifact Id** as `spring-webmvc`, and **Version** as `4.0.3.RELEASE`. Select **Scope** as `compile` and then click on the **OK** button, as shown in the following screenshot:

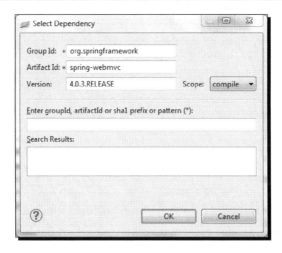

4. Similarly, add the dependency for **JavaServer Pages Standard Tag Library (JSTL)** by clicking on the same **Add** button; this time, enter **Group Id** as `javax.servlet`, **Artifact Id** as `jstl`, **Version** as `1.2`, and select **Scope** as `compile`.

5. Finally, add one more dependency for **servlet-api**; repeat the same step with **Group Id** as `javax.servlet`, **Artifact Id** as `javax.servlet-api`, and **Version** as `3.1.0`, but this time, select **Scope** as `provided` and then click on the **OK** button.

6. As a last step, don't forget to save the `pom.xml` file.

What just happened?

In the Maven world, `pom.xml` (Project Object Model) is the configuration file that defines the required dependencies. While building our project, Maven will read that file and try to download the specified jars from the Maven central binary repository. You need Internet access in order to download jars from Maven's central repository. Maven uses an addressing system to locate a jar in the central repository, which consists of **Group Id**, **Artifact Id**, and **Version**.

Every time we add a dependency, an entry will be made within the `<dependencies>` `</ dependencies>` tags in the `pom.xml` file. For example, if you go to the **pom.xml** tab after finishing step 3, you will see an entry for `spring-mvc` as follows within the `<dependencies>` `</ dependencies>` tag:

```
<dependency>
    <groupId>org.springframework</groupId>
    <artifactId>spring-webmvc</artifactId>
    <version>4.0.3.RELEASE</version>
</dependency>
```

We added the dependency for spring-mvc in step 3, and in step 4, we added the dependency for JSTL. JSTL is a collection of useful JSP tags that can be used to write JSP pages easily. Finally, we need a servlet-api jar in order to use servlet-related code; this is what we added in step 5.

However, there is a little difference in the scope of the servlet-api dependency compared to the other two dependencies. We only need servlet-api while compiling our project. While packaging our project as `war`, we don't want to the ship servlet-api jar as part of our project. This is because the Tomcat web server would provide the servlet-api jar while deploying our project. This is why we selected the scope as **provided** for the servlet-api.

After finishing step 6, you will see all the dependent jars configured in your project, as shown in the following screenshot, under the **Maven Dependencies** library:

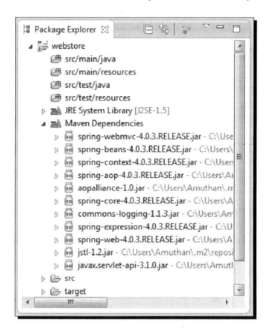

We added only three jars as our dependencies, but if you notice in our Maven dependency library list, you will see more than three jar entries. Can you guess why? What if our dependent jars have a dependency on other jars and so on?

For example, our spring-mvc jar is dependent on the spring-core, spring-context, and spring-aop jars, but we have not specified those jars in our `pom.xml` file; this is called **transitive dependencies** in the Maven world. In other words, we can say that our project is transitively dependent on these jars. Maven will automatically download all these transitive dependent jars; this is the beauty of Maven. It will take care of all the dependency management automatically; we need to inform Maven only about the first level dependencies.

Time for action – adding Java version properties in pom.xml

We successfully added all the required jars to our project, but we need to perform one small configuration in our `pom.xml` file, that is, telling Maven to use Java Version 7 while building our project. How do we tell Maven to do this? Simply add two property entries in `pom.xml`. Let's do this.

1. Open `pom.xml`. You will see some tabs at the bottom of `pom.xml`; select the **Overview** tab from the bottom of `pom.xml`, expand the **properties** accordion, and click on the **Create** button.

2. Now, an **Add property** window will appear; enter **Name** as `maven.compiler.source` and **Value** as `1.7`.

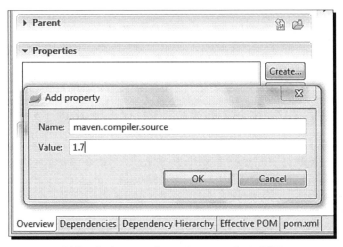

Adding the Java compiler version properties to POM

3. Similarly, create one more property with **Name** as `maven.compiler.target` and **Value** as `1.7`.

4. Finally, save `pom.xml`.

A jump-start to MVC

We created our project and added all the required jars, so we are ready to code. We are going to incrementally build an online web store throughout this book, chapter by chapter. As a first step, let's create a home page in our project to welcome our customers.

Our aim is simple; when we enter the `http://localhost:8080/webstore/` URL on the browser, we would like to show a welcome page that is similar to the following screenshot:

Don't worry if you are not able to understand some of the code; we are going to take a look at each concept in detail in the upcoming chapters. As of now, our aim is to have quick hands-on experience of developing a simple web page using Spring MVC.

Time for action – adding a welcome page

To create and add a welcome page, we need to execute the following steps:

1. Create a `WEB-INF/jsp/` directory structure under the `src/main/webapp/` directory; create a jsp view file called `welcome.jsp` under the `src/main/webapp/WEB-INF/jsp/` directory, and add the following code snippets into it and save it:

```
<%@ taglib prefix="c" uri="http://java.sun.com/jsp/jstl/core"%>

<html>
<head>
<meta http-equiv="Content-Type" content="text/html;
charset=ISO-8859-1">
<link rel="stylesheet" href="//netdna.bootstrapcdn.com/
bootstrap/3.0.0/css/bootstrap.min.css">
<title>Welcome</title>
</head>
<body>
  <section>
    <div class="jumbotron">
      <div class="container">
        <h1> ${greeting} </h1>
        <p> ${tagline} </p>
```

```
        </div>
      </div>
    </section>
  </body>
</html>
```

2. Create a class called `HomeController` under the `com.packt.webstore.controller` package in the source directory `src/main/java`, and add the following code into it:

```
package com.packt.webstore.controller;

import org.springframework.stereotype.Controller;
import org.springframework.ui.Model;
import org.springframework.web.bind.annotation.RequestMapping;

@Controller
public class HomeController {

    @RequestMapping("/")
    public String welcome(Model model) {
        model.addAttribute("greeting", "Welcome to Web Store!");
        model.addAttribute("tagline", "The one and only amazing web
            store");

        return "welcome";
    }
}
```

What just happened?

In step 1, we just created a JSP view; the important thing we need to notice here is the `<h1>` tag and the `<p>` tag. Both the tags have some expression that is surrounded by curly braces and prefixed by the $ symbol:

```
<h1> ${greeting} </h1>
<p> ${tagline} </p>
```

So, what is the meaning of `${greeting}`? It means that `greeting` is a kind of variable; during the rendering of this JSP page, the value stored in the `greeting` variable will be shown in the header 1 style, and similarly, the value stored in the `tagline` variable will be shown as a paragraph.

So now, the next question of where we will assign values to those variables arises. This is where the controller will be of help; within the `welcome` method of the `HomeController` class, take a look at the following lines of code:

```
model.addAttribute("greeting", "Welcome to Web Store!");
model.addAttribute("tagline", "The one and only amazing web store");
```

You can observe that the two variable names, `greeting` and `tagline`, are passed as a first parameter of the `addAttribute` method and the corresponding second parameter is the value for each variable. So what we are doing here is simply putting two strings, `"Welcome to Web Store!"` and `"The one and only amazing web store"`, into the model with their corresponding keys as `greeting` and `tagline`. As of now, simply consider the fact that `model` is a kind of map. Folks with knowledge of servlet programming can consider the fact that `model.addAttribute` works exactly like `request.setAttribute`.

So, whatever value we put into the model can be retrieved from the view (jsp) using the corresponding key with the help of the `${}` placeholder expression notation.

The dispatcher servlet

We created a controller that can put values into the model, and we created the view that can read those values from the model. So, the model acts as an intermediate between the view and the controller; with this, we have finished all the coding part required to present the welcome page. So will we be able to run our project now? No; at this stage, if we run our project and enter the `http://localhost:8080/webstore/` URL on the browser, we will get an **HTTP Status 404** error. This is because we have not performed any servlet mapping yet. In a Spring MVC project, we must configure a front servlet mapping. The front servlet (sometimes called the front controller) mapping is a design pattern where all requests for a particular web application are directed to the same servlet. One such front servlet given by Spring MVC framework is the dispatcher servlet (`org.springframework.web.servlet.DispatcherServlet`). We have not configured a dispatcher servlet for our project yet; this is why we get the **HTTP Status 404** error.

Time for action – configuring the dispatcher servlet

The dispatcher servlet is what examines the incoming request URL and invokes the right corresponding controller method. In our case, the `welcome` method from the `HomeController` class needs to be invoked if we enter the `http://localhost:8080/webstore/` URL on the browser. So let's configure the dispatcher servlet for our project:

1. Create `web.xml` under the `src/main/webapp/WEB-INF/` directory in your project and enter the following content inside `web.xml` and save it:

```
<web-app version="3.0" xmlns="http://java.sun.com/xml/ns/javaee"
    xmlns:xsi="http://www.w3.org/2001/XMLSchema-instance"
```

```
      xsi:schemaLocation="http://java.sun.com/xml/ns/javaee
                    http://java.sun.com/xml/ns/javaee/web-app_3_0.
xsd">
  <servlet>
    <servlet-name>DefaultServlet</servlet-name>
    <servlet-class> org.springframework.web.servlet.
DispatcherServlet </servlet-class>
  </servlet>

  <servlet-mapping>
    <servlet-name>DefaultServlet</servlet-name>
    <url-pattern>/</url-pattern>
  </servlet-mapping>

</web-app>
```

2. Now create one more xml file called `DefaultServlet-servlet.xml` under the same `src/main/webapp/WEB-INF/` directory and enter the following content into it and save it:

```
<?xml version="1.0" encoding="UTF-8"?>
<beans xmlns="http://www.springframework.org/schema/beans"
  xmlns:xsi="http://www.w3.org/2001/XMLSchema-instance"
  xmlns:context="http://www.springframework.org/schema/context"
  xmlns:mvc="http://www.springframework.org/schema/mvc"
  xsi:schemaLocation="http://www.springframework.org/schema/beans
http://www.springframework.org/schema/beans/spring-beans.xsd
    http://www.springframework.org/schema/context http://www.
springframework.org/schema/context/spring-context-4.0.xsd
    http://www.springframework.org/schema/mvc http://www.
springframework.org/schema/mvc/spring-mvc-4.0.xsd">

  <mvc:annotation-driven />
  <context:component-scan base-package="com.packt.webstore" />

  <bean class="org.springframework.web.servlet.view.
InternalResourceViewResolver">
    <property name="prefix" value="/WEB-INF/jsp/" />
    <property name="suffix" value=".jsp" />
  </bean>

</beans>
```

What just happened?

If you know about servlet programming, you might be quite familiar with the servlet configuration and `web.xml`. In `web.xml`, we configured a servlet named `DefaultServlet`, which is more or less similar to any other normal servlet configuration. The only difference is that we have not created any servlet class for that configuration. Instead, the servlet class (`org.springframework.web.servlet.DispatcherServlet`) is provided by the Spring MVC framework, and we make use of it in `web.xml`. After this step, our configured `DispatcherServlet` (`DefaultServlet`) will be ready to handle any requests that come to our application on runtime and will dispatch the request to the correct controller's method.

However, `DispatcherServlet` should know where our controllers and view files are located in our project, and only then can it properly dispatch the request to the correct controllers. So we have to give some hint to `DispatcherServlet` to locate the controllers and view files. This is what we configured in step 2 through the `DispatcherServlet-servlet.xml` file.

Don't worry if you are not able to understand each and every configuration in `web.xml` and `DispatcherServlet-servlet.xml`; we will take a look at these configuration files in next chapter. As of now, just remember that this is a one-time configuration that is needed to run our project successfully.

Deploying our project

We successfully created the project in the last section, so you might be curious to know what would happen if we run our project now. As our project is a web project, we need a web server to run it.

Time for action – running the project

As we already configured the Tomcat web server in our STS, let's use Tomcat to deploy and run our project:

1. Right-click on your project from **Package Explorer** and navigate to **Run As | Run on Server**.

2. A server selection window will appear with all the available servers listed; just select the server that we have configured, **Tomcat v7.0**.

3. At the bottom of the window, you can see a checkbox with the caption that says
Always use this server when running this project; select this checkbox and enter
the **Finish** button, as shown in the following screenshot:

Configuring the default server for a Spring MVC project

4. Now you will see a web page that will show you a welcome message.

Summary

In this chapter, we saw how to install all the prerequisites that are needed to get started and run our first Spring MVC application, for example, installing JDK, the Maven build tool, the Tomcat servlet container, and STS IDE.

We also learned how to perform various configurations in our STS IDE for Maven and Tomcat, created our first Spring MVC project, and added all Spring-related dependent jars through the Maven configuration.

We had a quick hands-on experience of developing a welcome page for our web store application. During that course, we learned how to put values into a model and how to retrieve these values from the model.

Whatever we have seen so far is just a glimpse of Spring MVC, but there is much more to uncover, for example, how the model and view controller are connected to each other and how the request flow occurs. We are going to explore these topics in the next chapter, so see you there!

2

Spring MVC Architecture – Architecting Your Web Store

What we saw in the first chapter is nothing but a glimpse of Spring MVC; in the previous chapter, our total focus was just on getting it to run a Spring MVC application. Now, it's time for us to deep-dive into Spring MVC architecture.

By the end of this chapter, you will have a clear understanding of:

◆   The dispatcher servlet and request mapping

◆   The web application context and configuration

◆   The Spring MVC request flow and Web MVC

◆   The web application architecture

The dispatcher servlet

In the first chapter, we were introduced to the dispatcher servlet and saw how to define a dispatcher servlet in `web.xml`. We learned that every web request first comes to the dispatcher servlet. The dispatcher servlet is the one that decides the controller method that it should dispatch the web request to. In the previous chapter, we created a welcome page that will be shown whenever we enter the URL `http://localhost:8080/webstore/` on the browser. Mapping a URL to the appropriate controller method is the primary duty of a dispatcher servlet.

So the dispatcher servlet reads the web request URL and finds the appropriate controller method that can serve that web request and invokes it. This process of mapping a web request to a specific controller method is called request mapping, and the dispatcher servlet is able to do this with the help of the `@RequestMapping` annotation (`org.springframework.web.bind.annotation.RequestMapping`).

Time for action – examining request mapping

Let's observe what will happen when you change the `value` attribute of the `@RequestMapping` annotation by executing the following steps:

1. Open your STS and run the **webstore** project; just right-click on your project and choose **Run As | Run on Server**. You will be able to view the same welcome message on the browser.

2. Now, go to the address bar of the browser and enter the URL, `http://localhost:8080/webstore/welcome`.

3. You will see the **HTTP Status 404** error page on the browser, and you will also see the following warning in the console:

    ```
    WARNING: No mapping found for HTTP request with URI [/webstore/
    welcome] in DispatcherServlet with name ' DefaultServlet'
    ```

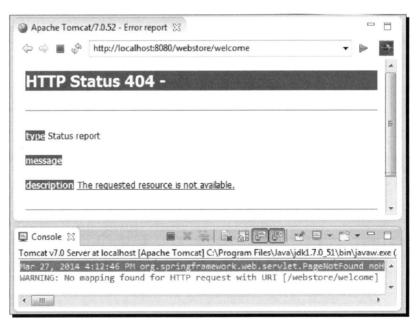

An error log displaying the "No mapping found" warning message

4. Now, open the `HomeController` class, change the `@RequestMapping` annotation's `value` attribute to `/welcome`, and save it. Basically, your new request mapping annotation will look like `@RequestMapping("/welcome")`.

5. Again, run the application and enter the same URL that you entered in step 2; now you will be able to see the same welcome message on the browser, without any request mapping error.

6. Finally, open the `HomeController` class and revert the changes that were made to the `@RequestMapping` annotation's value; just make it `@RequestMapping("/")` again and save it.

What just happened?

After starting our application, when we enter the URL `http://localhost:8080/webstore/welcome` on the browser, the dispatcher servlet (`org.springframework.web.servlet.DispatcherServlet`) immediately tries to find a matching controller method for the request path, `/welcome`.

In a Spring MVC application, the URL can logically be divided into five parts (see the following figure); the `@RequestMapping` annotation only matches against the URL request path. It omits the scheme, hostname, application name, and so on.

The `@RequestMapping` annotation has one more attribute called `method` to further narrow down the mapping based on the HTTP request method types (`GET`, `POST`, `HEAD`, `OPTIONS`, `PUT`, `DELETE`, and `TRACE`). If we do not specify the `method` attribute in the `@RequestMapping` annotation, the default method will be `GET`. We will learn more about the `method` attribute of the `@RequestMapping` annotation in *Chapter 4*, *Working with Spring Tag Libraries*, under the section on form processing.

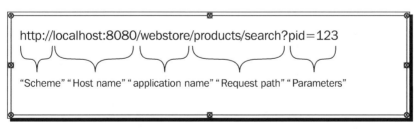

The logical parts of a typical Spring MVC application URL

Since we don't have a corresponding request mapping for the given URL path, `/welcome`, we get the **HTTP Status 404** error on the browser and the following error log on the console:

```
WARNING: No mapping found for HTTP request with URI [/webstore/welcome]
in DispatcherServlet with name 'DefaultServlet'
```

From the error log, we can clearly understand that there is no request mapping for the URL path, `/webstore/welcome`. So, we try to map this URL path to the existing controller method; that's why, in step 4, we put only the request path value, `/welcome`, in the `@RequestMapping` annotation as the `value` attribute. Now everything works perfectly fine.

Finally, we reverted our `@RequestMapping` annotation's value to / again in step 6. Why did we do this? Because we want it to show the welcome page under the web request URL `http://localhost:8080/webstore/` again. Observe carefully that here the last single character / is the request path. We will see more about request mapping in upcoming chapters.

Pop quiz – request mapping

Q1. If we have a Spring MVC application for library management called BookPedia and want to map a web request URL, `http://localhost:8080/BookPedia/category/fiction`, to a controller method, how will we form the `@RequestMapping` annotation?

1. `@RequestMapping("/fiction")`.
2. `@RequestMapping("/category/fiction")`.
3. `@RequestMapping("/BookPedia/category/fiction")`.

The web application context

In a Spring-based application, our application objects live within an object container. This container creates objects and associations between objects, and manages their complete life cycle. These container objects are called Spring-managed beans (or simply beans), and the container is called an application context in the Spring world.

A Spring container uses **dependency injection (DI)** to manage the beans that make up an application. An application context (`org.springframework.context.ApplicationContext`) creates beans and associate beans together based on the bean configuration and dispenses beans on request. A bean configuration can be defined via an XML file, annotation, or even via Java configuration classes. We will use only XML- and annotation-based bean configurations in our chapters.

A web application context is the extension of an application context, designed to work with the standard servlet context (`javax.servlet.ServletContext`). A web application context typically contains frontend-related beans, such as views and view resolvers. In the first chapter, we created an XML file called `DefaultServlet-servlet.xml`, which is nothing but a bean configuration file for our web application context.

Time for action – understanding the web application context

You have received enough of an introduction on the web application context; now, tweak a little bit with the name and location of the web application context configuration file (`DefaultServlet-servlet.xml`) and observe the effect. Perform the following steps:

1. Rename the `DefaultServlet-servlet.xml` file to `DispatcherServlet-servlet.xml`; you can find `DefaultServlet-servlet.xml` under the `src/main/webapp/WEB-INF/` directory.

2. Then, run your webstore project again and enter the URL, `http://localhost:8080/webstore/`; you will see an **HTTP Status 500** error message on your web page and a `FileNotFoundException` error in the stack trace as follows:

   java.io.FileNotFoundException: Could not open ServletContext resource [/WEB-INF/DefaultServlet-servlet.xml]

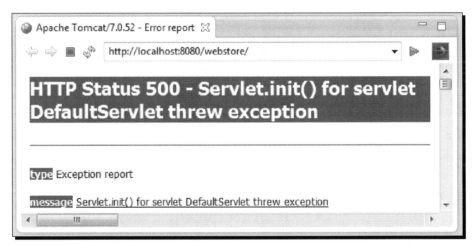

An error message displaying FileNotFoundException for DefaultServlet-servlet.xml

3. To fix this error, change the name of `DefaultServlet` to `DispatcherServlet` in `web.xml`; basically, after changing the name to `DispatcherServlet`, your servlet configuration will look like the following in the `web.xml` file:

```
<servlet>
    <servlet-name>DispatcherServlet</servlet-name>
```

```
    <servlet-class>org.springframework.web.servlet.
DispatcherServlet</servlet-class>
  </servlet>

  <servlet-mapping>
    <servlet-name>DispatcherServlet</servlet-name>
    <url-pattern>/</url-pattern>
  </servlet-mapping>
```

4. Now, run your application and enter the URL, `http://localhost:8080/webstore/`; you will see the welcome message again.

5. Rename your `DispatcherServlet-servlet.xml` file to `DispatcherServlet-context.xml` once more.

6. Next, create a directory structure `spring/webcontext/` under the `WEB-INF` directory and move the `DispatcherServlet-context.xml` file to the `src/main/webapp/WEB-INF/spring/webcontext/` directory.

7. Then, run your application, and you will see an **HTTP Status 500** error message on your web page again and a `FileNotFoundException` error message in the stack trace:

   java.io.FileNotFoundException: Could not open ServletContext resource [/WEB-INF/DispatcherServlet-servlet.xml]

8. To fix this error, add the following tags within the `<servlet>` and `</servlet>` tags in `web.xml` as shown in the following code:

```
<init-param>
  <param-name>contextConfigLocation</param-name>
  <param-value>
    /WEB-INF/spring/webcontext/DispatcherServlet-context.xml
  </param-value>
</init-param>
```

9. Now, run the application again and enter the URL, `http://localhost:8080/webstore/`; you will be able to see the welcome message again.

What just happened?

So, what we did first was renamed the `DefaultServlet-servlet.xml` file to `DispatcherServlet-servlet.xml`, and we got a `FileNotFoundException` error at runtime, as follows:

java.io.FileNotFoundException: Could not open ServletContext resource [/WEB-INF/DefaultServlet-servlet.xml]

To fix the error, we changed our dispatcher servlet configuration, as follows, in the `web.xml` file:

```
<servlet>
  <servlet-name>DispatcherServlet</servlet-name>
  <servlet-class> org.springframework.web.servlet.DispatcherServlet
  </servlet-class>
</servlet>

<servlet-mapping>
  <servlet-name>DispatcherServlet</servlet-name>
  <url-pattern>/</url-pattern>
</servlet-mapping>
```

We changed the servlet name to `DispatcherServlet` in order to align with the web application context configuration file named `DispatcherServlet-servlet.xml`. So, based on this exercise, we can learn that during the start-up of any Spring MVC project, the dispatcher servlet will look for a web application context configuration file of the pattern `<Configured dispatcher Servlet Name>-servlet.xml` under the `WEB-INF` directory. It is our responsibility to keep the web application context configuration file under the `WEB-INF` directory with the right name. However, what if we wish to keep the file in some other directory?

One of the important things to be noted in `<servlet-mapping>` is the value of the `<url-pattern>/</url-pattern>` tag. By assigning / as the URL pattern for the dispatcher servlet, we make `DispatcherServlet` the default servlet for our web application. So, every web request coming to our web application will be handled by `DispatcherServlet`.

For instance, in steps 5 and 6, we renamed the web application context configuration file and moved it to a completely new directory (`src/main/webapp/WEB-INF/spring/webcontext/`). In that case, how did we fix the **HTTP Status 500** error? The answer lies within a property called `contextConfigLocation`. For the dispatcher servlet to locate the web context configuration file easily, we gave the location of this file to the dispatcher servlet through a property called `contextConfigLocation`. That's why we added this property to the dispatcher servlet in step 8, as follows:

```
<servlet>
  <servlet-name>DispatcherServlet</servlet-name>
  <servlet-class>org.springframework.web.servlet.DispatcherServlet</servlet-class>
  <init-param>
```

```
      <param-name>contextConfigLocation</param-name>
      <param-value>
        /WEB-INF/spring/webcontext/DispatcherServlet-context.xml
      </param-value>
   </init-param>
 </servlet>
```

Now, we are able to run our application without any problem. Okay, we played a lot with the web application context configuration file and learned that the dispatcher servlet should know about the web application context configuration file during the start-up of our project. So the next question is: why is the dispatcher servlet looking for this web context configuration file, and what is defined inside this file? Let's find out the answer, but before that, you may answer the following pop quiz questions to make sure you understand the concept of the web application context configuration.

Pop quiz – the web application context

Q1. If the `contextConfigLocation` property was not configured in our dispatcher servlet configuration, under which location would Spring MVC look for the web application context configuration file?

1.   In the `WEB-INF` directory

2.   In `WEB-INF/spring`

3.   In `WEB-INF/spring/appServlet`

Q2. If we do not want to provide `contextConfigLocation` to the following dispatcher servlet configuration, how do we avoid the **HTTP Status 500** error?

```
<servlet>
  <servlet-name>FrontController</servlet-name>
  <servlet-class>org.springframework.web.servlet.DispatcherServlet</
servlet-class>

</servlet>
```

1.   By creating a context file called `FrontController-context.xml` in the `WEB-INF` directory

2.   By creating a file called `DispatcherServlet-context.xml` in `WEB-INF`

3.   By creating a file called `FrontController-servlet.xml` in `WEB-INF`

The web application context configuration

The web application context configuration file (`DispatcherServlet-context.xml`) is nothing but a simple Spring bean configuration file. Spring will create beans (objects) for every bean definition mentioned in this file during bootup of our application. If you open this web application context configuration file (`/WEB-INF/spring/webcontext/DispatcherServlet-context.xml`), you will find some configuration and bean definition as follows:

```xml
<?xml version="1.0" encoding="UTF-8"?>
<beans xmlns="http://www.springframework.org/schema/beans"
   xmlns:xsi="http://www.w3.org/2001/XMLSchema-instance"
   xmlns:context="http://www.springframework.org/schema/context"
   xmlns:mvc="http://www.springframework.org/schema/mvc"
   xsi:schemaLocation="http://www.springframework.org/schema/beans
http://www.springframework.org/schema/beans/spring-beans.xsd
    http://www.springframework.org/schema/context http://www.
springframework.org/schema/context/spring-context-4.0.xsd
    http://www.springframework.org/schema/mvc http://www.
springframework.org/schema/mvc/spring-mvc-4.0.xsd">


   <mvc:annotation-driven />
   <context:component-scan base-package="com.packt.webstore" />

   <bean class="org.springframework.web.servlet.view.
InternalResourceViewResolver">
      <property name="prefix" value="/WEB-INF/jsp/" />
      <property name="suffix" value=".jsp" />
   </bean>

</beans>
```

The first tag within the `<beans>` definition is `<mvc:annotation-driven />`. By this tag, we tell Spring MVC to configure the `DefaultAnnotationHandlerMapping`, `AnnotationMethodHandlerAdapter`, and `ExceptionHandlerExceptionResolver` beans. These beans are required for Spring MVC to dispatch requests to the controllers.

Actually `<mvc:annotation-driven />` does many things behind the screen. It also enables support for various convenient annotations such as `@NumberFormat` and `@DateTimeFormat` to format the form bean fields during form binding. Similarly, we have the `@Valid` annotation to validate the controller method's parameters. It also supports Java objects to/from an XML or JSON conversion via the `@RequestBody` and `@ResponseBody` annotations in the `@RequestMapping` or `@ExceptionHandler` method during form binding. We will see the usage of these annotations in later chapters. As of now, just remember that the `<mvc:annotation-driven />` tag is needed to enable annotations such as `@controller` and `@RequestMapping`.

What is the purpose of the second tag, `<context:component-scan>`? You need a bit of background information to understand the purpose of the `<context:component-scan>` tag. The `@Controller` annotation indicates that a particular class serves the role of a controller. We already learned that the dispatcher servlet searches such annotated classes for mapped methods (the `@RequestMapping` annotated methods) to serve a web request. In order to make the controller available for searching, we need to create a bean for this controller in our web application context.

We can create beans for controllers explicitly via the bean configuration (using the `<bean>` tag—you can see how we created a bean for the `InternalResourceViewResolver` class using the `<bean>` tag in the next section), or we can hand over that task to Spring via the autodetection mechanism. To enable the autodetection of the `@Controller` annotated classes, we need to add component scanning to our configuration using the `<context:component-scan>` tag. Now, you finally understand the purpose of the `<context:component-scan>` tag.

Spring will create beans (objects) for every `@Controller` class at runtime. The dispatcher servlet will search for the correct request mapping method in every `@Controller` bean based on the `@RequestMapping` annotation, to serve a web request. The `base-package` property of a `<context:component-scan>` tag indicates the package under which Spring should search for controller classes to create beans:

```
<context:component-scan base-package="com.packt.webstore" />
```

The preceding line instructs Spring to search for controller classes within the `com.packt.webstore` package and its subpackages.

 The `<context:component-scan>` tag not only recognizes controller classes, it also recognizes other stereotypes such as services and repository classes as well. We will learn more about services and repositories later.

Pop quiz – web application context configuration

Q1. What needs to be done to identify a class by Spring as a controller?

1. That particular class should have the `@Controller` annotation.

2. The `<mvc:annotation-driven />` and `<context:component-scan>` tags should be specified in the web application context configuration file.

3. That particular class should be put up in a package or subpackage that has been specified as a base package in the `<context:component-scan>` tag.

4. All of the above.

View resolvers

We saw the purpose of the first two tags that are specified within the web application context configuration file:

```
<mvc:annotation-driven />
<context:component-scan base-package="com.packt.webstore" />
```

Based on these tags, Spring creates the necessary beans to handle a web request and also creates beans for all the @Controller classes. However, to run a Spring MVC application successfully, Spring needs one more bean; this bean is called a view resolver.

A view resolver helps the dispatcher servlet identify the views that have to be rendered as the response for a specific web request. Spring MVC provides various view resolver implementations to identify views, and InternalResourceViewResolver is one such implementation. The final tag in the web application context configuration is the bean definition for the InternalResourceViewResolver class as follows:

```
<bean class="org.springframework.web.servlet.view.
InternalResourceViewResolver">
<property name="prefix" value="/WEB-INF/jsp/" />
    <property name="suffix" value=".jsp" />
</bean>
```

Through the preceding bean definition in the web application context configuration, we instruct Spring MVC to create a bean for the InternalResourceViewResolver class (org.springframework.web.servlet.view.InternalResourceViewResolver). We will learn more about the view resolver in *Chapter 5, Working with View Resolver*.

Time for action – understanding InternalResourceViewResolver

We instruct Spring to create a bean for an InternalResourceViewResolver class, but why? Who is going to use this bean? What is the role of the InternalResourceViewResolver bean in Spring MVC? Find the answer to these questions through the following exercise:

1. Open DispatcherServlet-context.xml; you can find this file under the src/main/webapp/WEB-INF/spring/webcontext/ directory in your project.

2. Change the prefix property value of the InternalResourceViewResolver bean as follows:

```
<property name="prefix" value="/WEB-INF/views/" />
```

3. Now, run your `webstore` project again and enter the URL `http://localhost:8080/webstore/`. You will see an **HTTP Status 404** error message in your browser as shown in the following screenshot:

An error page displaying the no resource found message

4. Then, rename the `jsp` directory (`/src/main/webapp/WEB-INF/jsp`) to `views`.

5. Finally, run your application and enter the URL, `http://localhost:8080/webstore/`. You will see the welcome message again.

What just happened?

After changing the `prefix` property value of the `InternalResourceViewResolver` bean, we got an **HTTP Status 404** error when we entered the URL, `http://localhost:8080/webstore/`, in the browser. The **HTTP Status 404** error means that the server could not find the web page that we asked for. If that is the case, then which web page did we ask for?

As a matter of fact, we didn't ask for any web page from the server directly; instead, the dispatcher servlet asks a particular web page from the server. What we already learned is that the dispatcher servlet invokes a method in any of the controller beans that can serve this web request. In our case, this method is nothing but the `welcome` method of our `HomeController` class, because this is the only request mapping method that can match the request path of the given URL, `http://localhost:8080/webstore/`, in its `@RequestMapping` annotation.

Now, observe the following:

- The `prefix` property value of the `InternalResourceViewResolver` bean definition in `DispatcherServlet-context.xml`; that is, `/WEB-INF/views/`
- The return value of the `welcome` method from the `HomeController` class; that is, `welcome`
- Finally, the suffix property value of the `InternalResourceViewResolver` bean, that is, `.jsp`

If you combine these three values together, you will get a web page request URL: `/WEB-INF/views/welcome.jsp`. Now, note the error message in the previous screenshot, showing the **HTTP Status 404** error for the same web page URL: `/WEB-INF/views/welcome.jsp` under the application name, `webstore/`.

So, the conclusion is that `InternalResourceViewResolver` resolves the actual view file path by prepending the configured `prefix` value and appending the `suffix` value with the view name—the view name is the value usually returned by the controller method. So, the controller method doesn't return the path of the actual view file; it returns only the logical view name. It is the job of `InternalResourceViewResolver` to form the URL of the actual view file correctly.

Who is going to use this final formed URL? The answer is the dispatcher servlet. After getting the final formed URL of the view file from the view resolver, the dispatcher servlet will try to get the view file from the server. During this time, if the formed URL is found to be wrong, then you will get the **HTTP Status 404** error.

Usually, after invoking the controller method, the dispatcher servlet will wait to get the logical view name from it. Once the dispatcher servlet gets the logical view name, it gives this name to the view resolver (`InternalResourceViewResolver`) to get the URL path of the actual view file; once the view resolver returns the URL path to the dispatcher servlet, the rendered view file is served to the client browser as a web page by the dispatcher servlet.

However, why did we get the error in step 3? Since we changed the `prefix` property of the `InternalResourceViewResolver` bean in step 2, the URL path value returned from `InternalResourceViewResolver` became `/WEB-INF/views/welcome.jsp` in step 3, which is an invalid path value (there is no directory called `views` under `WEB-INF`). That's why, we renamed the directory `jsp` to `views` in step 4 to align it with the path generated by `InternalResourceViewResolver` so that everything works fine again.

Model View Controller

So far, we have seen lots of concepts, such as the dispatcher servlet, request mapping, controllers, and view resolver; it would be good to see the overall picture of the Spring MVC request flow so that we can understand each component's responsibilities. However, before that, we need to understand the **Model View Controller (MVC)** concept some more. Every enterprise-level application's presentation layer can logically be divided into the following three major parts:

- The part that manages the data (Model)
- The part that creates the user interface and screens (View)
- The part that handles interactions between the user, user interface, and data (Controller)

The following diagram will help you understand the event flow and command flow within an MVC pattern:

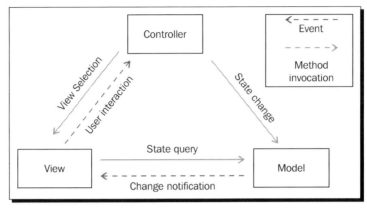

The classic MVC pattern

Whenever a user interacts with the view by clicking on a link or button, the view issues an event notification to the controller, and the controller issues a command notification to the model to update the data. Similarly, whenever the data in the model gets updated or changed, a change notification event is issued to the view by the model in response, and the view issues a state query command to the model to get the latest data from the model. Here, the model and view can interact directly; this pattern is called the classic MVC pattern. However, what Spring MVC employs is something called a **web MVC** pattern due to the limitations in the HTTP protocol.

Web applications rely on the HTTP protocol, which is a stateless pull protocol. This means that no request implies no reply; every time, we need to request the application to know its state. The MVC design pattern requires a push protocol for the views to be notified by the model. So in web MVC, the controller takes more responsibility for the state changing, state querying, and change notification.

In web MVC, every interaction between the model and view is taken through the controller only. So, the controller acts as a bridge between the model and view. There is no direct interaction between the model and view, as in the classic MVC pattern.

An overview of the Spring MVC request flow

The main entry point for a web request in a Spring MVC application is via the dispatcher servlet. The dispatcher servlet acts as the front controller and dispatches the requests to the other controller. The front controller's main duty is to find the appropriate controller to hand over the request for further processing. The following diagram shows an overview of the request flow in a Spring MVC application:

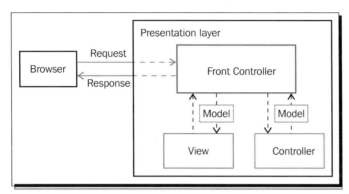

The Spring MVC request flow

Now, let's review the Spring MVC request flow in short:

1. When we enter a URL in the browser, the request comes to the dispatcher servlet. The dispatcher servlet then acts as a centralized entry point to the web application.

2. The dispatcher servlet determines a suitable controller that is capable of handling the request and dispatching this request to the controller.

3. The controller method updates objects in the model and returns the logical view name and updated model to the dispatcher servlet.

4. The dispatcher servlet consults with the view resolver to determine which view to render and passes the model data to that view.

5. The view furnishes the dynamic values in the web page using the model data, renders the final web page, and returns this web page to the dispatcher servlet.

6. At the end, the dispatcher servlet returns the final, rendered page as a response to the browser.

The web application architecture

Now, we understand the overall request flow and responsibility of each component in a typical Spring MVC application. However, this is not enough for us to build an online web store application. We also need to know the best practices to develop an enterprise-level web application. One of the best practices in a typical web application is to organize source code into layers, which will improve reusability and loose coupling. A typical web application normally has four layers: the presentation, domain, services, and persistence. So far, whatever we have seen, such as the dispatcher servlet, controllers, view resolvers, and so on, is considered a part of the presentation layer components. Let's understand the remaining layers and components one by one.

The domain layer

Let's start with the domain layer. A domain layer typically consists of a domain model. So, what is a domain model? A domain model is a representation of the data storage types required by the business logic. It describes the various domain objects (entities); their attributes, roles, and relationships; plus the constraints that govern the problem domain. Take a look at the following domain model diagram for order processing to get a quick idea about the domain model:

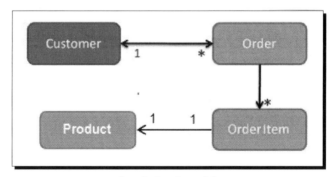

Sample domain model

Each block in the preceding diagram represents a business entity, and the lines represent the associations between the entities. Based on the preceding domain model diagram, we can understand that, in an order processing domain, a customer can have many orders, each order can have many order items, and each order item represents a single product.

During coding, the domain model will be converted into corresponding domain objects and associations by a developer. A domain object is a logical container of pure domain information. Since we are going to build an online web store application, in our domain, the primary domain object might be a product. So, let's start with the domain object to represent a product.

Time for action – creating a domain object

So far, in your webstore, you have showed only a welcome message. It is now time for you to show your first product on the web page. Do this by creating a domain object, as follows, to represent the product information:

1. Create a class called `Product` under the `com.packt.webstore.domain` package in the source folder `src/main/java`. Now, add the following code into it:

```
package com.packt.webstore.domain;

import java.math.BigDecimal;

public class Product {

    private String productId;
    private String name;
    private BigDecimal unitPrice;
    private String description;
    private String manufacturer;
    private String category;
    private long unitsInStock;
    private long unitsInOrder;
    private boolean discontinued;
private String condition;

    public Product() {
        super();
    }

    public Product(String productId, String name, BigDecimal
    unitPrice) {
        this.productId = productId;
        this.name = name;
        this.unitPrice = unitPrice;
    }
```

```java
// add setters and getters for all the fields here

@Override
public boolean equals(Object obj) {
  if (this == obj)
    return true;
  if (obj == null)
    return false;
  if (getClass() != obj.getClass())
    return false;
  Product other = (Product) obj;
  if (productId == null) {
    if (other.productId != null)
      return false;
  } else if (!productId.equals(other.productId))
    return false;
  return true;
}

@Override
public int hashCode() {
  final int prime = 31;
  int result = 1;
  result = prime * result
      + ((productId == null) ? 0 : productId.hashCode());
  return result;
}

@Override
public String toString() {
  return "Product [productId=" + productId + ", name=" + name +
"]";
  }
}
```

Add setters and getters for all of the fields in the preceding class. I have omitted it to make the code compact, but it is a must, so please do add it.

2. Now, create one more class called `ProductController` under the `com.packt.webstore.controller` package in the source folder `src/main/java` and add the following code into it:

```java
package com.packt.webstore.controller;

import java.math.BigDecimal;
```

```
import org.springframework.stereotype.Controller;
import org.springframework.ui.Model;
import org.springframework.web.bind.annotation.RequestMapping;
import com.packt.webstore.domain.Product;

@Controller
public class ProductController {

  @RequestMapping("/products")
  public String list(Model model) {
    Product iphone = new Product("P1234","iPhone 5s", new
BigDecimal(500));
    iphone.setDescription("Apple iPhone 5s smartphone with 4.00-
inch 640x1136 display and 8-megapixel rear camera");
    iphone.setCategory("Smart Phone");
    iphone.setManufacturer("Apple");
    iphone.setUnitsInStock(1000);

    model.addAttribute("product", iphone);

    return "products";
  }
}
```

3. Finally, add one more JSP view file called `products.jsp` under the directory `src/main/webapp/WEB-INF/views/`, add the following code snippets into it, and save it:

```
<%@ taglib prefix="c" uri="http://java.sun.com/jsp/jstl/core"%>

<html>
<head>
<meta http-equiv="Content-Type" content="text/html;
charset=ISO-8859-1">
<link rel="stylesheet"
  href="//netdna.bootstrapcdn.com/bootstrap/3.0.0/css/bootstrap.
min.css">
<title>Products</title>
</head>
<body>
  <section>
    <div class="jumbotron">
      <div class="container">
        <h1>Products</h1>
        <p>All the available products in our store</p>
      </div>
    </div>
  </section>
```

```
<section class="container">
  <div class="row">
    <div class="col-sm-6 col-md-3" style="padding-bottom: 15px">
      <div class="thumbnail">
        <div class="caption">
          <h3>${product.name}</h3>
          <p>${product.description}</p>
<p>${product.unitPrice} USD</p>
 <p>Available ${product.unitsInStock} units in stock</p>
        </div>
      </div>
    </div>
  </div>
</section>
</body>
</html>
```

4. Finally, run the application and enter the URL http://localhost:8080/
   webstore/products. You will be able to see a web page displaying the product
   information as shown in the following screenshot:

The Products page displaying the product information

What just happened?

Our aim is to show the details of a product on our web page; thus, in order to do this, we first need a domain object to hold the details of the product. That's what we did in step 1; we just created a class called `Product` (`Product.java`) to store information about the product, such as the name, description, price, and so on.

As we have already learned from the *An overview of the Spring MVC request flow* section, to show any dynamic data on a web page, prior to this, we need to put this data in a model; only then will the view be able to read this data from the model and render it on the web page. So, to put the product information in a model, we just created one more controller called `ProductController` (`ProductController.java`) in step 3.

In the `ProductController` class, we just have a single method called `list` whose responsibility is to create a product domain object to hold the information about the Apple iPhone 5s and add that object to the model. And finally, we return the view name as `products`. That's what we were doing through the following lines in the `list` method of `ProductController`:

```
model.addAttribute("product", iphone);
return "products";
```

Since we configured `InternalResourceViewResolver` as our view resolver in the web application context configuration file, in the process of resolving the view file for the given view name (in our case, the view name is `products`), the view resolver will try to look for a file `products.jsp` under `/WEB-INF/views/`. That's why, we created `products.jsp` in step 4. If you skip step 4, you will get the **HTTP Status 404** error when running the project.

For a better visual experience, `products.jsp` contains lots of `div` tags with Bootstrap CSS styles applied (Bootstrap is an open source CSS framework), so don't think that `products.jsp` is very complex; as a matter of fact, it is very simple. You need not bother about the `div` tags. These are present just for the appeal. You only need to observe the following four tags carefully in `products.jsp` to understand data retrieval from the model:

```
<h3>${product.name}</h3>
<p>${product.description}</p>
<p>${product.unitPrice} USD</p>
<p>Available ${product.unitsInStock} units in stock</p>
```

Note the `${product.unitPrice}` expression carefully; the text `product` in the expression is the name of the key that we used to store the `iphone` object in the model. (Remember this line `model.addAttribute("product", iphone);` from the `ProductController` class.) The text `unitPrice` is nothing but one of the fields from the `Product` domain class (`Product.java`). Similarly, we show some important fields of the `product` domain class in the `products.jsp` file.

When I say that `price` is the field name, I am actually making an assumption here that you have followed the standard Java bean naming conventions for the getters and setters of your domain class.

This is because, when Spring evaluates the expression `${product.unitPrice}`, it is actually trying to call the getter method of the field to get the value, so it will expect a `getUnitPrice()` method in the `Product.java` file.

After completing step 4, if we run our application and enter the URL `http://localhost:8080/WebStore/products`, we will be able to see a web page displaying the product information as shown in the previous screenshot.

So, we have created a domain class to hold information about a product, created a single product object in the controller, and added it to the model. Finally, we showed the product information in the view.

The persistence layer

Since we had a single product, we just instantiated it in the controller itself and displayed this product information on our web page successfully. However, a typical webstore contains thousands of products; all the information for these products is usually stored in a database. So, we need to make our `ProductController` class smart enough to load all the product information from the database into the model. However, if we write all the data retrieval logic in the `ProductController` class itself to retrieve product information from the database, our `ProductController` class will blow down into a big chunk of file. Logically speaking, data retrieval is not the duty of the controller because the controller is a presentation layer component. Moreover, we need to organize data retrieval code in a separate layer so that we can reuse this logic as much as possible from other controllers and layers.

How do we retrieve data from the database the Spring MVC way? There comes the concept of the persistence layer. A persistence layer usually contains repository objects to access domain objects. A repository object makes queries to the data source for the data, thereafter maps the data from the data source to a domain object, and finally, persists the changes in the domain object to the data source. So, a repository object is typically responsible for CRUD operations (`Create`, `Read`, `Update`, and `Delete`) on domain objects. The `@Repository` annotation (`org.springframework.stereotype.Repository`) is an annotation that marks a specific class as a repository. The `@Repository` annotation also indicates that the SQL exceptions thrown from the repository object's methods should be translated into Spring's `DataAccessExceptions`. Let's create a repository layer for our application.

Time for action – creating a repository object

Perform the following steps to create a repository class to access your product domain objects:

1. Create an interface called ProductRepository under the package com.packt. webstore.domain.repository in the source folder src/main/java. Add a single method declaration in it, as follows:

```
List <Product> getAllProducts();
```

2. Create a class called InMemoryProductRepository under the package com. packt.webstore.domain.repository.impl in the source folder src/main/ java. Now, add the following code into it:

```
package com.packt.webstore.domain.repository.impl;

import java.math.BigDecimal;
import java.util.ArrayList;
import java.util.List;
import org.springframework.stereotype.Repository;
import com.packt.webstore.domain.Product;
import com.packt.webstore.domain.repository.ProductRepository;

@Repository
public class InMemoryProductRepository implements
ProductRepository{

   private List<Product> listOfProducts = new ArrayList<Product>();

   public InMemoryProductRepository() {
      Product iphone = new Product("P1234","iPhone 5s", new
BigDecimal(500));
      iphone.setDescription("Apple iPhone 5s smartphone with 4.00-
inch 640x1136 display and 8-megapixel rear camera");
      iphone.setCategory("Smart Phone");
      iphone.setManufacturer("Apple");
      iphone.setUnitsInStock(1000);

      Product laptop_dell = new Product("P1235","Dell Inspiron", new
BigDecimal(700));
      laptop_dell.setDescription("Dell Inspiron 14-inch Laptop
(Black) with 3rd Generation Intel Core processors");
      laptop_dell.setCategory("Laptop");
```

```
    laptop_dell.setManufacturer("Dell");
    laptop_dell.setUnitsInStock(1000);

    Product tablet_Nexus = new Product("P1236","Nexus 7", new
BigDecimal(300));
    tablet_Nexus.setDescription("Google Nexus 7 is the lightest
7 inch tablet With a quad-core Qualcomm Snapdragon™ S4 Pro
processor");
    tablet_Nexus.setCategory("Tablet");
    tablet_Nexus.setManufacturer("Google");
    tablet_Nexus.setUnitsInStock(1000);

    listOfProducts.add(iphone);
    listOfProducts.add(laptop_dell);
    listOfProducts.add(tablet_Nexus);

  }

  public List<Product> getAllProducts() {
    return listOfProducts;
  }
}
```

3. Open `ProductController` from the package `com.packt.webstore.controller` in the source folder `src/main/java`, and add a private reference to `ProductRepository` with the `@Autowired` annotation (`org.springframework.beans.factory.annotation.Autowired`), as follows:

```
@Autowired
private ProductRepository productRepository;
```

4. Now, alter the body of the `list` method, as follows, in `ProductController`:

```
@RequestMapping("/products")
public String list(Model model) {
  model.addAttribute("products", productRepository.
getAllProducts());
  return "products";
}
```

5. Then, open the view file `products.jsp` from `src/main/webapp/WEB-INF/views/`, and remove all of the existing code and replace it with the following code snippet:

```
<%@ taglib prefix="c" uri="http://java.sun.com/jsp/jstl/core"%>

<html>
```

```
<head>
    <meta http-equiv="Content-Type" content="text/html;
charset=ISO-8859-1">
    <link rel="stylesheet"
    href="//netdna.bootstrapcdn.com/bootstrap/3.0.0/
css/bootstrap.min.css">
    <title>Products</title>
</head>
<body>
    <section>
      <div class="jumbotron">
        <div class="container">
          <h1>Products</h1>
          <p>All the available products in our store</p>
        </div>
      </div>
    </section>

    <section class="container">
      <div class="row">
        <c:forEach items="${products}" var="product">
          <div class="col-sm-6 col-md-3" style="padding-bottom:
15px">
            <div class="thumbnail">
              <div class="caption">
                <h3>${product.name}</h3>
                <p>${product.description}</p>
                <p>$${product.unitPrice}</p>
                <p>Available ${product.unitsInStock} units in
stock</p>
              </div>
            </div>
          </div>
        </c:forEach>
      </div>
    </section>
  </body>
</html>
```

> **6.** Finally, run the application and enter the URL `http://localhost:8080/webstore/products`. You will see a web page displaying the product information as shown in the following screenshot:

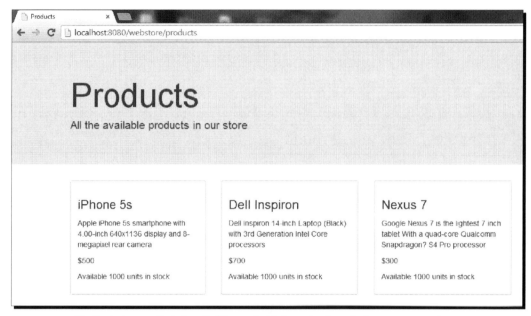

The Products page displaying all of the product information from the in-memory repository

What just happened?

Since we don't want to write all of the data retrieval logic inside `ProductController` itself, we delegated this task to another class called `InMemoryProductRepository`. The `InMemoryProductRepository` class has a single method called `getAllProducts()`, which returns a list of product domain objects.

As the name implies, `InMemoryProductRepository` is just a dummy, in-memory product repository. It does not retrieve any real product domain object information from any database as such; rather, it just instantiates a list of product domain objects in its constructor. So, in step 2, we just created the `InMemoryProductRepository` class, added a single method `getAllProducts()` to it, and instantiated some products in the constructor.

You may wonder, then, what we did in step 1. In step 1, we just created an interface called `ProductRepository`, which defines the expected behavior of a product repository. As of now, the only expected behavior of a `ProductRepository` interface is to return a list of product domain objects (`getAllProducts`), and our `InMemoryProductRepository` class is just an implementation of this interface.

Writing real data retrieval code is beyond the scope of this book, so I have created `InMemoryProductRepository` just for demonstration purposes. However, it is possible to replace the `InMemoryProductRepository` class with any other real implementation that can retrieve real data from the database.

Why do we have an interface and an implementation for the product repository? Remember that we are actually creating a persistence layer for our application. Who is going to use our persistence layer repository object? It will possibly be used by a controller object (in our case, `ProductController`) from the controller layer, so it is not the best practice to connect two layers (controller and persistence) with a direct reference. Instead, we can, in future, have an interface reference in the controller so that we can easily switch to different implementations of the repository without doing any code changes in the controller class, if we want.

That's the reason why we had the `ProductRepository` reference in our `ProductController` class in step 3, and not the `InMemoryProductRepository` class reference. Note the following lines in `ProductController`:

```
@Autowired
private ProductRepository productRepository;
```

What is the need of the `@Autowired` annotation here? If you observe the `ProductController` class carefully, you may wonder why we didn't instantiate any object for the reference, `productRepository`. Nowhere could we see a single line saying something like `productRepository = new InMemoryProductRepository();`.

So how come the execution of the line `productRepository.getAllProducts()` works just fine without any `NullPointerException` error in the `list` method of the `ProductController` class?

```
model.addAttribute("products", productRepository.getAllProducts() );
```

Who assigns the `InMemoryProductRepository` object to the `productRepository` reference? The answer is that the Spring Framework assigns the `InMemoryProductRepository` object to the `productRepository` reference.

Remember we learned that Spring creates and manages beans (objects) for every `@controller` class? Similarly, Spring creates and manages beans for `@Repository` classes as well. As soon as Spring sees the `@Autowired` annotation on top of the `ProductRepository` reference, it assigns the object of `InMemoryProductRepository` to this reference since Spring already created and holds the `InMemoryProductRepository` object in its object container (the web application context).

If you remember, we configured a component scan through the following tag in the web application context configuration file:

```
<context:component-scan base-package=" com.packt.webstore" />
```

Also, we learned earlier that if we configure our web application context as mentioned, it not only detects controllers (@controller), but it also detects other stereotypes such as repositories (@Repository) and services (@Service).

Since we added the @Repository annotation on top of the InMemoryProductRepository class, Spring knows that if any reference of the type productRepository has an @Autowired annotation on top of it, then it should assign the implementation object InMemoryProductRepository to that reference. This process of managing the dependency between classes is called dependency injection or wiring in the Spring world. So, to mark any class as a repository object, we need to annotate that class with the @Repository annotation (org.springframework.stereotype.Repository).

We understand how the persistence layer works, but after the repository object returns a list of products, how do we show it on the web page? If you remember how we added our first product to the model, it is very similar to that. Instead of a single object, this time we add a list of objects to the model through the following line in the list method of ProductController:

```
model.addAttribute("products", productRepository.getAllProducts() );
```

In the preceding code, productRepository.getAllProducts() just returns a list of product domain objects (List<Product>), and we directly add this list to the model.

In the corresponding view file (products.jsp), using the <C:forEach> tag, we loop through the list and display the information for each product inside a styled div tag:

```
<c:forEach items="${products}" var="product">
  <div class="col-sm-6 col-md-3" style="padding-bottom: 15px">
    <div class="thumbnail">
      <div class="caption">
        <h3>${product.name}</h3>
        <p>${product.description}</p>
        <p>${product.unitPrice} USD</p>
        <p> Available ${product.unitsInStock} units in stock </p>
      </div>
    </div>
  </div>
</c:forEach>
```

Again, note that the text products in the expression ${products} is nothing but the key that we used when adding the product list to the model from the ProductController class.

The `for each` loop is a special JSTL looping tag that will run through the list of products and assign each product to a variable called `product` (var=`"product"`) on each iteration. From the `product` variable, we fetch information such as the name, description, and `unitPrice` of the product and display it within the `<h3>` and `<p>` tags. That's how we are finally able to see the list of products on the products web page.

The service layer

So far so good; we created a presentation layer that contains a controller, dispatcher servlet, view resolvers, and so on. Then, we created a domain layer that contains a single domain class, `Product`. Finally, we created the persistence layer, which contains a repository interface and an implementation to access our `Product` domain objects.

However, we are still missing one more concept called the service layer. Why do we need the service layer? We saw how a persistence layer deals with all of the logic related to data access (CRUD) and the presentation layer deals with all of the activities related to the web request and view; the domain layer contains classes to hold information that is retrieved from database records / the persistence layer. However, where can we put the code for business operations?

The service layer exposes business operations that could be composed of multiple CRUD operations. These CRUD operations are usually performed by the repository objects. For example, you could have a business operation to process a customer order, and in order to perform such a business operation, you would need to perform the following operations:

1. First, ensure that all of the products in the requested order are available in your store.

2. Second, have a sufficient quantity of these products in your store.

3. Finally, update the product inventory by reducing the available count for each product that was ordered.

Service objects are good candidates for such business operations logic. The service operations could also represent the boundaries of SQL transactions; this means that all of the elementary CRUD operations performed inside the business operation should be inside a transaction: either all of them should succeed or they should roll back in case of error.

Time for action – creating a service object

Perform the following steps to create a service object that will perform the simple business operation of order processing:

1. Open the interface `ProductRepository` from the package `com.packt.webstore.domain.repository` in the source folder `src/main/java`, and add one more method declaration on it, as follows:

```
Product getProductById(String productID);
```

2. Open the implementation class `InMemoryProductRepository` and add an implantation for the previously declared method, as follows:

```
public Product getProductById(String productId) {
    Product productById = null;

    for(Product product : listOfProducts) {
        if(product!=null && product.getProductId()!=null && product.
getProductId().equals(productId)){
            productById = product;
            break;
        }
    }

    if(productById == null){
        throw new IllegalArgumentException("No products found with
the product id: "+ productId);
    }

    return productById;
}
```

3. Create an interface called `OrderService` under the package `com.packt.webstore.service` in the source folder `src/main/java`. Now, add a method declaration in it as follows:

```
void processOrder(String  productId, int count);
```

4. Create a class called `OrderServiceImpl` under the package `com.packt.webstore.service.impl` in the source folder `src/main/java`. Then, add the following code into it:

```
package com.packt.webstore.service.impl;

import org.springframework.beans.factory.annotation.Autowired;
```

```
import org.springframework.stereotype.Service;
import com.packt.webstore.domain.Product;
import com.packt.webstore.domain.repository.ProductRepository;
import com.packt.webstore.service.OrderService;
```

```
@Service
public class OrderServiceImpl implements OrderService{

   @Autowired
   private ProductRepository productRepository;

   public void processOrder(String productId, long quantity) {
      Product productById = productRepository.
getProductById(productId);

      if(productById.getUnitsInStock() < quantity){
         throw new IllegalArgumentException("Out of Stock. Available
Units in stock"+ productById.getUnitsInStock());
      }

      productById.setUnitsInStock(productById.getUnitsInStock() -
quantity);
   }
}
```

5. Now, create one more controller class called `OrderController` under the package `com.packt.webstore.controller` in the source folder `src/main/java`, and add the following code into it:

```
package com.packt.webstore.controller;

import org.springframework.beans.factory.annotation.Autowired;
import org.springframework.stereotype.Controller;
import org.springframework.ui.Model;
import org.springframework.web.bind.annotation.RequestMapping;
import com.packt.webstore.service.OrderService;

@Controller
public class OrderController {

   @Autowired
   private OrderService orderService;

   @RequestMapping("/order/P1234/2")
   public String process() {
```

```
        orderService.processOrder("P1234", 2);
        return "redirect:/products";
    }
}
```

6. Finally, run the application and enter the URL `http://localhost:8080/webstore/order/P1234/2`. You will be able to see a web page displaying the product information as shown in the following screenshot (note that the available units in stock for iPhone 5s show as **Available 998 units in stock**):

The Products page displaying the product information after the stock was updated via a service call

What just happened?

Before going through the steps, I just want to remind you of a fact regarding repository objects: all of the data access (CRUD) operations on a domain object should be carried through repository objects only. Fact number two is that service objects rely on repository objects to carry out all operations related to data access. That's why, before creating the actual service interface/implementation, we created a repository interface / implementation method (`getProductById`) in steps 1 and 2.

The `getProductById` method from the `InMemoryProductRepository` class just returns a product domain object for the given product ID. We need this method when we write the logic for our service object method (`processOrder`) in the `OrderServiceImpl` class. If the product is not found for the given ID, then `InMemoryProductRepository` throws `IllegalArgumentException`.

Now, let's review steps 3 and 4, where we created the actual service definition and implementation. In step 3, we created an interface called `OrderService` to define all of the expected responsibility of an order service. We defined only one responsibility, as of now, within that interface; that is, to process the order via the method, `processOrder`. The `processOrder` method has two parameters: one is `productId` and the other is `quantity`. In step 4, we implemented the `processOrder` method within the `OrderServiceImpl` class, where we reduced the amount of stock available for the given `productId` by the `quantity` parameter.

In the previous exercise, within the `ProductController` class, we connected controller and repository through the `ProductRepository` interface reference to maximize loose coupling. Similarly, we have now connected the service layer and repository layer through the `ProductRepository` interface reference, as follows, in the `OrderServiceImpl` class:

```
@Autowired
private ProductRepository productRepository;
```

As we have already learned, Spring assigned the `InMemoryProductRepository` object to the `productRepository` reference in the previously mentioned code because the `productRepository` reference has the `@Autowired` annotation, and we know that Spring creates and manages all of the `@Service` and `@Repository` objects. Note that `OrderServiceImpl` has the `@Service` annotation (`org.springframework.stereotype.Service`) on top of it. We used the `productRepository` reference to get the product for the given ID within the `processOrder` method of the `OrderServiceImpl` class as follows:

```
public void processOrder(String productId, long quantity) {
    Product productById = productRepository.getProductById(productId);

    if(productById.getUnitsInStock() < quantity){
        throw new IllegalArgumentException("Out of Stock. Available Units
in stock"+ productById.getUnitsInStock());
    }

    productById.setUnitsInStock(productById.getUnitsInStock() -
quantity);
}
```

To ensure transactional behavior, Spring provides the @Transactional annotation (org.springframework.transaction.annotation. Transactional). We need to annotate service methods with the @ Transactional annotation to define transaction attributes, and we need to do some more configuration in our application context for transactional behavior to take effect.

However, since we are using dummy, in-memory repositories to mimic data access, to annotate service methods with the @Transactional annotation is meaningless. To know more about transaction management in Spring, refer to http://docs.spring.io/spring/docs/current/spring-framework-reference/html/transaction.html.

We already created the service layer, and now it is ready to be consumed from the presentation layer. It is time for us to connect our service layer with the controller. In step 5, we created one more controller, OrderController, with a request mapping method called process in it that is shown in the following code snippet:

```
@RequestMapping("/order/P1234/2")
public String process() {
    orderService.processOrder("P1234", 2);
    return "redirect:/products";
}
```

The process method from the OrderController class uses our orderService reference to process the order for the product ID, P1234. After successfully executing the process method of OrderController, the available units in stock should get reduced by 2 for the product with the ID, P1234.

You will also notice that we mapped the /order/P1234/2 URL path to the process method using the @RequestMapping annotation. So, when we finally try to hit the URL http://localhost:8080/webshop/order/P1234/2, we will be able to see that the available units in stock get reduced by two for the product, P1234.

Have a go hero – accessing the product domain object via a service

In our ProductController class, we only have the ProductRepository reference to access the Product domain object. However, to access ProductRepository directly from ProductController is not the best practice; it is always good to access the persistence layer repository via the service object. However, we have not created any service object to mediate between ProductController and ProductRepository.

Why don't you create a service layer to mediate between `ProductController` and `ProductRepository`? The following are some of the things you can try out:

1. Create an interface called `ProductService` with a method declaration, `List <Products> getAllProducts();`.

2. Create an implementation class, `ProductServiceImpl`, for the `ProductService` interface.

3. Autowire the `ProductRepository` reference in the `ProductServiceImpl` class and use this reference within the `getAllProducts` method to get all of the products from `ProductRepository`.

4. Replace the `ProductRepository` reference with the `ProductService` reference in the `ProductController` class. Accordingly, change the list method in the `ProductController` class.

5. After finishing this, you will be able to see the same product listings under the URL, `http://localhost:8080/webshop/products/`.

An overview of the web application architecture

So far, we have seen how to organize our code into layers so that we can avoid tight coupling between various code files, and improve reusability and the separation of concerns. We just created one domain class, one repository class, and one service class for demonstration purposes, but a typical, real-world MVC application may contain as many domain, repository, and service classes as required. Each layer is usually connected through interfaces and always controller access domain objects from the repository via the service interface only.

Every typical, enterprise-level Spring MVC application will logically have four layers: presentation, domains, persistence, and services. The domain layer is sometimes called the model layer. The following block diagram will help you conceptualize this idea:

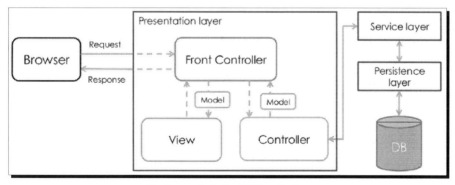

The layers of a Spring MVC application

So, we learned how to create a service layer object and repository layer object; what we saw in the service layer and repository layer was just a glimpse. Spring has extensive support to deal with databases and transactions; handling these is a very vast topic and deserves its own book. In the upcoming chapters, we will concentrate more on the presentation layer, which contains most of the concepts related to Spring MVC rather than those related to the database and transaction.

Have a go hero – listing all our customers

It is great that you have listed all of the products in your web application under the URL, `http://localhost:8080/webstore/products`, but in order to become a successful web store, maintaining only the product information is not enough. You need to maintain information about the customer as well so that you can attract them by giving special discounts based on their purchase history.

Why don't you maintain customer information in your application? Execute the following steps to make some improvements to your application to maintain customer information:

1. Add one more domain class called the `Customer` domain class in the same package where the product exists.

2. Add fields such as `customerId`, `name`, `address`, and `noOfOrdersMade` to the `Customer` class.

3. Create a persistence layer to return all customers.

4. Create an interface called `CustomerRepository` with a method declaration, `List <Customers> getAllCustomers();`.

5. Create an implementation `InMemoryCustomerRepository` for `CustomerRepository` and instantiate a dummy customer in the constructor of `InMemoryCustomerRepository`, as you did for `InMemoryProductRepository`.

6. Create a service layer to get all of the customers from the repository.

7. Create an interface called `CustomerService` with a method declaration, `List <Customers> getAllCustomers()`.

8. Create an implementation `CustomerServiceImpl` for `CustomerService`.

9. Create one more controller called `CustomerController`.

10. Add a request mapping method to map the URL, `http://localhost:8080/webstore/customers`.

11. Create a view file called `customers.jsp`.

After finishing this exercise, you will be able to see all of your customers under the URL, `http://localhost:8080/webstore/customers`. This is very similar to the way we listed all of our products under the URL, `http://localhost:8080/webstore/products`.

Summary

At the start of this chapter, we learned the duty of a dispatcher servlet and how it maps a request using the `@RequestMapping` annotation. Next, we saw what a web application context is and how to configure it for our web application. After that, we got a little introduction about view resolvers and how `InternalResourceViewResolver` resolves the view file for the given logical view name. We also learned the concept of MVC and the overall request flow of a Spring MVC application, and then we learned about web application architecture. In the web application architecture section, we saw how to create and organize code under the various layers of a Spring MVC application, such as the domain layer, persistence layer, and service layer. At the same time, we saw how to retrieve product domain objects from the repository and present them on the web page using the controller. We also learned where a service object fits in. Finally, we saw an overview of the web application architecture.

I hope you got a good overview of Spring MVC and the various components involved in developing a Spring MVC application. In the next chapter, we are specifically going to learn more about controllers and related concepts. Meet you in the next chapter!

3
Control Your Store with Controllers

In Chapter 2, Spring MVC Architecture – Architecting Your Web Store, we learned the overall architecture of a Spring MVC application. We didn't go into any of the concepts in detail; our total aim was to understand the overall flow. In this chapter, we are going to have an in-depth look at the controllers in Spring MVC as they have an important role.

This chapter will cover the following concepts:

◆ Defining a controller
◆ URI template patterns
◆ Matrix variables
◆ Request parameters

Defining a controller

Controllers are presentation layer components that are responsible for responding to user actions. These actions could be entering a particular URL on the browser, clicking on a link, submitting a form on a web page, and so on. Any regular Java class can be transformed into a controller by simply being annotated with the `@Controller` annotation (`org.springframework.stereotype.Controller`).

And we had already learned that the `@Controller` annotation supports Spring's autodetection mechanism for auto-registering the bean definition in the web application context. To enable such auto-registering, we must add the `<context:component-scan>` tag in the web application context configuration file; we have seen how to do that in the *The web application context configuration* section of *Chapter 2, Spring MVC Architecture – Architecting Your Web Store*.

A controller class is made up of request-mapped methods, also called handler methods. Handler methods are annotated with the `@RequestMapping` annotation (`org.springframework.web.bind.annotation.RequestMapping`). The `@RequestMapping` annotation is used to map URLs to particular handler methods. In *Chapter 2, Spring MVC Architecture – Architecting Your Web Store*, we saw a brief introduction on the `@RequestMapping` annotation and learned how to apply the `@RequestMapping` annotation on the handler method level. However, in Spring MVC, we can even specify the `@RequestMapping` annotation at the controller class level. In that case, Spring MVC will consider the controller class level `@RequestMapping` annotation value before mapping the URL to the handler methods. This feature is called relative request mapping.

The terms **request mapped method**, **mapped method**, **handler method**, and **controller method** all mean the same thing; these terms are used to specify the controller method with an `@RequestMapping` annotation. They have been used interchangeably in this book.

Time for action – adding class-level request mapping

Let's add a `@RequestMapping` annotation on our `ProductController` class to demonstrate the relative request mapping feature. However, before that, we just want to ensure that you have already replaced the `ProductRepository` reference with the `ProductService` reference in the `ProductController` class as part of the previous chapter's *Time for action – creating a service object* section. Because contacting the persistence layer directly from the presentation layer is not a best practice, all access to the persistence layer should go through the service layer. Perform the following steps (those who have completed this exercise can directly start from step 5; others please continue from step 1):

1. Create an interface called `ProductService` under the `com.packt.webstore.service` package in `src/main/java` and add two method declarations in it as follows:

   ```
   List<Product> getAllProducts();
   Product getProductById(String productID);
   ```

2. Create a class called `ProductServiceImpl` under the `com.packt.webstore.service.impl` package in `src/main/java` and add the following code into it:

   ```
   package com.packt.webstore.service.impl;

   import java.util.List;
   import org.springframework.beans.factory.annotation.Autowired;
   ```

```
import org.springframework.stereotype.Service;
import com.packt.webstore.domain.Product;
import com.packt.webstore.domain.repository.ProductRepository;
import com.packt.webstore.service.ProductService;

@Service
public class ProductServiceImpl implements ProductService{

    @Autowired
    private ProductRepository productRepository;

    public List<Product> getAllProducts() {
        return productRepository.getAllProducts();
    }

    public Product getProductById(String productID) {
        return productRepository.getProductById(productID);
    }
}
```

3. Open `ProductController`, remove the existing `ProductRepository` reference, and add the `ProductService` reference as follows:

```
@Autowired
private ProductService productService;
```

4. Now, alter the body of the `list` method in the `ProductController` class as follows (note that this time we used the `productService` reference to get all of the products):

```
@RequestMapping("/products")
public String list(Model model) {
    model.addAttribute("products",
        productService.getAllProducts());

    return "products";
}
```

5. In the `ProductController` class, add the following annotation on top of the class:

```
@RequestMapping("/products")
```

6. From the `list` method's `@RequestMapping` annotation, remove the `value` attribute completely; so now, the `list` method will have a plain `@RequestMapping` annotation without any attributes as follows:

```
@RequestMapping
public String list(Model model) {
```

7. Now, add one more handler method in the `ProductController` class as follows:

```
@RequestMapping("/all")
public String allProducts(Model model) {
    model.addAttribute("products", productService.getAllProducts());

    return "products";
}
```

8. Finally, run the application again and enter the URL `http://localhost:8080/webstore/products/all` in the browser to view all of the products.

What just happened?

What we have demonstrated here is a simple concept called relative request mapping. We did the following three things in the `ProductController` class:

- We added an `@RequestMapping` annotation at the class level with a `value` attribute defined as `"/products"` in step 5

- We removed the `value` attribute from the `@RequestMapping` annotation of the `list` method in step 6

- Finally, we added one more handler method called `allProducts`, which also puts the same list of products on the model as the `list` method, but under a different URL mapping—`@RequestMapping("/all")`

In all our previous examples, we annotated the `@RequestMapping` annotations only at the controller method level, but Spring MVC also allows us to specify request mapping at the controller class level. In this case, Spring MVC maps a specific URL path at the method level that is relative to the class level `@RequestMapping` URL value.

In step 5, we just added the `@RequestMapping` annotation at the `ProductController` class level with the URL mapping value `/products`. And in step 7, we added a new handler method called `allProducts` with a URL mapping value `/all`. So, the final request path for the `allProducts` method is formed by combining the class and method request mapping values, which is `/products/all`. So, if we defined any class level request mapping, Spring MVC would consider that class level request path before mapping the request to the method.

Steps 1 to 4 just teach you how to create and connect a service layer object with the `ProductController` class. As of now, the `ProductServiceImpl` class does not have any distinguishable business logic in it; rather, it simply delegates the call to the persistence layer's repository object (`ProductRepository`) to access the `Product` domain object. So as of now, there is no real meaning to have a service layer for `ProductRepository`; however, in future, if we decide to replace the `InMemoryProductRepository` object with a real database backed repository object, we will definitely need this service layer to write code to handle transaction-related tasks. So, just to maintain the industry's best practices, I have retained the service layers in most of the examples in this book.

In step 6, we simply didn't specify any request path value in the `@RequestMapping` annotation of the `list` method. By doing so, we made the `list` method the default request mapping method for the `ProductController` class. So, whenever a request URL ends up with the controller class level request path value without any further relative path, Spring MVC invokes this method as a response to the request.

So, finally in our case, the URL `http://localhost:8080/webstore/products` will be mapped to the `list` method and `http://localhost:8080/webstore/products/all` will be mapped to the `allProducts` method.

 If you specify more than one default mapping method inside a controller, you will get `IllegalStateException` with the message **Ambiguous mapping found**. So, a controller can have only one default request mapping method at most.

Pop quiz – class-level request mapping

Q1. In a web application called `library` that has the following request mapping at a controller class level and in the method level, which is the appropriate request URL to map the request to the `books` method?

```
@RequestMapping("/books")
public class BookController {
...

@RequestMapping(value = "/list")
public String books(Model model) {
...
```

1.   `http://localhost:8080/library/books/list`
2.   `http://localhost:8080/library/list`

3. `http://localhost:8080/library/list/books`

4. `http://localhost:8080/library/`

Q2. If we have another handler method called `bookDetails` under `BookController` as follows, what will the URL that maps to that method be?

```
@RequestMapping()
public String bookDetails(Model model) {
...
```

1. `http://localhost:8080/library/books/details`

2. `http://localhost:8080/library/books`

3. `http://localhost:8080/library/details`

4. `http://localhost:8080/library/`

The role of a controller in Spring MVC

In Spring MVC, controller methods are the final destination point that a web request can reach. After being invoked, the controller method starts to process the web request by interacting with the service layer to complete the work that needs to be done. Usually, the service layer executes some business operations on domain objects and calls the persistence layer to update the domain objects. After the processing has been completed by the service layer object, the controller is responsible for updating and building up the `model` object and chooses a view for the user to see next as a response.

Remember that Spring MVC always keeps the controllers unaware of any view technology used. That's why the controller returns only a logical view name; later, `DispatcherServlet` consults with `ViewResolver` to find out the exact view to be rendered. According to the controller, `Model` is a collection of arbitrary objects and `View` is specified with a logical name.

In all our previous exercises, the controllers used to return the logical view name and update the model via the model parameter available in the controller method. There is another, seldom used way of updating the model and returning the view name from the controller with the help of the `ModelAndView` object (`org.springframework.web.servlet.ModelAndView`). Look at the following code snippet, for example:

```
@RequestMapping("/all")
public ModelAndView allProducts() {
    ModelAndView modelAndView = new ModelAndView();

    modelAndView.addObject("products", productService.getAllProducts());
```

```
modelAndView.setViewName("products");

return modelAndView;
}
```

The preceding code snippet just shows how we can encapsulate the model and view using the `ModelAndView` object.

Handler mapping

We have learned that `DispatcherServlet` is the one that dispatches the request to the handler methods based on the request mapping; however, in order to interpret the mappings defined in the request mapping, `DispatcherServlet` needs a `HandlerMapping` implementation (`org.springframework.web.servlet.HandlerMapping`). The `DispatcherServlet` consults with one or more `HandlerMapping` implementations to find out which `controller (handler)` can handle the request. So, `HandlerMapping` determines which controller to call.

The `HandlerMapping` interface provides the abstraction for mapping requests to handlers. The `HandlerMapping` implementations are capable of inspecting the request and coming up with an appropriate controller. Spring MVC provides many `HandlerMapping` implementations, and the one we are using to detect and interpret mappings from the `@RequestMapping` annotation is the `RequestMappingHandlerMapping` class (`org.springframework.web.servlet.mvc.method.annotation.RequestMappingHandlerMapping`). To start using `RequestMappingHandlerMapping`, we have to add the `<mvc:annotation-driven>` element in our web application context configuration file so that Spring MVC can create and register a bean for `RequestMappingHandlerMapping` in our web application context. We already configured `<mvc:annotation-driven>` in *Chapter 2, Spring MVC Architecture – Architecting Your Web Store*, in the *The web application context configuration* section.

Using URI template patterns

In the previous chapters, we saw how to map a particular URL to a controller method; for example, if the URL entered was `http://localhost:8080/webstore/products`, we mapped that request to the `list` method of `ProductController` and listed all the product information on the web page.

What if we want to list only a subset of the products based on category, for instance, we want to display only the products that fall under the category of laptops if the user entered the URL `http://localhost:8080/webstore/products/laptop`? Similarly, what if the URL is `http://localhost:8080/webstore/products/tablet` and we would like to show only tablets on the web page?

One way to do this is to have a separate request mapping method in the controller for every unique category. However, it won't scale if we have hundreds of categories; in that case, we'll have to write a hundred request mapping methods in the controller. So how do we do this in an elegant way?

We use the Spring MVC URI template pattern feature. If you note the following URLs, the only part that changes in the URL is the category type (laptop and tablet); other than that, everything remains the same:

- `http://localhost:8080/webstore/products/laptop`
- `http://localhost:8080/webstore/products/tablet`

So, we can define a common URI template for the previously mentioned URLs, which might look like `http://localhost:8080/webstore/products/{category}`. Spring MVC can leverage this fact and make that template portion (`{category}`) of the URL a variable, called a path variable in the Spring world.

Time for action – showing products based on category

Let's add a category view to the products page using the path variable:

1. Open the `ProductRepository` interface and add one more method declaration on its `getProductsByCategory` method:

```
List<Product> getProductsByCategory(String category);
```

2. Open the implementation class `InMemoryProductRepository` and add an implementation for the previously declared method as follows:

```
public List<Product> getProductsByCategory(String category) {
  List<Product> productsByCategory = new ArrayList<Product>();

  for(Product product: listOfProducts) {
    if(category.equalsIgnoreCase(product.getCategory())){
      productsByCategory.add(product);
    }
  }

  return productsByCategory;
}
```

3. Similarly, open the `ProductService` interface and add one more method declaration on its `getProductsByCategory` method:

```
List<Product> getProductsByCategory(String category);
```

4. Open the service implementation class `ProductServiceImpl` and add an implementation as follows:

```
public List<Product> getProductsByCategory(String category) {
   return productRepository.getProductsByCategory(category);
}
```

5. Open the `ProductController` class and add one more request mapping method as follows:

```
@RequestMapping("/{category}")
public String getProductsByCategory(Model model,
@PathVariable("category") String productCategory) {
   model.addAttribute("products", productService.getProductsByCateg
ory(productCategory));
   return "products";
}
```

6. Run the application and enter the URL `http://localhost:8080/webstore/products/tablet`; you will see something as specified in the following screenshot:

Showing products by category with the help of path variables

What just happened?

Step 5 is the most important in the whole sequence from the previous list, because all the steps prior to step 5 are the prerequisites for step 5. What we are doing in step 5 is nothing but adding a list of `product` objects to the model like we normally would:

```
model.addAttribute("products",
   productService.getProductsByCategory(ProductCategory));
```

One thing we need to note here is the `getProductsByCategory` method from `productService`; we need this method to get the list of products for the given category, and `productService` as such cannot give the list of products for the given category. It will ask the repository. That's why, in step 4, we used the `productRepository` reference to get the list of products by category within the `ProductServiceImpl` class. Note the following code snippet from `ProductServiceImpl`:

```
return productRepository.getProductsByCategory(category);
```

Another important thing to be noted in the code snippet from step 5 is the `@RequestMapping` annotation's request path value as follows:

```
@RequestMapping("/{category}")
```

By enclosing a portion of a request path within curly braces, we indicate to the Spring MVC that it is a URI template variable. According to Spring MVC documentation, a URI template is a URI-like string that contains one or more variable names. When you substitute values for these variables, the template becomes a URI.

For example, the URI template `http://localhost:8080/webstore/products/` `{category}` contains the variable `category`. Assigning the value `laptop` to the variable yields `http://localhost:8080/webstore/products/laptop`. In Spring MVC, we can use the `@PathVariable` annotation (`org.springframework.web.bind.annotation.` `PathVariable`) to read a URI template variable.

Since we have the `@RequestMapping("/products")` annotation at the `ProductController` level, the actual request path of the `getProductsByCategory` method will be `/products/{category}`. So at runtime, if we give a web request URL as `http://localhost:8080/webstore/products/laptop`, then the `category` path variable will have the value `laptop`. Similarly, for the web request `http://` `localhost:8080/webstore/products/tablet`, the `category` path variable will have the value `tablet`.

How do we retrieve the value stored in the URI template path variable `category`? As we already mentioned, the `@PathVariable` annotation will help us read that variable. All we need to do is simply annotate the `getProductsByCategory` method parameter with the `@PathVariable` annotation as follows:

```
public String getProductsByCategory(@PathVariable("category")
  String productCategory, Model model) {
```

So, Spring MVC will read whatever value is present in the `category` URI template variable and assign it to the method parameter `productCategory`. So, we have the category value in a variable, and we just pass it to `productService` to get the list of products in that category. Once we get that list of products, we simply add it to the model and return the same view name that we have used to list all the products.

The value attribute in the `@PathVariable` annotation should be the same as the variable name in the path expression of the `@RequestMapping` annotation. For example, if the path expression is `"/products/{identity}"`, then to retrieve the path variable identity, you have to form the `@PathVariable` annotation as `@PathVariable("identity")`.

>
> If the `@PathVariable` annotation has been specified without any value attribute, it will try to retrieve a path variable with the same name as that of the variable that it has been annotated with.
>
> For example, if you specify simply `@PathVariable String productId`, then Spring will assume that it should look for a URI template variable `"{productId}"` in the URL. A request mapping method can have any number of `@PathVariable` annotations.

Finally, in step 6, when we enter the URL `http://localhost:8080/webstore/products/tablet`, we see information about Google's Nexus 7, which is a tablet. Similarly, if we enter the URL `http://localhost:8080/webstore/products/laptop`, we see information about Dell's Inspiron laptop.

Pop quiz – request path variable

Q1. In a web application called WebStore that has the following request mapping at a controller class level and in the method level, which is the appropriate request URL that can be used?

```
@RequestMapping("/items")
public class ProductController {
...
@RequestMapping(value = "/type/{type}", method = RequestMethod.GET)
public String productDetails(@PathVariable("type") String
  productType, Model model) {
```

1. `http://localhost:8080/WebStore/items/electronics`
2. `http://localhost:8080/WebStore/items/type/electronics`
3. `http://localhost:8080/WebStore/items/productType/electronics`
4. `http://localhost:8080/WebStore/type/electronics`

Q2. For the following request mapping annotation, which are the correct method signatures to retrieve the path variables?

```
@RequestMapping(value="/manufacturer/{ manufacturerId}
   /product/{productId}")
```

1. ```
   public String productByManufacturer(@PathVariable String
   manufacturerId, @PathVariable String productId, Model model)
   ```
2. ```
   public String productByManufacturer (@PathVariable String
   manufacturer, @PathVariable String product, Model model)
   ```
3. ```
   public String productByManufacturer
   (@PathVariable("manufacturer") String manufacturerId,
   @PathVariable("product") String productId, Model model)
   ```
4. ```
   public String productByManufacturer
   (@PathVariable("manufacturerId") String manufacturer,
   @PathVariable("productId") String product, Model model)
   ```

Using matrix variables

In the last section, we saw the URI template facility to bind variables in the URL request path. However, there is one more way to bind variables in the request URL in a name-value pair style; these bound variables are referred to as matrix variables within Spring MVC. Look at the following URL:

```
http://localhost:8080/webstore/products/filter/price;low=500;high=1000
```

In this URL, the actual request path is just up to `http://localhost:8080/webstore/products/filter/price`, after which we have something like `low=500;high=1000`; here, `low` and `high` are just matrix variables. However, what makes matrix variables so special is the ability to assign multiple values for a single variable; this means that we can assign a list of values to a URI variable. Take a look at the following URL:

```
http://localhost:8080/webstore/products/filter/ByCriteria;brand=googl
e,dell;category=tablet,laptop
```

In the given URL, we have two variables, namely, `brand` and `category`; both have multiple values, `brand=google, dell` and `category=tablet, laptop`. How do we read these variables from the URL during request mapping? We use the special binding annotation `@MatrixVariable` (`org.springframework.web.bind.annotation.MatrixVariable`). One cool thing about the `@MatrixVariable` annotation is that it allows us to collect the matrix variables in a map of collections (`Map<String, List<String>>`), which will be more helpful when we are dealing with complex web requests.

Time for action – showing the products based on filter

Consider a situation where we want to filter the product list based on the `brand` and `category` variables. For example, you want to list all the products that fall under the category `laptop` and `tablets` and from the manufacturers `google` and `dell`. With the help of the matrix variables, we can form a URL to bind the `brand` and `category` variables' values into the URL as follows:

```
http://localhost:8080/webstore/products/filter/ByCriteria;brand=googl
e,dell;category=tablet,laptop
```

Let's map this URL to a handler method with the help of the `@MatrixVariable` annotation:

1. Open the `ProductRepository` interface and add one more method declaration, `getProductsByFilter`, on it:

    ```
    Set<Product> getProductsByFilter(Map<String,
      List<String>> filterParams);
    ```

2. Open the implementation class, `InMemoryProductRepository`, and add the following method implementation for `getProductsByFilter`:

    ```
    public Set<Product> getProductsByFilter(Map<String, List<String>>
    filterParams) {
        Set<Product> productsByBrand = new HashSet<Product>();
        Set<Product> productsByCategory = new HashSet<Product>();

        Set<String> criterias = filterParams.keySet();

        if(criterias.contains("brand")) {
          for(String brandName: filterParams.get("brand")) {
            for(Product product: listOfProducts) {
              if(brandName.equalsIgnoreCase(product.
                getManufacturer())){
                productsByBrand.add(product);
              }
            }
          }
        }

        if(criterias.contains("category")) {
          for(String category: filterParams.get("category")) {
            productsByCategory.addAll(this.
              getProductsByCategory(category));
    ```

```
        }
    }

    productsByCategory.retainAll(productsByBrand);

    return productsByCategory;
}
```

3. Open the interface `ProductService` and add one more method declaration on it called `getProductsByFilter` as follows:

```
Set<Product> getProductsByFilter(Map<String,
    List<String>> filterParams);
```

4. Open the service implementation class, `ProductServiceImpl`, and add the following method implementation for `getProductsByFilter`:

```
public Set<Product> getProductsByFilter(Map<String,
    List<String>> filterParams) {
        return productRepository.getProductsByFilter(filterParams);
}
```

5. Open `ProductController` and add one more request mapping method as follows:

```
@RequestMapping("/filter/{ByCriteria}")
    public String getProductsByFilter(@MatrixVariable(pathVar=
        "ByCriteria") Map<String,List<String>> filterParams,
        Model model) {
        model.addAttribute("products",
            productService.getProductsByFilter(filterParams));
        return "products";
}
```

6. Open the web application context configuration file (`DispatcherServlet-context.xml`) from `src/main/webapp/WEB-INF/spring/webcontext/` and enable matrix variable support by setting `enable-matrix-variables` to `true` in the `<mvc:annotation-driven>` tag as follows:

```
<mvc:annotation-driven enable-matrix-variables="true"/>
```

7. Finally, run the application and enter the URL `http://localhost:8080/webstore/products/filter/ByCriteria;brand=google,dell;catego ry=tablet,laptop;` you will see the product listing as shown in the following screenshot:

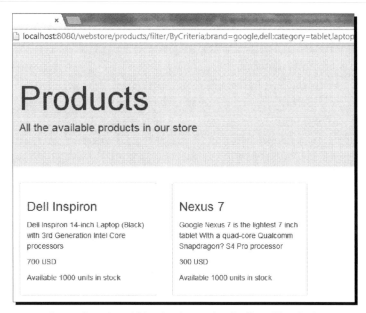

Usage of matrix variables showing product list filtered by criteria

What just happened?

Our aim is to retrieve the matrix variable values from the URL and do something useful; in our case, the URL we are trying to map is `http://localhost:8080/webstore/products/filter/ByCriteria;brand=google,dell;category=tablet,lapt op`, where we want to extract the matrix variables `brand` and `category`. The `brand` and `category` variables have the values `google`, `dell` and `tablet`, `laptop`, respectively. In the previous URL, the request path is up to `http://localhost:8080/webstore/products/filter/ByCriteria` only. That's why, in step 5, we annotated our `getProductsByFilter` request mapping method as follows:

```
@RequestMapping("/filter/{ByCriteria}")
```

However, you may wonder why we have a URI template (`/{ByCriteria}`) in the `@RequestMapping` annotation, which is like mapping to a path variable. It is because if our request URL contains the matrix variable, then we will have to form the `@RequestMapping` annotation with a URI template to identify the starting of matrix variable's segments within URL. That's why we defined `ByCriteria` as a URI template in the request mapping annotation (`@RequestMapping("/filter/{ByCriteria}")`).

A URL can have multiple matrix variables; each matrix variable will be separated with a ; (semicolon). To assign multiple values to a single variable, each value must be separated by a "," (comma), or we can repeat the variable name. See the following URL, which is a repeated variable version of the same URL that we used in our example:

```
http://localhost:8080/webstore/products/filter/
ByCategory;brand=google;brand=dell;category=tablet;
category=laptop
```

Note that we repeated the variables brand and category twice in the URL.

We mapped the web request to the getProductsByFilter method, but how do we retrieve the value from the matrix variables? The answer is the @MatrixVariable annotation. It is quite similar to the @PathVariable annotation; if you notice the getProductsByFilter method signature in step 5, we annotated the method parameter filterParams with the @MatrixVariable annotation as follows:

```
public String getProductsByFilter(@MatrixVariable(pathVar=
   "ByCriteria") Map<String,List<String>> filterParams, Model model)
```

So, Spring MVC will read all the matrix variables found in the URL after the {ByCriteria} URI template and place those matrix variables into the map of the method parameter filterParams. The filterParams map will have each matrix variable name as key and the corresponding list will contain the multiple values assigned for the matrix variable. The pathVar attribute from the @MatrixVariable annotation is used to identify the matrix variable segment in the URL; that's why it has the value ByCriteria, which is nothing but the URI template value that we used in our request mapping URL.

A URL can have multiple matrix variable segments. Take a look at the following URL:

```
http://localhost:8080/webstore/products/filter/ByCriteria;brand=googl
e,dell;category=tablet,laptop/BySpecification;dimention=10,20,15;colo
r=red,green,blue
```

It contains two matrix variable segments, each identified by the prefixes ByCriteria and BySpecification, respectively. So in order to capture each matrix variable segment into a map, we have to form the controller method signature as follows:

```
@RequestMapping("/filter/{ByCriteria}/{BySpecification}")
public String filter(@MatrixVariable(pathVar="ByCriteria")
   Map<String,List<String>> criteriaFilter, @MatrixVariable(pathVar=
   " BySpecification") Map<String,List<String>> specFilter,
   Model model) {
```

We got the value of the matrix variables into the method parameter `filterParams`, but what did we do with that `filterParams` map? We simply passed it as a parameter to the service method to retrieve the products based on criteria as follows:

```
productService.getProductsByFilter(filterParams)
```

Again, the service passes that map to the repository to get the list of products based on the criteria. Once we get the list, we simply add that list to the model and return the same view name that was used to list the products.

To enable the use of matrix variables in Spring MVC, we set the `enable-matrix-variables` attribute of the `<mvc:annotation-driven>` tag to `true`; we did this in step 6. Finally, we were able to view the products based on the specified criteria in step 7 on our product listing page.

Understanding request parameters

Matrix variables and path variables are a great way of binding variables in the URL request path. However, there is one more way to bind variables in the HTTP request, not only as a part of the URL but also in the body of the HTTP web request, which are the so-called HTTP parameters. You might have heard about the GET or POST parameters. GET parameters have been used for years as a standard way to bind variables in the URL, and POST parameters are used to bind variables in the body of the HTTP request. We will learn about POST parameters in the next chapter during form submission.

Okay, now let's see how to read GET request parameters using the Spring MVC style. To demonstrate the use of the request parameter, let's add a product details page to our application.

Time for action – adding the product details page

So far in our product listing page, we have only shown product information such as the product's name, description, price, and available units in stock. However, we haven't shown information such as the manufacturer's name, category, product ID, and so on. Let's create a product details page displaying this information as follows:

1. Open the `ProductController` class and add one more request mapping method as follows:

```
@RequestMapping("/product")
public String getProductById(@RequestParam("id")
  String productId, Model model) {
  model.addAttribute("product",
    productService.getProductById(productId));
  return "product";
}
```

2. Add one more JSP view file called `product.jsp` under the directory `src/main/webapp/WEB-INF/views/`, and add the following code snippet into it and save it:

```jsp
<%@ taglib prefix="c" uri="http://java.sun.com/jsp/jstl/core"%>

<html>
<head>
<meta http-equiv="Content-Type" content="text/html;
charset=ISO-8859-1">
<link rel="stylesheet"
  href="//netdna.bootstrapcdn.com/bootstrap/3.0.0/css/
    bootstrap.min.css">
<title>Products</title>
</head>
<body>
  <section>
    <div class="jumbotron">
      <div class="container">
        <h1>Products</h1>
      </div>
    </div>
  </section>
  <section class="container">
    <div class="row">
      <div class="col-md-5">
        <h3>${product.name}</h3>
        <p>${product.description}</p>
        <p>
          <strong>Item Code : </strong><span class=
            "label label-warning">${product.productId}</span>
        </p>
        <p>
          <strong>manufacturer</strong> :
            ${product.manufacturer}
        </p>
        <p>
          <strong>category</strong> : ${product.category}
        </p>
        <p>
          <strong>Availble units in stock </strong> :
            ${product.unitsInStock}
        </p>
        <h4>${product.unitPrice} USD</h4>
        <p>
          <a href="#" class="btn btn-warning btn-large"> <span
            class="glyphicon-shopping-cart glyphicon">
              </span> Order Now
          </a>
```

```
    </p>
   </div>
  </div>
 </section>
</body>
</html>
```

3. Now, run the application and enter the URL http://localhost:8080/ webstore/products/product?id=P1234; you will see the product details page as shown in the following screenshot:

Usage of request parameter showing product details page

What just happened?

What we did in step 1 is very similar to what we did in the getProductsByCategory method of ProductController. We just added a product object to the model that is returned by the service object as follows:

```
model.addAttribute("product",
   productService.getProductById(productId));
```

However, the important question here is, who is giving the value of the parameter productId? The answer is simple, as you guessed; since we annotated the parameter productId with the @RequestParam("id") annotation (org.springframework.web. bind.annotation.RequestParam), Spring MVC will try to read a GET request parameter with the name id from the URL and assign it to the getProductById method parameter, productId.

The @RequestParam annotation also follows the same convention for other binding annotations; that is, if the name of the GET request parameter and the name of the variable it is annotated with are the same, then there will be no need to specify the value attribute in the @RequestParam annotation.

Finally, in step 6, we added one more view file called product.jsp because we wanted a detailed view of the product so that we could display all the information about the product. Nothing fancy in this product.jsp; as usual, we get the value from the model and show it within HTML tags using the usual JSTL expression language notation ${} as follows:

```
<h3>${product.name}</h3>
    <p>${product.description}</p>
... ...
```

We saw how to retrieve a GET request parameter from the URL, but how do we pass more than one GET request parameter in the URL? The answer is that we need to delimit each parameter value pair with an & symbol; for example, if we want to pass category and price as GET request parameters in a URL, we have to form the URL as follows:

```
http://localhost:8080/WebStore/products/product?category=laptop&pri
ce=700
```

Similarly, to map the preceding URL in a request mapping method, our request mapping method should have at least two parameters with the @RequestParam annotation:

```
public String getProducts(@RequestParam String category,
   @RequestParam String price) {
```

Pop quiz – the request parameter

Q1. Which is the appropriate request URL for the following request mapping method signature?

```
@RequestMapping(value = "/products", method = RequestMethod.GET)
public String productDetails(@RequestParam String rate, Model model)
```

1. http://localhost:8080/webstore/products/rate=400

2. http://localhost:8080/webstore/products?rate=400

3. http://localhost:8080/webstore/products?rate/400

4. http://localhost:8080/webstore/products/rate=400

Time for action – implementing a master detail view

A master detail view is nothing but the display of very important information on a master page. Once we select an item in the master view, a detailed page of the selected item will be shown in the detail view page. Let's build a master detail view for our product listing page so that when we click on any product, we see the detailed view of that product.

We have already implemented the product listing page (`http://localhost:8080/ webshop/products`) and product details page (`http://localhost:8080/webstore/ products/product?id=P1234`), so the only thing needed is to connect these two views to make a master detail view. Perform the following steps:

1. Open `products.jsp`; you can find `products.jsp` under `src/main/webapp/ WEB-INF/views/` in your project and add the following `spring` tag lib reference on top of the file:

    ```
    <%@ taglib prefix="spring"
      uri="http://www.springframework.org/tags" %>
    ```

2. Add the following lines after the **Available units in stock** paragraph tag in `products.jsp`:

    ```
    <p>
    <a href=" <spring:url value=
      "/products/product?id=${product.productId}" /> " class=
      "btn btn-primary">
    <span class="glyphicon-info-sign glyphicon"/></span> Details
    </a>
    </p>
    ```

3. Now, open `product.jsp`; you can find `product.jsp` under `src/main/webapp/ WEB-INF/views/` in your project and add the following `spring` tag lib reference on top of the file:

    ```
    <%@ taglib prefix="spring" uri=
      "http://www.springframework.org/tags" %>
    ```

    And, add the following lines just before the **Order Now** link in `product.jsp`:

    ```
    <a href="<spring:url value="/products" />" class="btn btn-
    default">
       <span class="glyphicon-hand-left glyphicon"></span> back
    </a>
    ```

4. Run the application and enter the URL `http://localhost:8080/webstore/products`; you will be able to see a product list page that has a **Details** button with every product, as specified in the following screenshot:

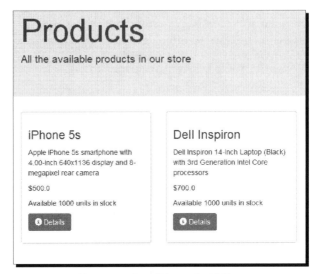

The master view of the product listing

5. Finally, click on any product's **Details** button, and you will be able to see the detail view with the back button link to the product listing page.

What just happened?

What we did is simple. In step 2, we added a hyperlink using the following tag in `products.jsp`:

```
<a href=" <spring:url value=
  "/products/product?id=${product.productId}" /> " htmlEscape=
  "true" />" class="btn btn-primary">
  <span class="glyphicon-info-sign glyphicon"/></span> Details
</a>
```

Note the `href` attribute of the `<a>` tag as follows, which has a `<spring:url>` tag as the value:

```
<spring:url value="/products/product?id=${product.productId}" />
```

This `<spring:url>` tag is used to construct a valid Spring URL. We needed this `<spring:url>` to be used in step 2; that's why we added a reference to the `spring` tag library in step 1. Observe the value attribute of the `<spring:url>` tag; we can note that for the `id` URL parameter, we assigned the expression `${product.productId}`. So, while rendering this link, Spring MVC will assign the corresponding product ID in that expression.

For example, while rendering the link of the first product, Spring MVC will assign the value `P1234` for the product ID. So, the final URL value within `<spring:url>` will become `/products/product?id=P1234`, which is nothing but the request mapping path of the product details page. So, when you click on this link, you land on the details page of that product.

Similarly, we need a link to the product listing page from the product details page; that's why we added another link in the `product.jsp` tag in step 4 as follows:

```
<a href="<spring:url value="/products" />" class="btn btn-default">
   <span class="glyphicon-hand-left glyphicon"></span> back
</a>
```

Note that the `span` tag is just for styling the button with the icon, so you needn't mind it that much. The only interesting thing for us is the `href` attribute of the `<a>` tag, which has the `<spring:url>` tag with the value attribute `/products` on it.

Have a go hero – adding multiple filters to list products

It is good that we learned various techniques to bind parameters with URLs, such as using path variables, matrix variables, and GET parameters. We saw how to get products of a particular category using path variables, how to get products within a particular price range, and finally, we saw how to get a particular product by the product ID.

Now, imagine that you want to apply multiple criteria to view a desired product; for example, what if you want to view a product that falls under the `tablet` category, is within the price range of $200 to $400, and has been manufactured by Google?

To retrieve a product that can satisfy all of the previously mentioned criteria, we can form a URL as follows:

```
http://localhost:8080/webstore/products/tablet/price;low=200;high=400
?manufacturer="Google"
```

Why don't you write a corresponding controller method to serve the preceding request URL? Here are some hints to accomplish the requirement:

◆ Create a repository layer method to return all the products based on manufacturer. For this, add a method declaration in the `productRepository` interface to get the products by manufacturer as follows:

```
List <Product> getProductsByManufacturer(String manufacturer);
```

Add an implementation for the `getProductsByManufacturer()` method in `InMemoryProductRepository`. It is like the `getProductsByCategory()` method; the only difference is that instead of the category, we fetch the products by manufacturer name.

◆ Extend the `productService` interface with the `getProductsByManufacturer()` method and implement the same method in the `productServiceImpl` class.

◆ Create one more request mapping method called `filterProducts` in the `productController` class to map the following URL:

```
http://localhost:8080/webstore/products/tablet/price;low=200;hi
gh=400?manufacturer="Google"
```

Remember that this URL contains the matrix variables `low` and `high` to represent the price range, the GET parameter `manufacturer` to identify the manufacturer, and finally, a URI template path variable `tablet` to represent the category.

◆ Use the same view file `products.jsp` to list the filtered products.

Remember that `getProductsByCategory` from `productService` returns products based on category, the `getProductsBypriceFilter` method returns products within a certain price range, and finally, our newly introduced method, `getProductsByManufacturer`, returns products belonging to a particular manufacturer. You have to combine these three method results before updating the model with the product list in the `filterProducts` controller method. You can probably use `java.util.Set` to combine the results of these three service methods to avoid duplication. Good luck!

Summary

In this chapter, we learned how to define a controller and the usage of the `@Controller` annotation. After that, we learned the concept of relative request mapping, where we saw how to define request mapping at the controller level and understood how Spring relatively maps a web request to the controller request mapping method. We then learned about the role of a controller in Spring MVC and about how the dispatcher servlet uses handler mapping to find out the exact handler methods. We also saw various parameter binding techniques, such as URI template patterns, matrix variables, and HTTP GET request parameters to bind parameters with URLs. Finally, we saw how to implement a master detail view.

In the next chapter, we are going to explore various Spring tags that are available in the `spring` tag library. We will also learn more about form processing and how to bind form data with the HTTP POST parameter. Get ready for the next chapter!

4
Working with Spring Tag Libraries

In previous chapters, we learned how to put data into the model from the controller, but we haven't seen how to do this the other way around. This means that we haven't learned how to put the data from the view into the model. In Spring MVC, the process of putting an HTML form element's values into model data is called form binding.

Spring MVC provides some JSP tag libraries to make it easier to bind form elements to model data. Spring tag libraries also support various other common functionalities, such as, externalizing messages and error handling. In this chapter, we are going to learn more about how to make use of these predefined tag libraries of Spring.

After finishing this chapter, we will have a good idea about the following topics:

- Serving and processing web forms
- Form binding and whitelisting
- Spring tag libraries

Serving and processing forms

Spring supports different view technologies, but if we are using JSP-based views, we can make use of the Spring tag library tags to make up our JSP pages. These tags provide many useful, common functionalities such as form binding, evaluating errors outputting internationalized messages, and so on. In order to use these tags, we must add references to this tag library in our JSP pages as follows:

```
<%@taglib prefix="form" uri=
  "http://www.springframework.org/tags/form" %>
```

```
<%@taglib prefix="spring" uri=
  "http://www.springframework.org/tags" %>
```

In all of our previous chapters' examples, we saw that the data transfer took place from model to view via the controller. The following line is a typical example of how we put data into the model from a controller:

```
model.addAttribute(greeting, "Welcome")
```

Similarly the next line shows how we retrieve that data in the view using the JSTL expression:

```
<p> ${greeting} </p>
```

> **JavaServer Pages Standard Tag Library (JSTL)** is also a tag library provided by Oracle. And it is a collection of useful JSP tags that encapsulates the core functionality common to many JSP pages. We can add a reference to the JSTL tag library in our JSP pages as `<%@ taglib prefix="c" uri="http://java.sun.com/jsp/jstl/core"%>`.

However, what if we want to put data into the model from the view? How do we retrieve that data from the controller? For example, consider a scenario where an admin of our store wants to add new product information in our store by filling and submitting an HTML form. How can we collect the values filled in the HTML form elements and process it in the controller? This is where the Spring tag library tags help us to bind the HTML tag element's values to a form-backing bean in the model. Later, the controller can retrieve the form-backing bean from the model using the `@ModelAttribute` annotation (`org.springframework.web.bind.annotation.ModelAttribute`).

> Form-backing beans (sometimes called form beans) are used to store form data. We can even use our domain objects as form beans; this works well when there's a close match between the fields on the form and the properties on our domain object. Another approach is to create separate classes for form beans, which are sometimes called **Data Transfer Objects (DTOs)**.

Time for action – serving and processing forms

The Spring tag library provides some special `<form>` and `<input>` tags that are more or less similar to HTML form and input tags, but it has some special attributes to bind the form elements data with the form-backing bean. Let's create a Spring web form in our application to add new products to our product list by performing the following steps:

1. We open our `ProductRepository` interface and add one more method declaration in it as follows:

   ```
   void addProduct(Product product);
   ```

2. We then add an implementation for this method in the
`InMemoryProductRepository` class as follows:

```
public void addProduct(Product product) {
    listOfProducts.add(product);
}
```

3. We open our `ProductService` interface and add one more method declaration in
it as follows:

```
void addProduct(Product product);
```

4. And, we add an implementation for this method in the `ProductServiceImpl` class
as follows:

```
public void addProduct(Product product) {
    productRepository.addProduct(product);
}
```

5. We open our `ProductController` class and add two more request mapping
methods as follows:

```
@RequestMapping(value = "/add", method = RequestMethod.GET)
public String getAddNewProductForm(Model model) {
    Product newProduct = new Product();
    model.addAttribute("newProduct", newProduct);
    return "addProduct";
}

@RequestMapping(value = "/add", method = RequestMethod.POST)
public String processAddNewProductForm(
    @ModelAttribute("newProduct") Product newProduct) {
    productService.addProduct(newProduct);
    return "redirect:/products";
}
```

6. Finally, we add one more JSP view file called `addProduct.jsp` under `src/main/`
`webapp/WEB-INF/views/` and add the following tag reference declaration in it as
the very first line:

```
<%@ taglib prefix="c" uri="http://java.sun.com/jsp/jstl/core"%>
<%@ taglib prefix="form" uri=
    "http://www.springframework.org/tags/form"  %>
```

7. Now, we add the following code snippet under the tag declaration line and save
`addProduct.jsp` (note that I have skipped the `<form:input>` binding tags for
some of the fields of the product domain object, but I strongly encourage that you
add binding tags for the skipped fields when you try out this exercise):

```
<html>
<head>
<meta http-equiv="Content-Type" content=
  "text/html; charset=ISO-8859-1">
<link rel="stylesheet"
  href="//netdna.bootstrapcdn.com/bootstrap/3.0.0/css/
  bootstrap.min.css">
<title>Products</title>
</head>
<body>
  <section>
    <div class="jumbotron">
      <div class="container">
        <h1>Products</h1>
        <p>Add products</p>
      </div>
    </div>
  </section>
  <section class="container">
    <form:form  modelAttribute="newProduct" class=
      "form-horizontal">
    <fieldset>
      <legend>Add new product</legend>

      <div class="form-group">
        <label class="control-label col-lg-2 col-lg-2" for=
          "productId">Product Id</label>
        <div class="col-lg-10">
          <form:input id="productId" path="productId" type=
            "text" class="form:input-large"/>
        </div>
      </div>

      <!-- Similarly bind <form:input> tag for name,
        unitPrice,manufacturer,category,unitsInStock and
        unitsInOrder fields-->

      <div class="form-group">
        <label class="control-label col-lg-2" for=
          "description">Description</label>
```

```
          <div class="col-lg-10">
            form:textarea id="description" path=
              "description" rows = "2"/>
          </div>
        </div>

        <div class="form-group">
          <label class="control-label col-lg-2" for=
            "discontinued">Discontinued</label>
          <div class="col-lg-10">
            <form:checkbox  id="discontinued" path=
              "discontinued"/>
          </div>
        </div>

        <div class="form-group">
          <label class="control-label col-lg-2" for=
            "condition">Condition</label>
          <div class="col-lg-10">
            <form:radiobutton path="condition" value=
              "New" />New
            <form:radiobutton path="condition" value=
              "Old" />Old
            <form:radiobutton path="condition" value=
              "Refurbished" />Refurbished
          </div>
        </div>

        <div class="form-group">
          <div class="col-lg-offset-2 col-lg-10">
            <input type="submit" id="btnAdd" class=
              "btn btn-primary" value ="Add"/>
          </div>
        </div>
      </fieldset>
    </form:form>
  </section>
</body>
</html>
```

8. Now, we run our application and enter the URL `http://localhost:8080/webstore/products/add`. We will be able to see a web page that displays a web form where we can add the product information as shown in the following screenshot:

Add the product's web form

9. Now, we enter all the information related to the new product that we want to add and click on the **Add** button; we will see the new product added in the product listing page under the URL `http://localhost:8080/webstore/products`.

What just happened?

In the whole sequence, steps 5 and 6 are very important steps that need to be observed carefully. Whatever is mentioned prior to step 5 is familiar as we have seen it in previous recipes; anyhow, I will give you a brief note on what we have done in steps 1 to 4.

In step 1, we created a method declaration `addProduct` in our `ProductRepository` interface to add new products. In step 2, we implemented the `addProduct` method in our `InMemoryProductRepository` class; the implementation is just to update the existing `listOfProducts` by adding a new product to the list. Steps 3 and 4 are just a service layer extension for `ProductRepository`. In step 3, we declared a similar method, `addProduct`, in our `ProductService` interface and implemented it in step 4 to add products to the repository via the `productRepository` reference.

Okay, coming back to the important step; we have done nothing but added two request mapping methods, namely, `getAddNewProductForm` and `processAddNewProductForm`, in step 5 as follows:

```
@RequestMapping(value = "/add", method = RequestMethod.GET)
public String getAddNewProductForm(Model model) {
    Product newProduct = new Product();
    model.addAttribute("newProduct", newProduct);
    return "addProduct";
}


@RequestMapping(value = "/add", method = RequestMethod.POST)
public String processAddNewProductForm(
    @ModelAttribute("newProduct") Product productToBeAdded) {
    productService.addProduct(productToBeAdded);
    return "redirect:/products";
}
```

If you observe these methods carefully, you will notice a peculiar thing, which is that both the methods have the same URL mapping value in their `@RequestMapping` annotation (`value = "/add"`). So, if we enter the URL `http://localhost:8080/webstore/products/add` in the browser, which method will Spring MVC map that request to?

The answer lies in the second attribute of the `@RequestMapping` annotation (`method = RequestMethod.GET` and `method = RequestMethod.POST`). If you will notice again, even though both methods have the same URL mapping, they differ in request method.

So, what is happening behind the screen is that when we enter the URL `http://localhost:8080/webstore/products/add` in the browser, it is considered as a GET request. So, Spring MVC maps this request to the `getAddNewProductForm` method, and within this method, we simply attach a new empty `Product` domain object to the model under the attribute name, `newProduct`.

```
Product newProduct = new Product();
model.addAttribute("newProduct", newProduct);
```

So in the view `addproduct.jsp`, we can access this model object, `newProduct`. Before jumping into the `processAddNewProductForm` method, let's review the `addproduct.jsp` view file for some time so that we are able to understand the form processing flow without confusion. In `addproduct.jsp`, we have just added a `<form:form>` tag from the Spring tag library using the following line of code:

```
<form:form  modelAttribute="newProduct" class="form-horizontal">
```

Since this special `<form:form>` tag is acquired from the Spring tag library, we need to add a reference to this tag library in our JSP file. That's why we have added the following line at the top of the `addProducts.jsp` file in step 6:

```
<%@ taglib prefix="form" uri=
  "http://www.springframework.org/tags/form"  %>
```

In the Spring `<form:form>` tag, one of the important attributes is `modelAttribute`. In our case, we assigned the value `newProduct` as the value of `modelAttribute` in the `<form:form>` tag. If you recall correctly, you will notice that this value of `modelAttribute` and the attribute name we used to store the `newProduct` object in the model from our `getAddNewProductForm` method are the same. So, the `newProduct` object that we attached to the model in the controller method (`getAddNewProductForm`) is now bound to the form. This object is called the **form-backing bean** in Spring MVC.

Okay, now notice each `<form:input>` tag inside the `<form:form>` tag shown in the following code. You will observe that there is a common attribute in every tag. This attribute name is `path`:

```
<form:input id="productId" path="productId" type=
  "text" class="form:input-large"/>
```

The `path` attribute just indicates the field name that is relative to the form-backing bean. So, the value that is entered in this input box at runtime will be bound to the corresponding field of the form bean.

Okay, now is the time to come back and review our `processAddNewProductForm` method. When will this method be invoked? This method will be invoked once we press the submit button of our form. Yes, since every form submission is considered as a POST request, this time the browser will send a POST request to the same URL, that is, `http://localhost:8080/webstore/products/add`.

So, this time, the `processAddNewProductForm` method will get invoked since it is a POST request. Inside the `processAddNewProductForm` method, we simply call the service method `addProduct` to add the new product to the repository, as follows:

```
productService.addProduct(productToBeAdded);
```

However, the interesting question here is, how is the `productToBeAdded` object populated with the data that we entered in the form? The answer lies within the `@ModelAttribute` annotation (`org.springframework.web.bind.annotation.ModelAttribute`). Note the method signature of the `processAddNewProductForm` method shown in the following line of code:

```
public String processAddNewProductForm(@ModelAttribute("newProduct")
  Product productToBeAdded)
```

Here, if you notice the value attribute of the `@ModelAttribute` annotation, you will observe a pattern. The values of the `@ModelAttribute` annotation and `modelAttribute` from the `<form:form>` tag are the same. So, Spring MVC knows that it should assign the form-bound `newProduct` object to the `productToBeAdded` parameter of the `processAddNewProductForm` method.

The `@ModelAttribute` annotation is not only used to retrieve an object from a model, but if we want to, we can even use it to add objects to the model. For instance, we rewrite our `getAddNewProductForm` method to something like the following code with the use of the `@ModelAttribute` annotation:

```
@RequestMapping(value = "/add", method = RequestMethod.GET)
  public String getAddNewProductForm(
    @ModelAttribute("newProduct") Product newProduct) {
    return "addProduct";
}
```

You can notice that we haven't created any new empty `Product` domain object and attached it to the model. All we have done was added a parameter of the type `Product` and annotated it with the `@ModelAttribute` annotation so that Spring MVC would know that it should create an object of `Product` and attach it to the model under the name `newProduct`.

One more thing that needs to be observed in the `processAddNewProductForm` method is the logical view name, `redirect:/products`, that it returns. So, what are we trying to tell Spring MVC by returning a string `redirect:/products`? To get the answer, observe the logical view name string carefully. If we split this string with the `:` (colon) symbol, we will get two parts; the first part is the prefix `redirect` and the second part is something that looks like a request path, `/products`. So, instead of returning a view name, we simply instruct Spring to issue a redirect request to the request path, `/products`, which is the request path for the `list` method of our `ProductController` class. So, after submitting the form, we list the products using the `list` method of `ProductController`.

 As a matter of fact, when we return any request path with the `redirect:` prefix from a request mapping method, Spring uses a special view object, `RedirectView` (`org.springframework.web.servlet.view.RedirectView`), to issue a redirect command behind the screen. We will see more about `RedirectView` in the upcoming chapter.

Instead of landing in a web page after the successful submission of a web form, we are spawning a new request to the request path `/products` with the help of `RedirectView`. This pattern is called *Redirect After Post*, which is a common pattern to use with web-based forms. We are using this pattern to avoid double submission of the same form; sometimes, if we press the browser's refresh button or back button after submitting the form, there are chances that the same form will be resubmitted.

Customizing data binding

In the last section, we saw how to bind data submitted by an HTML form or by query string parameters to a form-backing bean. In order to do the binding, Spring MVC internally uses a special binding object called `WebDataBinder` (`org.springframework.web.bind.WebDataBinder`).

The `WebDataBinder` object extracts the data out of the `HttpServletRequest` object, converts it to a proper data format, loads it into a form-backing bean, and validates it. To customize the behavior of the data binding, we can initialize and configure the `WebDataBinder` object in our controller. The `@InitBinder` annotation (`org.springframework.web.bind.annotation.InitBinder`) helps us do this. The `@InitBinder` annotation designates a method to initialize `WebDataBinder`.

Let's see a practical way of customizing `WebDataBinder`. Since we are using the actual domain object itself as the form-backing bean, during form submission, there is a chance of security vulnerability. Since Spring automatically binds HTTP parameters to form bean properties, an attacker could bind suitably named HTTP parameters with form properties that weren't intended for binding. To address this problem, we can explicitly tell Spring which fields are allowed for form binding. Technically speaking, the process of explicitly specifying the allowed fields for form binding is called whitelisting form fields in Spring MVC; we can do whitelisting using `WebDataBinder`.

Time for action – whitelisting form fields

In the previous exercise, while adding a new product, we bound every field of the `Product` domain in the form. However, it is meaningless to specify the `unitsInOrder` and `discontinued` values during the addition of a new product because nobody can make an order before adding the product to the store, and similarly, the `discontinued` products need not be added in our product list. So, we should not allow these fields to be bound to the form bean while adding a new product to our store. However, all the other fields of the `Product` domain object need to be bound. Let's see how to do this with the following steps:

1. We open our `ProductController` class and add a method as follows:

```
@InitBinder
public void initialiseBinder(WebDataBinder binder) {
    binder.setDisallowedFields("unitsInOrder", "discontinued");
}
```

2. We then add an extra parameter of the type `BindingResult` (`org.springframework.validation.BindingResult`) to the `processAddNewProductForm` method as follows:

```
public String processAddNewProductForm(
```

```
@ModelAttribute("newProduct") Product productToBeAdded,
BindingResult result)
```

3. In the same `processAddNewProductForm` method, we add the following condition just before the line where we saved the `productToBeAdded` object:

```
String[] suppressedFields = result.getSuppressedFields();
if (suppressedFields.length > 0) {
    throw new RuntimeException("Attempting to bind
        disallowed fields: " + StringUtils.
        arrayToCommaDelimitedString(suppressedFields));
}
```

4. Now, we run our application and enter the URL `http://localhost:8080/webstore/products/add`; we will be able to see a web page that displays a web form where we can add new product information. Let's fill every field, particularly **Units in order** and **Discontinued**.

5. Now, click on the **Add** button. You will see an **HTTP Status 500** error on the web page, as shown in the following screenshot:

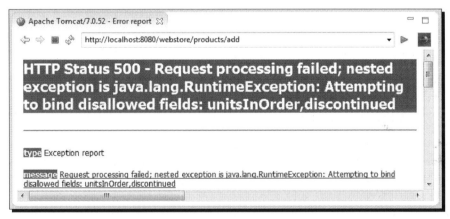

Add product page showing error for disallowed fields

6. Now, we open `addProduct.jsp` from `/webstore/src/main/webapp/WEB-INF/views/` in our project and remove the input tags that are related to the **Units in order** and **Discontinued** fields. Basically, we need to remove the following block of code:

```
<div class="form-group">
    <label class="control-label col-lg-2" for=
        "unitsInOrder">Units In
        Order</label>
    <div class="col-lg-10">
```

```
        <form:input id="unitsInOrder" path="unitsInOrder"  type=
          "text" class="form:input-large"/>
      </div>
   </div>

   <div class="form-group">
      <label class="control-label col-lg-2" for=
        "discontinued">Discontinued</label>
      <div class="col-lg-10">
        <form:checkbox  id="discontinued" path="discontinued"/>
      </div>
   </div>
```

7. Now, we run our application again and enter the URL `http://localhost:8080/webstore/products/add`. We will be able to see a web page that displays a web form where we can add a new product, but this time, without the **Units in order** and **Discontinued** fields.

8. Now, we enter all of the information related to the new product and click on the **Add** button; we will see the new product added in the product listing page under the URL `http://localhost:8080/webstore/products`.

What just happened?

Our intention was to put some restrictions on binding the HTTP parameters with the form-backing bean. As we already discussed, the automatic binding feature of Spring could lead to a potential security vulnerability, in case we used the domain object itself as the form bean. So, we have to explicitly specify to Spring MVC what the only allowed fields are. That's what we did in step 1.

The `@InitBinder` annotation designates a controller method as a hook method to do some custom configuration regarding data binding on `WebDataBinder`. And, `WebDataBinder` is the one that does the data binding at runtime, so we need to specify to `WebDataBinder` only the fields allowed for binding. If you observe our `initialiseBinder` method from `ProductController`, it has a parameter called `binder`, which is of the type `WebDataBinder`. We simply call the `setAllowedFields` method on the `binder` object and pass the fields' names that are allowed for binding. Spring MVC calls this method to initialize `WebDataBinder` before binding since it has the `@InitBinder` annotation.

 The `WebDataBinder` class also has a method called `setDisallowedFields` to strictly specify the disallowed fields for binding. If you use this method, Spring MVC allows any HTTP request parameters to be bound, except that these field names are specified in the `setDisallowedFields` method.

Okay, we configured which fields are allowed for binding, but we need to verify whether any other fields other than the ones allowed are bound with the form-backing bean. That's what we did in steps 2 and 3.

We changed `processAddNewProductForm` by adding one extra parameter called `result`, which is of the type `BindingResult`. Spring MVC will fill this object with the result of the binding. If any attempt is made to bind anything other than the allowed fields, the `getSuppressedFields` count of the `BindingResult` object will be greater than zero. That's why, we checked suppressed field count and threw `RuntimeException` as follows:

```
if (suppressedFields.length > 0) {
throw new RuntimeException("Attempting to bind disallowed fields:
  " + StringUtils.arrayToCommaDelimitedString(suppressedFields));
}
```

We wanted to ensure that our binding configuration is working; that's why, we ran our application without changing the view file `addProduct.jsp` in step 4. As expected, we got the **HTTP Status 500** error saying **Attempting to bind disallowed fields** when we submitted the add product form with the `unitsInOrder` and `discontinued` fields filled. We realized that our binder configuration is working, so we changed our view file to not bind the disallowed fields. That's what we did in step 6; we just removed the input field elements that are related to the disallowed fields from the `addProduct.jsp` file.

After this, our page for adding new products works just fine, as expected. In case any of the outside attackers try to tamper the POST request and attach a HTTP parameter with the same field name of the form-backing bean, they will get `RuntimeException`.

Whitelisting is just an example of how we can customize the binding with the help of `WebDataBinder`. However, using `WebDataBinder`, we can do other types of binding customizations as well. For example, `WebDataBinder` internally uses many `PropertyEditor` (`java.beans.PropertyEditor`) implementations to convert HTTP request parameters to the target field of the form-backing bean. We can even register the custom `PropertyEditor` objects with `WebDataBinder` to convert more complex data types. For instance, take a look at the following code snippet that shows how to register the custom `PropertyEditor` class to convert a `Date` type:

```
@InitBinder
public void initialiseBinder (WebDataBinder binder) {
  DateFormat dateFormat = new SimpleDateFormat("MMM d, YYYY");
  CustomDateEditor orderDateEditor = new CustomDateEditor(dateFormat,
    true);
  binder.registerCustomEditor(Date.class, orderDateEditor);
}
```

There are many advanced configurations we can do with `WebDataBinder` in terms of data binding, but for a beginner level, we don't need to go so deep.

Externalizing text messages

So far, in all our view files, we hardcoded text values for all of the labels. For instance, take our `addProduct.jsp` file for the product ID input tag; we have a label tag with a hardcoded text value as `ProductId`, as follows:

```
<label class="control-label col-lg-2 col-lg-2" for=
    "productId">Product Id</label>
```

Externalizing these texts from a view file into a properties file will help us have single, centralized control of all the label messages, and moreover, it will help us make our web pages ready for internationalization. We will see more about internationalization in *Chapter 6, Intercept Your Store with Interceptor*, but in order to do internationalization, we need to externalize the label messages first. So now, we are going to see only how to externalize the locale-sensitive text messages from our web page.

Time for action – externalizing messages

Let's see how to externalize the label texts in our `addProduct.jsp` file:

1. We open our `addProduct.jsp` file and add the following `taglib` reference at the top:

    ```
    <%@ taglib prefix="spring" uri=
        "http://www.springframework.org/tags" %>
    ```

2. Change the product ID `<label>` tag's value as `<spring:message code="addProdcut.form.productId.label"/>`, as shown as follows:

    ```
    <label class="control-label col-lg-2 col-lg-2" for=
        "productId"> <spring:message code=
        "addProduct.form.productId.label"/> </label>
    ```

3. We create a file called `messages.properties` under `/src/main/resources` in our project and add the following line in it:

    ```
    addProduct.form.productId.label = New Product ID
    ```

4. Now, we open our web application context configuration file `DispatcherServlet-context.xml` from `src/main/webapp/WEB-INF/spring/webcontext/` and add the following bean definition in it:

    ```
    <bean id= "messageSource" class=
        "org.springframework.context.support.
        ResourceBundleMessageSource">
        <property name="basename" value="messages"/>
    </bean>
    ```

5. Now, we run our application again and enter the URL `http://localhost:8080/webstore/products/add`. We will be able to see the add product page with the product ID label **New Product ID**.

What just happened?

Spring MVC has a special a tag called `<spring:message>` to externalize texts from JSP files. In order to use this tag, we need to add a reference to the Spring tag library, which is what we did in step 1. We just added a reference to the Spring tag library in our `addProduct.jsp` file as follows:

```
<%@ taglib prefix="spring" uri=
   "http://www.springframework.org/tags" %>
```

In step 2, we used this tag to externalize the label text of the `productId` input tag, as follows:

```
<label class="control-label col-lg-2 col-lg-2" for=
   "productId"> <spring:message code=
   "addProduct.form.productId.label"/> </label>
```

Here, an important thing that needs to be noted is the `code` attribute of the `<spring:message>` tag that we have assigned the value `addProduct.form.productId.label` as the code for this `<spring:message>` tag. This `code` attribute is a kind of key, and at runtime, Spring will try to read the corresponding value for the given key (`code`) from a message source property file.

We said that Spring will read the message value from a message source property file, so we need to create that property file, which is what we did in step 3. We just created a property file with the name `messages.properties` under the resource directory. Inside this file, we assigned the `label` text value to the message tag `code` as follows:

```
addProduct.form.productId.label = New Product ID
```

Note that for demonstration purposes, I just externalized a single label, but a typical web application will have externalized messages almost for all of the labels. In that case, the `messages.properties` file will have many code-value pair entries.

Okay, we have created the message source property file and added the `<spring:message>` tag in our JSP file. However, to connect these two, we need to create one more Spring bean in our web application context for the `org.springframework.context.support.ResourceBundleMessageSource` class with the name `messageSource`. We did this in step 4 as follows:

```
<bean id= "messageSource" class=
   "org.springframework.context.support.ResourceBundleMessageSource">
   <property name="basename" value="messages"/>
</bean>
```

One important property that needs to be noted here is the `basename` property. We assigned the value `messages` for that property; if you remember, this is the name of the property file that we created in step 3.

That is all that we have done to enable the externalization of messages in a JSP file. Now, if we run the application and open up the add product page, we can see that the product ID label has the same text as that assigned to the code `addProduct.form.productId.label` in the `messages.properties` file.

Using Spring Security tags

At the start of this chapter, we saw how to serve and process web forms. In that exercise, we created a web page to add products. Anyone with access to the add products page can add new products to our web store. However, in a typical web store, only the administrator can add products. So, how do we restrict other users from accessing the add products page? There comes Spring Security to help us.

Spring Security is a vast topic, so we are not going to see all of the capabilities of Spring Security; instead, we are only going to see how to add basic authentication to our web pages.

Time for action – adding a login page

We are going to use Spring Security features to restrict access to the add products page. Only an authorized user with a valid username and password will be able to access the add products page. Let's see how we can do this in Spring MVC with the following steps:

1. We open `pom.xml`, which can be found under the project root folder itself.

2. We will be able to see some tabs at the bottom, under the `pom.xml` file; we select the **Dependencies** tab and click on the **Add** button of the **Dependencies** section.

3. A **Select Dependency** window will appear; here, we enter **Group Id** as `org.springframework.security`, **Artifact Id** as `spring-security-config`, **Version** as `3.1.4.RELEASE`, and select **Scope** as `compile` and click on the **OK** button.

4. Similarly, we add one more dependency **Group Id** as `org.springframework.security`, **Artifact Id** as `spring-security-web`, **Version** as `3.1.4.RELEASE`, and select **Scope** as `compile` and click on the **OK** button. And most importantly, we save `pom.xml`.

5. Now, we go to the adjacent tab, which is the **Dependency Hierarchy** tab in pom. xml. We can see the **Resolved Dependencies** section on the right, which lists all the resolved dependency entries.

6. We just right-click on the entry with the name spring-asm:3.0.7.RELEASE[compile] from the **Resolved Dependencies** list and choose the **Exclude Maven Artifact...** option and click on **OK**. Then, we save pom.xml.

7. Now, we create one more controller class called LoginController under the com.packt.webstore.controller package in src/main/java and add the following code into it:

```
package com.packt.webstore.controller;

import org.springframework.stereotype.Controller;
import org.springframework.ui.Model;
import org.springframework.web.bind.annotation.RequestMapping;
import org.springframework.web.bind.annotation.RequestMethod;

@Controller
public class LoginController {

  @RequestMapping(value="/login", method = RequestMethod.GET)
  public String login() {
    return "login";
  }

  @RequestMapping(value="/loginfailed", method =
    RequestMethod.GET)
  public String loginerror(Model model) {

    model.addAttribute("error", "true");
    return "login";

  }

  @RequestMapping(value="/logout", method = RequestMethod.GET)
  public String logout(Model model) {
    return "login";
  }
}
```

8. And, we add one more JSP view file called `login.jsp` under `src/main/webapp/`
`WEB-INF/views/` and add the following code snippet into it and save it:

```jsp
<%@ taglib prefix="c" uri="http://java.sun.com/jsp/jstl/core"%>
<%@ taglib prefix="form" uri="http://www.springframework.org/tags/
form"  %>
<%@ taglib prefix="spring" uri="http://www.springframework.org/
tags"  %>


<html>
<head>
<meta http-equiv="Content-Type" content=
  "text/html; charset=ISO-8859-1">
<link rel="stylesheet"
  href="//netdna.bootstrapcdn.com/bootstrap/3.0.0/css/
  bootstrap.min.css">
<title>Products</title>
</head>
<body>
  <section>
    <div class="jumbotron">
      <div class="container">
        <h1>Products</h1>
        <p>Add products</p>
      </div>
    </div>
  </section>
<div class="container">
    <div class="row">
    <div class="col-md-4 col-md-offset-4">
        <div class="panel panel-default">
          <div class="panel-heading">
            <h3 class="panel-title">Please sign in</h3>
          </div>
          <div class="panel-body">
          <c:if test="${not empty error}">
          <div class="alert alert-danger">
            <spring:message code=
              "AbstractUserDetailsAuthenticationProvider.
              badCredentials"/><br />
          </div>
          </c:if>
              <form action="<c:url value=
              "/j_spring_security_check"></c:url>" method=
              "post">
```

```
        <fieldset>
      <div class="form-group">
        <input class="form-control" placeholder=
          "User Name" name='j_username' type="text">
      </div>
      <div class="form-group">
        <input class="form-control" placeholder=
          "Password" name='j_password'  type=
          "password" value="">
      </div>
      <input class="btn btn-lg btn-success btn-block"
        type="submit" value="Login">
      </fieldset>
        </form>
      </div>
    </div>
   </div>
  </div>
 </div>
</body>
```

9. Now, we open our `addProduct.jsp` file and add the following code tag within the `jumbotron` div tag:

    ```
    <a href="<c:url value="/j_spring_security_logout" />" class=
      "btn btn-danger btn-mini pull-right">logout</a>
    ```

10. Then, we open our message source file `messages.properties` from `/src/main/resources` and add the following line in it:

    ```
    AbstractUserDetailsAuthenticationProvider.badCredentials=
      The username or password you entered is incorrect.
    ```

11. Now, we create one more bean configuration file called `security-context.xml` under `src/main/webapp/WEB-INF/spring/webcontext` and add the following content into it and save it:

    ```
    <?xml version="1.0" encoding="UTF-8"?>
    <beans xmlns="http://www.springframework.org/schema/beans"
      xmlns:xsi="http://www.w3.org/2001/XMLSchema-instance"
      xmlns:context="http://www.springframework.org/schema/context"
      xmlns:mvc="http://www.springframework.org/schema/mvc"
      xmlns:security=
        "http://www.springframework.org/schema/security"
      xsi:schemaLocation="http://www.springframework.org/schema/mvc
        http://www.springframework.org/schema/mvc/spring-mvc-
        3.2.xsd
    ```

```
     http://www.springframework.org/schema/security
       http://www.springframework.org/schema/security/spring-
       security-3.1.xsd
     http://www.springframework.org/schema/beans http:
       //www.springframework.org/schema/beans/spring-beans.xsd
     http://www.springframework.org/schema/context
       http://www.springframework.org/schema/context/spring-
       context-3.2.xsd">

  <security:http auto-config="true">
    <security:intercept-url pattern="/products/add" access=
      "ROLE_ADMIN" />

    <security:form-login login-page="/login"
            default-target-url="/products/add"
            authentication-failure-url="/loginfailed"/>
        <security:logout logout-success-url="/logout" />
  </security:http>

  <security:authentication-manager>
    <security:authentication-provider>
      <security:user-service>
        <security:user name="Admin" password=
          "Admin123" authorities="ROLE_ADMIN" />
      </security:user-service>
    </security:authentication-provider>
  </security:authentication-manager>
</beans>
```

12. Then, we add the following tags in `web.xml` under the `<web-app>` tag:

```
<context-param>
    <param-name>contextConfigLocation</param-name>
    <param-value>
/WEB-INF/spring/webcontext/security-context.xml
</param-value>
</context-param>

  <listener>
<listener-class>
org.springframework.web.context.ContextLoaderListener
</listener-class>
  </listener>
```

13. Now, we also add the following tags in web.xml under the `<web-app>` tag and save it:

```
<filter>
  <filter-name>springSecurityFilterChain</filter-name>
  <filter-class>
     org.springframework.web.filter.DelegatingFilterProxy
  </filter-class>
</filter>

<filter-mapping>
  <filter-name>springSecurityFilterChain</filter-name>
  <url-pattern>/*</url-pattern>
</filter-mapping>
```

14. We run our application and enter the URL http://localhost:8080/webstore/ products/add. We will be able to see a login page, as shown in the following screenshot:

The login page showing an error message for invalid credentials

15. Now, we enter **User Name** as Admin and **Password** as Admin123 and click on the **Login** button. Finally, we will be able to see the regular add products page with a **Logout** button.

What just happened?

As usual, in order to use Spring Security in our project, we need some Spring Security related jars; from steps 1 to 4, we just added those jars as Maven dependencies. However, we did something unusual in steps 5 and 6. We excluded the spring- asm dependency (spring-asm:3.0.7.RELEASE[compile]) from the resolved dependencies list.

From the Spring 3.2 version onwards, the `spring-asm` module had already been included in the `spring-core` module, so there is no need to have `spring-asm` as a separate transitive dependency. If you have skipped steps 5 and 6, you will get `java.lang.IncompatibleClassChangeError` when starting up the project.

In step 7, we created one more controller (`LoginController`) to handle all our login-related web requests that contain simply three request mapping methods correspondingly to handle login, login failure, and log out requests. All three methods return the same view name, out of which the `loginerror` method sets a model variable `error` to `true` in the model.

Since in step 7, all the request mapping methods return the view name `login`, we need to create a view file `login.jsp`, which is what we did in step 8.

The `login.jsp` file contains many tags with a Bootstrap-style class applied to enhance the look and feel of the login form; we don't need to concentrate on these tags. However, there are some important tags out there that can be used to understand the flow; the first one is the `<c:if>` tag, as shown in the following code:

```
<c:if test="${not empty error}">
  <div class="alert alert-danger">
    <spring:message code=
      "AbstractUserDetailsAuthenticationProvider.badCredentials"/>
  </div>
</c:if>
```

The `<c:if>` tag is a special JSTL tag used to check a condition; it is more like an `if` condition that we use in our programming language. Using this `<c:if>` tag, we simply check whether the model variable error contains any value. If the model variable error is not empty, we simply show an error message within the `div` tag using the `<spring:message>` tag.

Remember that from the `Externalizing text messages` exercise, we already learned how to externalize messages. In this recipe, we simply used the predefined error key, `AbstractUserDetailsAuthenticationProvider.badCredentials`, of Spring Security as the message key. Since we did this, we just overrode the default error message in step 10.

Okay, coming back to step 8, what are the other important tags in the `login.jsp` file? The next important tag is the `form` tag, which represents the login form. Note the `action` attribute of the `form` tag shown in the following code:

```
<form action="<c:url value="/j_spring_security_check"></c:url>"
  method="post">
```

We simply post our login form values, such as `username` and `password`, to the Spring Security authentication handler URL, which is `/j_spring_security_check`. Here, the special `<c:url>` JSTL tag is used to format the URL.

While posting the username and password to the Spring Security authentication handler, Spring expects these values to be bound under the variable names `j_username` and `j_password` correspondingly. That's why, if you notice the input tag for the username and password, it carries the name attributes as `j_username` and `j_password`, as follows:

```
<input class="form-control" placeholder="User Name" name=
  'j_username' type="text">
<input class="form-control" placeholder="Password" name=
  'j_password'  type="password" value="">
```

Similarly, Spring handles the logout operation under the `j_spring_security_logout` URL; that's why, in step 9, we formed the logout link on the add products page as follows:

```
<a href="<c:url value="/j_spring_security_logout" />" class=
  "btn btn-danger btn-mini pull-right">logout</a>
```

We are almost done with the coding to incorporate Spring Security into our project, but still we need to do some more configuration to get it up and running with the basic authentication for the add products page. For the first configuration, we need to define our authentication manager and specify the authenticated users and roles to Spring Security. We did this with the help of a security context file.

A security context file is more similar to a web application context configuration file. Based on the configuration and bean definition found in this file, Spring creates and manages the necessary beans related to Spring Security. We created such a security context file in step 11. The first configuration tag that is found in this security context file (`security-context.xml`) is `<security:http>`, as follows:

```
<security:http auto-config="true">
    <security:intercept-url pattern="/products/add" access=
      "ROLE_ADMIN" />

    <security:form-login login-page="/login"
                         default-target-url="/products/add"
                         authentication-failure-url=
                           "/loginfailed"/>
        <security:logout logout-success-url="/logout" />
    </security:http>
```

The `<security:http>` tag contains a lot of information, and we will see them one by one. The first configuration within the `<security:http>` tag is as follows:

```
<security:intercept-url pattern="/products/add" access=
  "ROLE_ADMIN" />
```

This instructs Spring to intercept every web request that is received by the request path `/products/add` and only allows access to whichever user has the role of `ROLE_ADMIN`. If you recall, `/products/add` is nothing but the request path for our add products page.

The next configuration within the `<security:http>` tag is as follows:

```
<security:form-login login-page="/login"
            default-target-url="/products/add"
            authentication-failure-url="/loginfailed"/>
```

Here, the `login-page` attribute denotes the URL that it should forward the request to, to get the login form; remember that this request path should be the same as the request mapping of the `login()` method of `LoginController`. Also, `default-target-url` denotes the default landing page after a successful login, and the final attribute `authentication-failure-url` indicates the URL that the request needs to be forwarded to in the case of a login failure.

The final configuration, `<security:logout logout-success-url="/logout" />`, denotes where the request needs to be forwarded after a logout. Remember that this also carries the same request mapping value, which is the value of the `logout` method, from the `LoginController` class.

The next configuration tag in the security context file is the `<security:authentication-manager>` tag; refer to the following code:

```
<security:authentication-manager>
  <security:authentication-provider>
    <security:user-service>
      <security:user name="Admin" password=
        "Admin123" authorities="ROLE_ADMIN" />
    </security:user-service>
  </security:authentication-provider>
</security:authentication-manager>
```

The important information configured under the authentication manager is who the users are, what their corresponding password is, and which roles they have, as follows:

```
<security:user name="Admin" password="Admin123" authorities=
  "ROLE_ADMIN" />
```

The preceding piece of configuration says that it is a user with the name `Admin` and has a password `Admin123` and a role `ROLE_ADMIN`. We can add as many roles as we want by separating them with a comma.

Okay, we defined the security-related configuration in the security context file, but Spring should know about this file and have to read this file before booting the application. Then only will it be able to create and manage the security-related beans. How do we instruct Spring to pick up this file? The answer is the same: the `contextConfigLocation` location property that we have used to locate the web application context configuration file. However, this time, we loaded the security context file through the `ContextLoaderListener` class and not through the dispatcher servlet. That's why, we initiated `ContextLoaderListener` in `web.xml` and gave `contextConfigLocation` via the `<context-param>` tag in step 12, as follows:

```xml
<context-param>
    <param-name>contextConfigLocation</param-name>
    <param-value>/WEB-INF/spring/webcontext/security-
       context.xml</param-value>
</context-param>

<listener>
    <listener-class>
       org.springframework.web.context.ContextLoaderListener
</listener-class>
</listener>
```

Based on the preceding configuration, the `ContextLoaderListener` class will load our security context file (`/WEB-INF/spring/webcontext/security-context.xml`) into the Spring runtime so that Spring can create the necessary beans while booting the application.

As a final step, we need to configure the Spring Security filter in our `web.xml` file so that every web request can be examined for user authentication. This is what we configured in step 13, as follows:

```xml
<filter>
  <filter-name>springSecurityFilterChain</filter-name>
  <filter-class>
    org.springframework.web.filter.DelegatingFilterProxy
  </filter-class>
</filter>

<filter-mapping>
  <filter-name>springSecurityFilterChain</filter-name>
  <url-pattern>/*</url-pattern>
</filter-mapping>
```

After finishing all the steps, if we access the URL `http://localhost:8080/WebStore/products/add`, Spring MVC will prompt us to provide the username and password. Since we have configured an admin user in step 11 with **User Name** as `Admin` and **Password** as `Admin123`, we have to provide these credentials to proceed to the add products page.

Summary

At the start of this chapter, we saw how to serve and process forms; we learned how to bind form data with a form-backing bean and read that bean in the controller. After that, we went a little deeper into form bean binding and configured the binder in our controller to whitelist some of the POST parameters from being bound to the form bean. We saw how to use one more special tag, `<spring:message>`, of Spring to externalize messages in a JSP file. Finally we also saw how to incorporate spring security to do basic authentication to access product add page.

In the next chapter, we will learn more about view and view resolvers.

5

Working with View Resolver

In the previous chapter, we learned how we can use some of the Spring tags that can only be used in JSP and JSTL views. However, Spring has excellent support for other view technologies as well, such as the XML view, JSON view, and so on. Spring MVC maintains a high level of decoupling between the view and controller. The controller knows nothing about view except the view name. It is the responsibility of the view resolver to map the correct view for the given view name.

In this chapter, we will take a deeper look into views and view resolvers. After finishing this chapter, you will have a clear idea about the following topics:

- Views and resolving views
- Static views
- The multipart view resolver
- Content negotiation
- The handler exception resolver

Resolving views

As we already mentioned, Spring MVC does not make any assumption about any specific view technology. According to Spring MVC, a view is identifiable as an implementation of the `org.springframework.web.servlet.View` interface, shown as follows:

```
public interface View {

    String getContentType();
```

```
    void render(Map<String, ?> model, HttpServletRequest request,
HttpServletResponse response) throws Exception;


}
```

The `render` method from the Spring MVC `View` interface defines the main responsibility of a view object. The responsibility is that it should render of proper content as a response (`javax.servlet.http.HttpServletResponse`) based on `Model` and request (`javax.servlet.http.HttpServletRequest`).

Because of the simplicity of Spring MVC's `View` interface, we can write our own view implementation if we want. However, Spring MVC provides many convenient view implementations that are ready for use by simply configuring it in our web application's context configuration file.

One such view is `InternalResourceView` (`org.springframework.web.servlet.view.InternalResourceView`), which renders the response as a JSP page. Similarly, there are other view implementations such as `RedirectView`, `TilesView`, `FreeMarkerView`, and `VelocityView`, which are available for specific view technologies. Spring MVC does not encourage coupling the view object with the controller as it will lead the controller method to tightly couple with one specific view technology. However, if you want to do so, you can do something similar to what is shown in the following code snippet:

```
@RequestMapping("/home")
public ModelAndView greeting(Map<String, Object> model) {

  model.put("greeting", "Welcome to Web Store!");
  model.put("tagline", "The one and only amazing web store");

  View view = new InternalResourceView("/WEB-INF/views/welcome.jsp");

  return new ModelAndView(view, model);
}
```

In the preceding code handler method, we haven't returned any logical view name; rather, we directly instantiated `InternalResourceView` out of `welcome.jsp` and composed it into the `ModelAndView` (`org.springframework.web.servlet.ModelAndView`) object. The preceding example is not encouraged since it has tightly coupled the greeting handler method with `InternalResourceView`. Instead, what we can do is return a logical view name and configure an appropriate view resolver of our choice in our web application's context to create a view object.

Spring comes with quite a few view resolvers to resolve various types of views. We already learned how we can configure `InternalResourceViewResolver` as our view resolver to resolve JSP views in *Chapter 2, Spring MVC Architecture – Architecting Your Web Store*, and we also learned how `InternalResourceViewResolver` resolves a particular logical view name into a view (see the *View resolvers* section, in *Chapter 2, Spring MVC Architecture – Architecting Your Web Store*). Anyhow, I will repeat it briefly here.

`InternalResourceViewResolver` will resolve the actual view's file path by prepending the configured prefix value and appending the suffix value with the logical view name; the logical view name is the value usually returned by the controller method. So, the controller method didn't return any actual view; it just returned the view name. It is the job of `InternalResourceViewResolver` to form the correct URL path of actual JSP view file for `InternalResourceView`.

The redirect view

In a web application, URL redirection or forwarding are the techniques to move visitors to a different web page than the one they request. Most of the time, this technique is used after submitting a web form to avoid resubmission of the same form due to the event of pressing the browser's back button or refresh button. Spring MVC has a special `View` object called Redirectview to handle redirection and forwarding. To use `Redirectview` (`org.springframework.web.servlet.view.Redirectview`) with our controller, we simply need to return the target URL string with the redirection prefix from the controller. There are two redirection prefixes available in Spring MVC, as shown in the following code snippet:

```
return redirect:/products/productDetail
```

And:

```
return forward:/products/productDetail
```

Time for action – examining RedirectView

Though both redirection and forwarding are used to present a different web page than the one requested, there is a little difference between them. Let's try to understand these by examining them:

1. Open our `HomeController` class and add one more request mapping method as follows:

```
@RequestMapping("/welcome/greeting")
public String greeting() {
  return "welcome";
}
```

2. Now, alter the `return` statement of the existing welcome request mapping method, and save it as follows:

```
return "forward:/welcome/greeting";
```

3. Now, run our application and enter `http://localhost:8080/webstore/`. You will be able to see a welcome message on the web page.

4. Now, alter the return statement of the existing welcome request mapping method again and save it as follows:

```
return "redirect:/welcome/greeting";
```

5. Now, run our application and enter `http://localhost:8080/webstore/`. You will see a blank page without any welcome message.

6. Finally, revert the return value of the `welcome` method of `HomeController` to the original value, shown as follows:

```
return "welcome";
```

What just happened?

So, what we have demonstrated here is how we can invoke the redirect view from the controller method. In step 1, we simply created a request mapping method called `greeting` for the `welcome/greeting` request path. This method simply returns a logical view name as `welcome`.

Since we returned the logical view name as `welcome`, the `welcome.jsp` file will be rendered by `InternalResourceView` at runtime. The `welcome.jsp` file expects two model attributes, namely `greeting` and `tagline`, during rendering. In step 2, we altered the `return` statement of the exiting request mapping method to return a redirected URL, as follows:

```
@RequestMapping("/")
public String welcome(Model model) {
    model.addAttribute("greeting", "Welcome to Web Store!");
    model.addAttribute("tagline", "The one and only amazing web store");

    return "forward:/welcome/greeting";
}
```

What we have done in step 2 is more important; instead of returning a logical view name, we simply return the request path value of the `greeting` handler method with the `forward:` keyword prefixed.

The moment Spring MVC sees this, it can understand that it is not a regular logical view name, so it won't search for any view file under the `src/main/webapp/WEB-INF/views/` directory; rather, it will consider this request for it to be forwarded to another request mapping method based on the request path attached after the `forward:` keyword.

One important thing to remember here is that the forwarded request is still the active original request, so whatever value we have put in the model at the start of the request would still be available. This is why we did not add any value to `Model` inside the `greeting` method. We simply return the view name as `welcome` and the `welcome.jsp` file on the assumption that there will be model attributes, namely `greeting` and `tagline`, available in the model. So, when we finally run our application, as mentioned in step 3, even though we issued the request to the URL `http://localhost:8080/webstore/`, the `RedirectView` will forward our request to `http://localhost:8080/webstore/welcome/greeting`, and we will able to see the welcome message on the web page.

Again in step 4, we simply changed the `return` statement of the `welcome` method with the `redirect:` prefix. This time, Spring will consider this request as a new request, so whatever value we have put in the model (inside the `welcome` method) at the start of the original request would have been gone. This is why you saw an empty welcome page in step 6, since the `welcome.jsp` page can't read the `greeting` and `tagline` model attributes from the model.

So, based on this exercise, we understand that `RedirectView` will get into the picture if we return a redirected URL with the appropriate prefix from the controller method. `RedirectView` will keep the original request or spawn a new request based on redirection or forwarding.

Pop quiz – redirect view

Consider the following customer controller:

```
@Controller("/customers")
public class CustomerController {

  @RequestMapping("/list")
  public String list(Model model) {
    return "customers";
  }

  @RequestMapping("/process")
  public String process(Model model) {
    // return
  }
}
```

Q1. If I want to get redirected to the `list` method from `process`, how should I form the return statement within the `process` method?

1. `return "redirect:list";.`

2. `return "redirect:/list";.`

3. `return "redirect:customers/list";.`

4. `return "redirect:/customers/list";.`

Serving static resources

So far, we have seen that every request goes through the controller and returns a corresponding view file for the request; most of the time, these view files contain dynamic content. By dynamic content, I mean the model values that are dynamically populated in the view file during the request processing. For example, if the view file is of the JSP type, then we populate model values in the JSP file using the JSP expression notation, `${ }`.

However, what if we have some static content that we want to serve to the client? For example, consider an image that is static content; we don't want to go through controllers in order to serve (fetch) an image as there is nothing to process or update any values in the model. We simply need to return the requested image.

Let's say we have a directory (`/resources/images/`) that contains some product images, and we want to serve these images upon request. For example, if the requested URL is `http://localhost:8080/webstore/resource/images/P1234.png`, then we would like to serve the image with the `P1234.png` name. Similarly, if the requested URL is `http://localhost:8080/webstore/resource/images/P1236.png`, then an image with the name `P1236.png` needs to be served.

Time for action – serving static resources

Let's see how we can serve static images with Spring MVC:

1. Place some images under the `src/main/webapp/resources/images/` directory; I have used three product images, namely `P1234.png`, `P1235.png`, and `P1236.png`.

2. Add the following tag in our web application context's configuration `DispatcherServlet-context.xml` file:

    ```
    <mvc:resources  location="/resources/"
    mapping="/resource/**"/>
    ```

3. Now, run our application and enter `http://localhost:8080/webstore/resource/images/P1234.png` (change the image name in the URL based on the images you placed in step 1).

4. You are now able to view the image you requested in the browser.

What just happened?

What just happened was simple; in step 1, we placed some image files under the `src/main/webapp/resources/images/` directory. In step 2, we just added the `<mvc:resources>` tag in the web application context configuration to tell Spring where these image files are located in our project so that spring can serve those files upon request. Consider the following code snippet:

```
<mvc:resources  location="/resources/"  mapping="/resource/**"/>
```

The location attribute of the `<mvc:resources>` tag defines the base directory location of static resources that you want to serve. In our case, we want to serve all images that are available under the `src/main/webapp/resources/images/` directory; you may wonder why we have given only `/resources/` as the location value instead of `src/main/webapp/resources/images/`. This is because we consider the `resources` directory as the base directory for all resources, we can have multiple subdirectories under `resources` directory to put our images and other static resource files

The second attribute, `mapping`, just indicates the request path that needs to be mapped to this resource directory. In our case, we have assigned `/resources/**` as the mapping value. So, if any web request starts with the `/resource` request path, then it will be mapped to the `resources` directory, and the `/**` symbol indicates the recursive look for any resource files underneath the base resource directory.

This is why, if you notice in step 3, we formed the URL as `http://localhost:8080/webstore/resource/images/P1234.png`. So, while serving this web request, Spring MVC will consider `/resource/images/P1234.png` as the request path. So, it will try to map `/resource` to the resource base directory, `resources`. From this directory, it will try to look for the remaining path of the URL, which is `/images/P1234.png`. Since we have the `images` directory under the `resources` directory, Spring can easily locate the image file from the `images` directory.

As a matter of fact, behind the screen, Spring MVC uses `org.springframework.web.servlet.resource.ResourceHttpRequestHandler` to serve the resources that are configured by the `<mvc:resources>` tag. So, in our application, if any request comes with the request path's `/resource` prefix in its URL, then Spring will look into the location directory that is configured in the `<mvc:resources>` tag and will return the requested file to the browser. Remember, Spring allows you to host not only images, but also any type of static files, such as PDFs, Word documents, Excel sheets, and so on in this fashion.

It is good that we are able to serve product images without adding any extra request mapping methods in the controller.

Pop quiz – static view

Consider the following resource configuration:

```
<mvc:resources  location="/pdf/"  mapping="/resources/**"/>
```

Q1. Under the `pdf` directory, if I have a sub directory such as `product/manuals/`, which contains a `.pdf` file called `manual-P1234.pdf`, how can I form the request path to access that `.pdf` file?

1. `/pdf/product/manuals/manual-P1234.pdf`.

2. `/resources/pdf/product/manuals/manual-P1234.pdf`.

3. `/product/manuals/manual-P1234.pdf`.

4. `/resource/pdf/product/manuals/manual-P1234.pdf`.

Time for action – adding images to the product detail page

Let's extend this technique to show product images in our product listing page and in the product detail page. Perform the following steps:

1. Open `products.jsp`; you can find `products.jsp` under the `/src/main/webapp/WEB-INF/views/` directory in your project. Now, add the following `<img>` tag after the `<div class="thumbnail">` tag:

    ```
    <img src="<c:url
    value="/resource/images/${product.productId}.png"></c:url>"
    alt="image"  style = "width:100%"/>
    ```

2. Similarly, open `product.jsp` and add the following `<img>` tag after the `<div class="row">` tag:

    ```
    <div class-"col-md-5">
      <img src="<c:url
      value="/resource/images/${product.productId}.png"></c:url>"
      alt="image"  style = "width:100%"/>
    </div>
    ```

3. Now, run our application and enter `http://localhost:8080/webstore/products`. You will be able to see the product list page with every product that has a product image, as shown in the following figure:

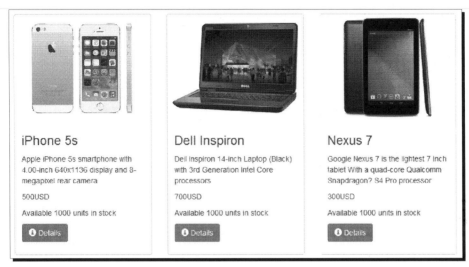

Product listings with the image attached

4. Now, click on the **Details** button of any product, and you will be able to see the corresponding view of the product details with the image attached to the details page, as follows:

The product detail page with the image attached

What just happened?

What we have done is simple. We learned how we can serve static resources and how we can host product images. During this exercise, we learned that in our application, if any request comes with the request path's /resource prefix, it would get mapped to the base resource directory, and any remaining URL path would lead to the static file.

We leveraged this fact, and formed the image's src URL accordingly; notice the src attribute of the <img> tag we added in step 1:

```
<img src="<c:url
value="/resource/images/${product.productId}.png"></c:url>"
alt="image"  style = "width:100%"/>
```

The src attribute value that we are forming in the preceding <img> tag has an expression language notation to fetch the product ID; after getting the product ID, we simply concatenate it to the existing value to form a valid request path, shown as follows:

```
/resource/images/${product.productId}.png
```

For example, if the product ID is P1234, then we would get an image request URL as /resource/images/P1234.png, which is nothing but one of the image file names that we have already put up in the /resources/images directory. So, Spring can easily return the image file that we showed using the <img> tag in steps 1 and 2.

The multipart request in action

In the preceding exercise, we learned how we can incorporate the static view to show product images in the products' details page. We simply put some images in a directory in the server and performed a configuration, and Spring MVC was able to pick up these files during the rendering of the page that had the product details. What if we automate this process? I mean instead of putting these images, what if we are able to upload images to the image directory?

How can we do this? There comes the multipart request. The multipart request is a type of HTTP request that sends the file and data to the server. Spring MVC has good support for a multipart request. Let's say we want to upload some files to the server. To accomplish this, we will have to form a multipart request.

Time for action – adding images to the product page

Let's add the image upload facility to our add products page:

1. Add a bean definition in our web application's context configuration file (DispatcherServlet-context.xml) for CommonsMultipartResolver, as follows:

```
<bean id="multipartResolver"
class="org.springframework.web.multipart.commons.
CommonsMultipartResolver">
  <property name="maxUploadSize" value="10240000"/>
</bean>
```

2. Open pom.xml; you can find pom.xml under the project root directory itself.

3. You will be able to see some tabs at the bottom of the pom.xml file. Select the **Dependencies** tab and click on the **Add** button of the **Dependencies** section.

4. A **Select Dependency** window will appear; enter **Group Id** as commons-fileupload, **Artifact Id** as commons-fileupload, **Version** as 1.2.2; select **Scope** as **compile**; and click on the **OK** button.

5. Similarly, add one more **Group Id** dependency as org.apache.commons, **Artifact Id** as commons-io, **Version** as 1.3.2; select **Scope** as **compile**; click on the **OK** button; and save the pom.xml file.

6. Open our product's domain class (Product.java) and add a reference to org.springframework.web.multipart.MultipartFile with the corresponding setters and getters as follows:

```
private MultipartFile  productImage;
```

7. Open addProduct.jsp; you can find addProduct.jsp under the /src/main/webapp/WEB-INF/views/ directory in your project. Add the following set of tags after the <form:input id="condition"> tag group:

```
<div class="form-group">
  <label class="control-label col-lg-2" for="productImage">
  <spring:message code="addProdcut.form.productImage.label"/>
  </label>
  <div class="col-lg-10">
    <form:input id="productImage" path="productImage"
      type="file" class="form:input-large" />
  </div>
</div>
```

8. Add an entry in our message bundle source (`messages.properties`) for the product's image label, as follows:

```
addProdcut.form.productImage.label = Product Image file
```

9. Now, set the `enctype` attribute to `multipart/form-data` in the `form` tag as follows and save `addProduct.jsp`:

```
<form:form  modelAttribute="newProduct" class="form-horizontal"
enctype="multipart/form-data">
```

10. Open our `ProductController.java` file and modify the `processAddNewProductForm` method's signature by adding an extra method parameter of the `HttpServletRequest` type (`javax.servlet.http.HttpServletRequest`); so basically, your `processAddNewProductForm` method signature should look like the following code snippet:

```
public String processAddNewProductForm(
@ModelAttribute("newProduct") Product newProduct, BindingResult
result, HttpServletRequest request) {
```

11. Add the following code snippet inside the `processAddNewProductForm` method just before `productService.addProduct(newProduct);`:

```
MultipartFile productImage =
  productToBeAdded.getProductImage();
String rootDirectory =
  request.getSession().getServletContext().getRealPath("/");

if (productImage!=null && !productImage.isEmpty()) {
  try {
    productImage.transferTo(new
      File(rootDirectory+"resources\\images\\"+
      productToBeAdded.getProductId() + ".png"));
  } catch (Exception e) {
    throw new RuntimeException("Product Image saving failed",
    e);
  }
}
```

12. Within the `initialiseBinder` method, add the `productImage` field to the whitelisting set as follows:

```
binder.setAllowedFields("productId",
  "name","unitPrice","description","manufacturer",
  "category","unitsInStock", "productImage");
```

13. Now, run our application and enter the URL `http://localhost:8080/webstore/products/add`. You will be able to see our `add products` page with an extra input field to choose a file to upload. Just fill every information as usual and more importantly, choose an image file of your choice to add a new image file, and click on the **Add** button. You will then be able to see that the image has been added to the products page and the product details page, as shown in the following screenshot:

Add product page with image selection option

What just happened?

Spring's `CommonsMultipartResolver` (`org.springframework.web.multipart.commons.CommonsMultipartResolver`) class determines whether the given request contains multipart content or not and parses the given HTTP request into multipart files and parameters. This is why we initiated this class within our servlet context in step 1. Through the `maxUploadSize` property, we have set a maximum of `10240000` bytes as the allowed file size to be uploaded:

```
<bean id="multipartResolver"
class="org.springframework.web.multipart.commons.
CommonsMultipartResolver">
  <property name="maxUploadSize" value="10240000"/>
</bean>
```

From steps 2 to 5, we added some of the `org.apache.commons` libraries as our maven dependency. This is because Spring uses these libraries internally to support the file uploading feature.

Since the image that we were uploading belongs to a product, it is better to keep that image as part of the product information; this is why in step 6, we added a reference to `MultipartFile` in our domain class (`Product.java`) and added corresponding setters and getters. This `MultipartFile` reference holds the actual product image file that we were uploading.

We want to incorporate the image uploading facility in our add products page; this is why, in the `addProduct.jsp` view file, we added a file input tag to choose the desired image, shown as follows:

```
<div class="form-group">
  <label class="control-label col-lg-2" for="productImage">
    <spring:message code="addProdcut.form.productImage.label"/>
  </label>
  <div class="col-lg-10">
    <form:input id="productImage" path="productImage" type="file"
      class="form:input-large" />
  </div>
</div>
```

In the preceding set of tag, the important one is the `<form:input>` tag. It has the `type` attribute as `file` so that it can have the **Choose File** button to display the file chooser window. As usual, we want this `form` field to be bound with the domain object field; this is why we have set the `path` attribute as `productImage`. If you remember correctly, this pathname is nothing but the same `MultipartFile` reference name that we added in step 6.

As usual, we want to externalize the label message for this file input tag as well, and that's why we added the `<spring:message>` tag, and in step 8, we added the corresponding message entry in the message source file (`messages.properties`).

Since our add product form is now capable of sending image files as well as part of the request, we need to encode the request as a multipart request. This is why, in step 9, we added the `enctype` attribute to the `<form:form>` tag and set its value as `multipart/form-data`. The `enctype` attribute indicates how the form data should be encoded when we are submitting it to the server.

We wanted to save the image file in the server under the location's `resources/images` directory; this directory structure would be available directly under the root directory of our web application at runtime. So, in order to get the root directory of our web application, we need `HttpServletRequest`. See the following code snippet:

```
String rootDirectory = request.getSession().getServletContext().
getRealPath("/");
```

This is why we added an extra method parameter called `request` of the `HttpServletRequest` type to our `processAddNewProductForm` method in step 10. Remember, Spring will fill this `request` parameter with the actual HTTP request.

In step 11, we simply read the image file from the domain object and wrote it into a new file with the product ID as the name, as shown in the following code snippet:

```
MultipartFile productImage = productToBeAdded.getProductImage();
String rootDirectory = request.getSession().getServletContext().
getRealPath("/");
if (productImage!=null && !productImage.isEmpty()) {
  try {
    productImage.transferTo(new
      File(rootDirectory+"resources\\images\\"+
      productToBeAdded.getProductId() + ".png"));
  } catch (Exception e) {
    throw new RuntimeException("Product Image saving failed", e);
  }
}
```

Remember, we purposely save the images with the product ID name because we have already designed our products (`products.jsp`) page and detail (`product.jsp`) page accordingly in order to display the right image based on the product ID.

As a final step, we added the newly introduced `productImage` file to the whitelisting set in the binder configuration within the `initialiseBinder` method.

Now, if you run our application and enter `http://localhost:8080/webstore/products/add`, you will be able to see our add products page with an extra input field to choose the file to upload.

Have a go hero – uploading product user manuals to the server

It is nice that we were able to upload the product image to the server while adding a new product. Why don't you extend this facility to upload a PDF file to server? For example, consider that every product has a user manual and you want to upload these user manuals as well while adding a product.

Here are some of the things you can do to upload PDF files:

◆ Create a directory with the `pdf` name under the `src/main/webapp/resources/` directory in your project.

◆ Add one more `MultipartFile` reference in your product domain class (`Product.java`) to hold the PDF file and change `Product.java` accordingly.

- ◆ Extend `addProduct.jsp`.
- ◆ Extend `ProductController.java` accordingly; don't forget to add the newly added field to the whitelist.
- ◆ So finally, you will be able to access the PDF under `http://localhost:8080/webstore/resource/pdf/P1237.pdf` if the newly added product id is `P1237`. Good luck!

Using ContentNegotiatingViewResolver

Content negotiation is a mechanism that makes it possible to serve a different representation of the same resource. For example, so far we have displayed our product detail page in a JSP representation. What if we want to represent the same content in an XML format, and similarly, what if we want the same content in a JSON format? There comes Spring MVC's `ContentNegotiatingViewResolver` (`org.springframework.web.servlet.view.ContentNegotiatingViewResolver`) to help us. The XML and JSON formats are popular data interchange formats that are used in web service communications heavily. So, using `ContentNegotiatingViewResolver`, we can incorporate many views such as `MappingJacksonJsonView` (for JSON) and `MarshallingView` (for XML) to represent the same product information as the XML/JSON format.

Time for action – configuring ContentNegotiatingViewResolver

`ContentNegotiatingViewResolver` does not resolve views itself but delegates them to other view resolvers based on the request. Now, let's add the content negotiation capability to our application:

1. Open `pom.xml`; you can find `pom.xml` under the project root directory itself.

2. You will be able to see some tabs at the bottom of `pom.xml` file. Select the **Dependencies** tab and click on the **Add** button of the **Dependencies** section.

3. A **Select Dependency** window will appear; enter **Group Id** as `org.springframework`, **Artifact Id** as `spring-oxm`, **Version** as `4.0.3.RELEASE`; select **Scope** as **compile**; and then click on the **OK** button.

4. Similarly, add one more dependency **Group Id** as `org.codehaus.jackson`, **Artifact Id** as `jackson-mapper-asl`, **Version** as `1.9.10`, and select **Scope** as **compile**. Then, click on the **OK** button and save `pom.xml`.

5. Add the bean configuration for `ContentNegotiatingViewResolver` in our web application's context configuration file, `DispatcherServlet-context.xml`, as follows:

```
<bean class=
"org.springframework.web.servlet.view.
ContentNegotiatingViewResolver">
```

```
      <property name="defaultViews">
        <list>
          <ref bean="jsonView"/>
          <ref bean="xmlView"/>
        </list>
      </property>
    </bean>
```

6. Now, add the bean configuration for the JSON view as follows:

```
<bean id="jsonView" class=
"org.springframework.web.servlet.view.json.
MappingJacksonJsonView">
    <property name="prettyPrint" value="true"/>
</bean>
```

7. Finally, add the bean configuration for the XML view as follows:

```
<bean id="xmlView" class=
"org.springframework.web.servlet.view.xml.MarshallingView">
    <constructor-arg>
      <bean class="org.springframework.oxm.jaxb.Jaxb2Marshaller">
        <property name="classesToBeBound">
          <list>
            <value>com.packt.webstore.domain.Product</value>
          </list>
        </property>
      </bean>
    </constructor-arg>
</bean>
```

8. Open our product domain class (`Product.java`), and add the `@XmlRootElement` annotation at the top of the class.

9. Similarly, add the `@XmlTransient` annotation at the top of the `getProductImage()` method and add another `@JsonIgnore` annotation on top of the `proudctImage` field.

10. Now, run our application and enter `http://localhost:8080/webstore/products/product?id=P1234`. You will now be able to view the detail page of the product with the `P1234` ID.

11. Now change the URL with the `.xml` extension (`http://localhost:8080/webstore/products/product.xml?id=P1234`). You will be able to see the same content in the XML format, as shown in the following screenshot:

```
This XML file does not appear to have any style
information associated with it. The document tree is
shown below.
─────────────────────────────────────────

▼<product>
   <category>Smart Phone</category>
  ▼<description>
     Apple iPhone 5s smartphone with 4.00-
     inch 640x1136 display and 8-megapixel
     rear camera
   </description>
   <discontinued>false</discontinued>
   <manufacturer>Apple</manufacturer>
   <name>iPhone 5s</name>
   <productId>P1234</productId>
   <unitPrice>500.0</unitPrice>
   <unitsInOrder>0</unitsInOrder>
   <unitsInStock>1000</unitsInStock>
</product>
```

The product detail page that shows the product information in the XML format

12. Similarly, this time change the URL with the `.json` extension (`http://localhost:8080/webstore/products/product.json?id=P1234`). You will be able to see the JSON representation of that content as shown in the following screenshot:

```
{
  "product" : {
    "productId" : "P1234",
    "name" : "iPhone 5s",
    "unitPrice" : 500,
    "description" : "Apple iPhone 5s smartphone
    "manufacturer" : "Apple",
    "category" : "Smart Phone",
    "unitsInStock" : 1000,
    "unitsInOrder" : 0,
    "discontinued" : false,
    "condition" : null
  }
}
```

The product detail page that shows the product information in the JSON format

What just happened?

Since we want an XML representation for our model data to convert our model objects into XML, we need Spring's object/XML mapping support. This is why we added the dependency for `spring-oxm.jar` in steps 1 to 3. The `spring-oxm` notation will help us convert an XML document to and from a Java object.

Similarly, to convert model objects into JSON, Spring MVC will use `jackson-mapper-asl.jar`, so we need that JAR in our project as well. In step 4, we just added the dependency configuration for that jar.

If you remember, we have already defined `InternalResourceViewResolver` in our web application context as our view resolver to resolve JSP-based views. However, this time, we want a view resolver to resolve XML and JSON views. This is why, in step 6 and 7, we configured `MappingJacksonJsonView` (for JSON) and `MarshallingView` (for XML) in our web application context.

As I already mentioned, `ContentNegotiatingViewResolver` does not resolve views itself. Instead, it delegates to other views based on the request, so we need to introduce other views to `ContentNegotiatingViewResolver`. We did that in step 5 through the `defaultViews` property in `ContentNegotiatingViewResolver`. Note that in the `ContentNegotiatingViewResolver` bean configuration, we just added the bean reference for the JSON view and XML view under the `defaultViews` property:

```
<bean class=
"org.springframework.web.servlet.view.ContentNegotiatingViewResolver">
  <property name="defaultViews">
    <list>
      <ref bean="jsonView"/>
      <ref bean="xmlView"/>
    </list>
  </property>
</bean>
```

We configured bean references for `jsonView` and `xmlView` inside `ContentNegotiatingViewResolver`.

The `xmlView` bean configuration, especially, has one important property called `classesToBeBound`, which lists the domain objects that needs XML conversion during the request processing. Since our product domain object needs the XML conversion, we added `com.packt.webstore.domain.Product` in the list of `classesToBeBound`, shown as follows:

```
<bean id="xmlView" class=
"org.springframework.web.servlet.view.xml.MarshallingView">
  <constructor-arg>
    <bean class="org.springframework.oxm.jaxb.Jaxb2Marshaller">
      <property name="classesToBeBound">
        <list>
          <value>
            com.packt.webstore.domain.Product
          </value>
        </list>
      </property>
    </bean>
  </constructor-arg>
</bean>
```

In order to convert to XML, we need to give one more hint to `MarshallingView` to identify the root XML element in the `Product` domain object. This is why, in step 8, we annotated our class with the `@XmlRootElement` annotation (`javax.xml.bind.annotation.XmlRootElement`).

In step 9, we added the `@XmlTransient` annotation (`javax.xml.bind.annotation.XmlTransient`) on top of the `getProductImage()` method and added another annotation, `@JsonIgnore` (`org.codehaus.jackson.annotate.JsonIgnore`), on top of the `productImage` field. This is because we don't want to represent the product image as part of the XML view or JSON view. Since both formats are purely text-based representation, it is not possible to represent images in texts.

In step 10, we simply accessed our product detail page in a regular way by firing the web request `http://localhost:8080/webstore/products/product?id=P1234` from the browser, and we will be able to see the normal JSP view, as expected.

In step 11, we just changed the URL slightly by adding a `.xml` extension to the `http://localhost:8080/webstore/products/product.xml?id=P1234` request path. This time, we will be able to see the same product information in the XML format.

Similarly, for the JSON view, we changed the extension by adding `.json` to the `http://localhost:8080/webstore/products/product.json?id=P1234` path, and we will be able to see the JSON representation of the same product information.

Working with the handler exception resolver

Spring MVC provides several approaches to exception handling. In Spring, one of the main exception handling constructs is the `HandlerExceptionResolver` interface (`org.springframework.web.servlet.HandlerExceptionResolver`). Any objects that implement this interface can resolve exceptions that are thrown during controller mapping or execution. The `HandlerExceptionResolver` implementers are typically registered as beans in the web application context.

Spring MVC creates two such `HandlerExceptionResolver` implementations by default to facilitate exception handling:

- `ResponseStatusExceptionResolver` is created to support the `@ResponseStatus` annotation

- `ExceptionHandlerExceptionResolver` is created to support the `@ExceptionHandler` annotation

Time for action – adding the response status exception

First, we will look at the `@ResponseStatus` annotation (`org.springframework.web.bind.annotation.ResponseStatus`). In *Chapter 3*, *Control Your Store with Controllers*, we created a request mapping method to display products by category under the URI template, `http://localhost:8080/webstore/products/{category}`. If no products were found under the given category, we would show an empty web page, which is not correct semantically. We should show an HTTP status error to indicate that no products exist under the given category. Let's see how we can do that with the help of the `@ResponseStatus` annotation:

1. Create a class called `NoProductsFoundUnderCategoryException` under the `com.packt.webstore.exception` package in the source folder, `src/main/java`. Now add the following code into it:

```
package com.packt.webstore.exception;

import org.springframework.http.HttpStatus;
import org.springframework.web.bind.annotation.ResponseStatus;

@ResponseStatus(value=HttpStatus.NOT_FOUND, reason="No products
found under this category")
public class NoProductsFoundUnderCategoryException extends
RuntimeException{

  private static final long serialVersionUID =
    3935230281455340039L;
}
```

2. Now, open our `ProductController` class and modify the `getProductsByCategory` method as follows:

```
@RequestMapping("/{category}")
public String getProductsByCategory(Model model,
@PathVariable("category") String category) {
  List<Product> products =
    productService.getProductsByCategory(category);

  if (products == null || products.isEmpty()) {
    throw new NoProductsFoundUnderCategoryException();
  }

  model.addAttribute("products", products);
  return "products";
}
```

3. Now run our application and enter `http://localhost:8080/webstore/products/HeadPhones`. You will see an HTTP status error that says **No products found under this category**, shown as follows:

The product category page that shows HTTP Status 404 for "No products found under this category"

What just happened?

In step 1, we just created a runtime exception called `NoProductsFoundUnderCategoryException` to indicate no products found under the given category. One of the important constructs that need to be noticed in the `NoProductsFoundUnderCategoryException` class is the `@ResponseStatus` annotation, which instructs the Spring MVC to return a specific HTTP status if this exception has been thrown from a request-mapping method.

We can configure the HTTP status that needs to be returned via the `value` attribute of the `@ResponseStatus` annotation; in our case, we configured `HttpStatus.NOT_FOUND` (`org.springframework.http.HttpStatus`), which indicates the familiar HTTP 404 response. The second attribute, `reason`, denotes the reason to be used for the HTTP response error.

In step 2, we just modified the `getProductsByCategory` method in the `ProductController` class to check whether the product list for the given category is empty. If so, we simply throw the exception we created in step 1, which causes the HTTP 404 status error to return to the client saying **No products found under this category**.

So finally, in step 3, we fired the web request, `http://localhost:8080/webstore/products/HeadPhones`, which would try to look for products under the **HeadPhones** category, but since we didn't have any products under the **HeadPhones** category, we got the HTTP 404 status error.

It is good that we have shown the HTTP status error for products not found under a given category, but sometimes, you may wish to have an error page where you want to show your error message in a detailed manner.

For example, run our application and enter the `http://localhost:8080/webstore/products/product?id=P1234` URL. You will be able to see a detailed view of **Iphone 5s**; now, change the product ID in the URL to an invalid one such as `http://localhost:8080/webstore/products/product?id=P1000`. You will see an error page.

Time for action – adding an exception handler

We must show a nice error message that says that no products were found with the given product ID. Let's do that with the help of `@ExceptionHandler`:

1. Create a class called `ProductNotFoundException` under the `com.packt.webstore.exception` package in the source folder `src/main/java`. Now, add the following code to it:

    ```
    package com.packt.webstore.exception;

    public class ProductNotFoundException extends RuntimeException{

        private static final long serialVersionUID =
          -694354952032299587L;

        private String productId;

        public ProductNotFoundException(String productId) {
          this.productId = productId;
    ```

```
        }

        public String getProductId() {
          return productId;
        }

    }
```

2. Now, open our `InMemoryProductRepository` class and modify the `getProductById` method as follows:

```
public Product getProductById(String productId) {
    Product productById = null;

    for(Product product : listOfProducts) {
      if(product!=null && product.getProductId()!=null &&
        product.getProductId().equals(productId)){
        productById = product;
        break;
      }
    }

    if(productById == null){
      throw new ProductNotFoundException("No products found with
        the product id: "+ productId);
    }

    return productById;
}
```

3. Add an exception handler method with the `@ExceptionHandler` annotation (`org.springframework.web.bind.annotation.ExceptionHandler`) as shown in the `ProductController` class:

```
@ExceptionHandler(ProductNotFoundException.class)
public ModelAndView handleError(HttpServletRequest req,
  ProductNotFoundException exception) {
  ModelAndView mav = new ModelAndView();
  mav.addObject("invalidProductId", exception.getProductId());
  mav.addObject("exception", exception);
  mav.addObject("url",
    req.getRequestURL()+"?"+req.getQueryString());
  mav.setViewName("productNotFound");
  return mav;
}
```

4. Finally, add one more JSP view file called `productNotFound.jsp`, under the `src/main/webapp/WEB-INF/views/` directory and add the following code snippets to it and save it:

```jsp
<%@ taglib prefix="c" uri="http://java.sun.com/jsp/jstl/core"%>
<%@ taglib prefix="spring" uri="http://www.springframework.org/
tags" %>

<html>
  <head>
    <meta http-equiv="Content-Type" content="text/html
      charset=ISO-8859-1">
    <link rel="stylesheet"
      href="//netdna.bootstrapcdn.com/bootstrap/3.0.0/
      css/bootstrap.min.css">
    <title>Welcome</title>
    </head>
  <body>
    <section>
      <div class="jumbotron">
        <div class="container">
          <h1 class="alert alert-danger"> There is no product
          found with the Product id ${invalidProductId}</h1>
        </div>
      </div>
    </section>

    <section>
      <div class="container">
        <p>${url}</p>
        <p>${exception}</p>
      </div>

      <div class="container">
        <p>
          <a href="<spring:url value="/products" />"
            class="btn btn-primary">
            <span class="glyphicon-hand-left glyphicon">
              </span> products
          </a>
        </p>
      </div>

    </section>
  </body>
</html>
```

5. Now, run our application and enter `http://localhost:8080/webstore/ products/product?id=P1000`. You will see an error page that says **There is no product found with the Product id P1000**, shown as follows:

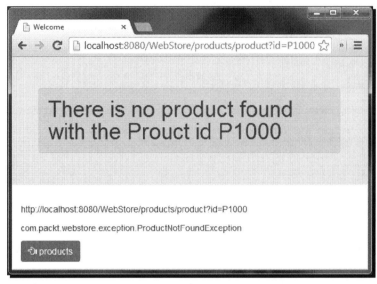

A product detail page that shows the custom error page for the invalid product id P1000

What just happened?

We thought of showing a custom-made error page instead of a raw exception in case the product is not found in the given product ID. So, in order to achieve this in step 1, we just created a runtime exception called `ProductNotFoundException` to be thrown when the product has not been found for the given product ID.

In step 2, we just modified the `getProductById` method of the `InMemoryProductRepository` class to check whether any products were found for the given product ID. If not, we simply throw the exception (`ProductNotFoundException`) we created in step 1.

In step 3, we added our exception handler method to handle `ProductNotFoundException` with the help of the `@ExceptionHandler` annotation. Within the `handleError` method, we just created a `ModelAndView` object (`org.springframework.web.servlet. ModelAndView`) and stored the requested invalid product ID, exception, and requested URL, and returned it with the view name, `productNotFound`:

```
@ExceptionHandler(ProductNotFoundException.class)
public ModelAndView handleError(HttpServletRequest req,
   ProductNotFoundException exception) {
   ModelAndView mav = new ModelAndView();
```

```
        mav.addObject("invalidProductId", exception.getProductId());
        mav.addObject("exception", exception);
        mav.addObject("url", req.getRequestURL()+"?"+req.getQueryString());
        mav.setViewName("productNotFound");
        return mav;
    }
```

Since we returned the `ModelAndView` object with the `productNotFound` view name, we must have a view file with the `productNotFound` name. This is why we created such a view file (`productNotFound.jsp`) in step 4. The `productNotFound.jsp` file just contains a CSS-styled `<h1>` tag to show the error message and a link button to the product listing page.

So, whenever we requested to show a product with an invalid ID such as `http://localhost:8080/webstore/products/product?id=P1000`, the `ProductController` class would throw `ProductNotFoundException`, which will be handled by the `handleError` method to show the custom error page (`productNotFound.jsp`).

Summary

In this chapter, we learned how `InternalResourceViewResolver` resolves views, and we learned how we can kick `RedirectView` from a controller method. We learned the important difference between `redirect` and `forward`. After that, we learned how we can host static resource files without going through the controllers' configuration. We also learned how to attach a static image file with the product details page. We learned how we can upload files to server. Finally, we saw how we can configure `ContentNegotiatingViewResolver` to give alternate XML and JSON views for the product domain object in our application. Finally, we learned how we can make use of `HandlerExceptionResolver` to resolve an exception.

In the next chapter, we will learn how we can intercept regular web requests with the help of an interceptor. See you in next chapter!

6

Intercept Your Store with Interceptor

In all the previous chapters, we have only learned how to map a request to a controller method. Once the request reaches the controller method, we execute some logic and return a logical view name that can be used by the view resolver to resolve views. However, what if we want to execute some logic before the actual request process is performed? Similarly, what if we want to execute another instruction before dispatching the response?

The Spring MVC interceptor can be used to intercept the actual request and response. Interceptors are a special web programming technique where one can execute a certain piece of logic before or after a web request is processed. In this chapter, we are going to learn more about the interceptor. We will learn the following:

- How to configure an interceptor
- How to add internalization support
- Data auditing using an interceptor
- Conditional redirecting using an interceptor

Working with interceptors

As I already mentioned, interceptors are used to intercept actual web requests before or after they are processed. We can relate the interceptor's concept in Spring MVC with the filter concept of servlet programming. In Spring MVC, interceptors are the special classes that must implement the `org.springframework.web.servlet.HandlerInterceptor` interface.

The `HandlerInterceptor` interface defines three important methods, as follows:

◆ `preHandle`: This method gets called just before the web request reaches the controller method to be executed

◆ `postHandle`: This method will get called just after the execution of the controller method

◆ `afterCompletion`: This method will get called after the completion of the entire web request cycle

Once we have created our own interceptor by implementing the `HandlerInterceptor` interface, we need to configure it in our web application context for it to take effect.

Time for action – configuring an interceptor

Every web request takes a certain amount of time to get processed in the server. In order to find out how much time it takes to process a web request, we need to calculate the time difference between the start time and end time of the web request process. We can achieve this using the interceptor concept. Let's configure our own interceptor in our project to log the execution time of each web request by performing the following steps:

1. Open `pom.xml`—you can find `pom.xml` under the root directory of the project itself.

2. You will be able to see some tabs at the bottom of the `pom.xml` file; select the **Dependencies** tab and click on the **Add** button of the **Dependencies** section.

3. A **Select Dependency** window will appear; enter **Group Id** as `log4j`, enter **Artifact Id** as `log4j`, enter **Version** as `1.2.12`, select **Scope** as **compile**, and click on the **OK** button to save `pom.xml`.

4. Create a class named `PerformanceMonitorInterceptor` under the `com.packt.webstore.interceptor` package in the source folder `src/main/java` and add the following code into it:

```
package com.packt.webstore.interceptor;

import java.text.DateFormat;
import java.text.SimpleDateFormat;
import java.util.Calendar;
import javax.servlet.http.HttpServletRequest;
import javax.servlet.http.HttpServletResponse;
import org.apache.log4j.Logger;
import org.springframework.util.StopWatch;
import org.springframework.web.servlet.HandlerInterceptor;
import org.springframework.web.servlet.ModelAndView;
```

```
public class PerformanceMonitorInterceptor implements
HandlerInterceptor {

  ThreadLocal<StopWatch> stopWatchLocal = new
    ThreadLocal<StopWatch>();
  Logger logger = Logger.getLogger(this.getClass());

  public boolean preHandle(HttpServletRequest request,
    HttpServletResponse response, Object handler) throws
    Exception {
    StopWatch stopWatch = new StopWatch(handler.toString());
    stopWatch.start(handler.toString());
    stopWatchLocal.set(stopWatch);

    logger.info("Accessing URL path: " + getURLPath(request));
    logger.info("Request processing started on: " +
      getCurrentTime());
    return true;
  }

  public void postHandle(HttpServletRequest arg0,
    HttpServletResponse response, Object handler, ModelAndView
    modelAndView) throws Exception {
    logger.info("Request processing ended on " +
      getCurrentTime());
  }

  public void afterCompletion(HttpServletRequest request,
    HttpServletResponse response, Object handler,
    Exception exception) throws Exception {
    StopWatch stopWatch = stopWatchLocal.get();
    stopWatch.stop();

    logger.info("Total time taken for processing: " +
      stopWatch.getTotalTimeMillis()+ " ms");
    stopWatchLocal.set(null);
    logger.info
("====================================================");
  }

  private String getURLPath(HttpServletRequest request) {
    String currentPath = request.getRequestURI();
    String queryString = request.getQueryString();
    queryString = queryString == null ? "" : "?" + queryString;
    return currentPath+queryString;
  }
```

```
    private String getCurrentTime() {
      DateFormat formatter = new SimpleDateFormat
        ("dd/MM/yyyy 'at' hh:mm:ss");
      Calendar calendar = Calendar.getInstance();
      calendar.setTimeInMillis(System.currentTimeMillis());
      return formatter.format(calendar.getTime());
    }


}
```

5. Now, open the web application context configuration file `DispatcherServlet-context.xml` from `src/main/webapp/WEB-INF/spring/webcontext/`, and add the following element in it and save the file:

```
<mvc:interceptors>
  <bean class=
  "com.packt.webstore.interceptor.
  PerformanceMonitorInterceptor"/>
</mvc:interceptors>
```

6. Create a property file named `log4j.properties` under the directory `src/main/resources` and add the following content to it. Then, save the file:

```
# Root logger option
log4j.rootLogger=INFO, file, stdout

# Direct log messages to a log file
log4j.appender.file=org.apache.log4j.RollingFileAppender
log4j.appender.file.File= C:\\webstore\\webstore-performance.log
log4j.appender.file.MaxFileSize=1MB
log4j.appender.file.MaxBackupIndex=1
log4j.appender.file.layout=org.apache.log4j.PatternLayout
log4j.appender.file.layout.ConversionPattern=%d{yyyy-MM-dd
HH:mm:ss} %-5p %c{1}:%L - %m%n

# Direct log messages to stdout
log4j.appender.stdout=org.apache.log4j.ConsoleAppender
log4j.appender.stdout.Target=System.out
log4j.appender.stdout.layout=org.apache.log4j.PatternLayout
log4j.appender.stdout.layout.ConversionPattern=%d{yyyy-MM-dd
HH:mm:ss} %-5p %c{1}:%L - %m%n
```

7. Now, run the application and enter `http://localhost:8080/webstore/products`. You will be able to see the performance logging in the console as follows:

```
 Console 23   Tasks  Display                                     ■ ✕ ✕ |  ▣ ▣ ▣ ▣  ▭ ▭ ▾ ▭ ▾ ▭ ▭
Tomcat v7.0 Server at localhost [Apache Tomcat] C:\Program Files\Java\jdk1.7.0_51\bin\javaw.exe (8 May, 2014 9:47:27 pm)
2014-05-08 21:47:35 INFO  PerformanceMonitorInterceptor:23 - Accessing URL path: /webstore/
2014-05-08 21:47:35 INFO  PerformanceMonitorInterceptor:24 - Request processing started on: 08/05/2014 at 09:47:35
2014-05-08 21:47:35 INFO  PerformanceMonitorInterceptor:29 - Request processing ended on 08/05/2014 at 09:47:35
2014-05-08 21:47:35 INFO  PerformanceMonitorInterceptor:36 - Total time taken for processing: 99 ms
2014-05-08 21:47:35 INFO  PerformanceMonitorInterceptor:38 - ====================================================
2014-05-08 21:48:07 INFO  PerformanceMonitorInterceptor:23 - Accessing URL path: /webstore/products
2014-05-08 21:48:07 INFO  PerformanceMonitorInterceptor:24 - Request processing started on: 08/05/2014 at 09:48:07
2014-05-08 21:48:07 INFO  PerformanceMonitorInterceptor:29 - Request processing ended on 08/05/2014 at 09:48:07
2014-05-08 21:48:07 INFO  PerformanceMonitorInterceptor:36 - Total time taken for processing: 116 ms
2014-05-08 21:48:07 INFO  PerformanceMonitorInterceptor:38 - ====================================================
```

The PerformanceMonitorInterceptor logging message is shown in the console

8. Just open `C:\webstore-performance.log`; you will see the same log message in the logging file as well.

What just happened?

Our intention was to record the execution time of every request that is being received by our web application; we decided to record the execution time in a logfile. So, in order to use a logger, we need the `log4j` library; we added the `log4j` library as a maven dependency in step 3.

In step 4, we just defined an interceptor class named `PerformanceMonitorInterceptor` by implementing the `HandlerInterceptor` interface. As mentioned previously, there are three methods that need to be implemented. We will see each method one by one. The first method is `preHandle()`, which is called before the execution of the controller method:

```java
public boolean preHandle(HttpServletRequest request,
HttpServletResponse response, Object handler) throws Exception {
   StopWatch stopWatch = new StopWatch(handler.toString());
   stopWatch.start(handler.toString());
   stopWatchLocal.set(stopWatch);

   logger.info("Accessing URL path: " + getURLPath(request));
   logger.info("Request processing started on: " + getCurrentTime());
return true;
}
```

In the preceding `preHandle` method, we just initiated a `StopWatch` class to start recording the time. In the next step, we put that `stopWatch` instance in a `ThreadLocal` variable called the `stopWatchLocal` for the purpose of retrieval later on.

> Java provides a `ThreadLocal` class that we can set/get thread scoped variables. The values stored in `ThreadLocal` are local to the thread, which means that each thread will have its own `ThreadLocal` variable. One thread cannot access/modify the `ThreadLocal` variables of other threads. Since Spring MVC is based on the servlet programming model, each web request is an individual thread.

Finally, we just logged the requested URL path and current server time with the help of `logger`. Therefore, whenever a request comes to our web application, it is first received through this `preHandle` method and initiates `stopWatch` before reaching the controller method.

The second method is `postHandle`, which will get called after the execution of the controller method:

```
public void postHandle(HttpServletRequest arg0, HttpServletResponse
response, Object handler, ModelAndView modelAndView) throws Exception
{
   logger.info("Request processing ended on " + getCurrentTime());
}
```

In the preceding method, we simply log the current time, which is considered the request processing finished time. Our final method is `afterCompletion`, which is called after the complete request has been processed:

```
public void afterCompletion(HttpServletRequest request,
   HttpServletResponse response, Object handler, Exception exception)
   throws Exception {
   StopWatch stopWatch = stopWatchLocal.get();
   stopWatch.stop();

   logger.info("Total time taken for processing: " +
     stopWatch.getTotalTimeMillis()+ " ms");
   stopWatchLocal.set(null);
   logger.info
   ("======================================================");
}
```

In the `afterCompletion` method, we retrieved the `stopwatch` instance from `ThreadLocal` and immediately stopped it; now, the `stopwatch` instance will have a record of the total time that was taken between the `preHandle` and `afterCompletion` methods, which is considered as the total time taken to complete a request. We simply logged this duration in milliseconds and removed `stopwatch` from `ThreadLocal`.

> If you don't want to implement all the methods from the `HandlerInterceptor` interface in your interceptor class, you may consider extending your interceptor from `org.springframework.web.servlet.handler.HandlerInterceptorAdapter`. This is a convenient class provided by Spring MVC as a default implementation of all of the methods from the `HandlerInterceptor` interface.

After creating `PerformanceMonitorInterceptor`, we need to register our interceptor with Spring MVC, which is what we did in step 5 through Spring's special interceptor configuration element:

```
<mvc:interceptors>
  <bean class=
  "com.packt.webstore.interceptor.PerformanceMonitorInterceptor"/>
</mvc:interceptors>
```

In step 6, we added a `log4j.properties` file in order to specify some of the logger-related configuration. You can see that we configured the logfile location in `log4j.properties` as follows:

```
log4j.appender.file.File= C:\\webstore\\webstore-performance.log
```

Finally, in step 7, we ran our application in order to record some of the performance logging, and we were able to see that the logger is working just fine via the console. You can open the logfile to view the performance logs.

So, we understood how to configure an interceptor and have seen `PerformanceMonitorInterceptor` in action. In the next exercise, we will learn how to use some of Spring's preconfigured interceptors.

Pop quiz – interceptor

Consider the following interceptor:

```
public class SecurityInterceptor extends HandlerInterceptorAdapter{

    @Override
    public void afterCompletion(HttpServletRequest request,
    HttpServletResponse response, Object handler, Exception ex)
```

```
   throws Exception {
     // just some code related to after completion
   }
 }
```

Q1. Is the mentioned `SecurityInterceptor` class a valid interceptor?

1. It is not valid because it does not implement the `HandlerInterceptor` interface.
2. It is valid because it extends the `HandlerInterceptorAdapter` class.

Q2. What is the order of execution within the interceptor methods?

1. `preHandle`, `afterCompletion`, `postHandle`.
2. `preHandle`, `postHandle`, `afterCompletion`.

Internationalization (i18n)

Internationalization means adapting computer software to different languages and regional differences. For example, if you are developing a web application for a Dutch-based company, they may expect all the web page text to be displayed in the Dutch language, use the Euro for currency calculations, expect a space as a thousand separator when displaying numbers, and "," (comma) as a decimal point. On the other hand, when the same Dutch company wants to open a market in America, they expect the same web application to be adapted for American locales; for example, the web pages should be displayed in English, dollars should be used for currency calculations, numbers should be formatted with "," (comma) as a thousand separator, and "." (dot) should be used as a decimal point, and so on.

The technique of designing a web application that can automatically adapt to different regions and countries without needing to be reengineered is called internationalization, sometimes shortened to i18N (I-eighteen letters-N).

In Spring MVC, we can achieve internationalization through `LocaleChangeInterceptor` (`org.springframework.web.servlet.i18n.LocaleChangeInterceptor`). The `LocaleChangeInterceptor` allows us to change the current locale on every web request via a configurable request parameter. In *Chapter 4, Working with Spring Tag Libraries*, we learned how to externalize text messages in the add products page. Now, we are going to add internationalization support for the same add products page (addProducts. jsp) because in Spring MVC, prior to internationalizing a label, we must externalize that label first. Since we already externalized all the label messages in the add products page (addProducts.jsp), we shall proceed to internationalize the add products page.

Time for action – adding internationalization

Technically, we can add as much language support as we want for internationalization, but for demonstration purposes, I am going to show you how to make an add product page for Dutch language support. Perform the following steps:

1. Create a file called `messages_nl.properties` under `/src/main/resources` in your project, add the following lines in it, and save the file:

    ```
    addProduct.form.productId.label = Nieuw product ID
    addProduct.form.name.label = Naam
    addProduct.form.unitPrice.label = Prijs unit
    addProduct.form.description.label = Beschrijving
    addProduct.form.manufacturer.label = Manufacturer
    addProduct.form.category.label = Fabrikant
    addProduct.form.unitsInStock.label = Aantal op voorraad
    addProduct.form.condition.label = Product Staat
    addProduct.form.productImage.label = Product image
    ```

2. Open the `addProduct.jsp` page and add the following set of tags right after the logout link:

    ```
    <div class="pull-right" style="padding-right:50px">
      <a href="?language=en" >English</a>|<a href="?language=nl"
      >Dutch</a>
    </div>
    ```

3. Now, open the web application context configuration file `DispatcherServlet-context.xml` from `src/main/webapp/WEB-INF/spring/webcontext/` and add one more bean definition for the locale resolver as follows:

    ```
    <bean id="localeResolver" class="org.springframework.web.servlet.
    i18n.SessionLocaleResolver">
      <property name="defaultLocale" value="en"/>
    </bean>
    ```

4. Now, configure one more interceptor in the web application context configuration; that means, add one more interceptor bean entry in the existing `<mvc:interceptors>` element for `LocaleChangeInterceptor` as follows:

    ```
    <mvc:interceptors>
      <bean class= "com.packt.webstore.interceptor.
    PerformanceMonitorInterceptor"/>
      <bean class= "org.springframework.web.servlet.i18n.
    LocaleChangeInterceptor">
      <property name="paramName" value="language"/>
      </bean>
    </mvc:interceptors>
    ```

5. Now, run the application and enter `http://localhost:8080/webstore/products/add`. You will be able to see the regular **Add products** page with two extra links in the top-right corner where you can choose the language:

The add product page displaying internationalization support to choose languages

6. Now, click on the **Dutch** link. You will see that the product ID label has transformed into the Dutch caption **Nieuw product ID**.

7. Since the configured `LocaleChangeInterceptor` will add a request parameter called `language` to the web request, you need to add this `language` request parameter to the whitelisting set in your `ProductController` page. Open the `ProductController` page, and within the `initialiseBinder` method, add the `language` request parameter to the whitelisting set as follows:

```
binder.setAllowedFields("productId","name","unitPrice",
"description","manufacturer","category","unitsInStock",
"productImage","language");
```

What just happened?

In step 1, we just created a property file called `messages_nl.properties`. This file acts as a Dutch-based message source for all our externalized label messages in the `addProducts.jsp` file. In order to display the externalized label messages, we used the `<spring:message>` tag in the `addProducts.jsp` file.

However, by default, the `<spring:message>` tag will read the messages from the `messages.properties` file only, but we need to make a provision for our end user to switch to the Dutch locale when they view the web page so that the label messages can come from the `messages_nl.properties` file. We provided this kind of a provision though a locale choosing link in `addProducts.jsp`, as mentioned in step 2. Consider the following code:

```
<a href="?language=en" >English</a>|<a href="?language=nl" >Dutch</a>
```

In step 2, we created two links each to choose either English or Dutch as the preferred locale. When the user clicks on these links, it will add a request parameter called `language` to the URL with the corresponding locale value. For example, when we click on the **English** link in the add products page at runtime, it will change the request URL to `http://localhost:8080/webstore/products/add?`**language=en**. Similarly, if we click on the **Dutch** link, it will change the request URL to `http://localhost:8080/webstore/products/add?`**language=nl**.

In step 3, we created a `SessionLocaleResolver` bean in our web application context as follows:

```
<bean id="localeResolver" class="org.springframework.web.servlet.i18n.
SessionLocaleResolver">
  <property name="defaultLocale" value="en"/>
</bean>
```

`SessionLocaleResolver` is the one that sets the locale attribute in the user session. One important property of `SessionLocaleResolver` is `defaultLocale`. We assigned `en` as the value for `defaultLocale`, which indicates that our page should use the language **English** as the default locale.

In step 4, we created a `LocaleChangeInterceptor` bean and configured it in the existing interceptor list, as follows:

```
<bean class= "org.springframework.web.servlet.i18n.
LocaleChangeInterceptor">
  <property name="paramName" value="language"/>
</bean>
```

We assigned the name `language` as the value of the `paramName` property in `LocaleChangeInterceptor`. The reason for this is because, if you notice in step 2, when we created the locale choosing link in the add products page (`addProduct.jsp`), we used the same parameter name as the request parameter within the `<a>` tag:

```
<a href="?language=en" >English</a>|<a href="?language=nl" >Dutch</a>
```

This way, we gave a hint to `LocaleChangeInterceptor` to choose the correct locale preferred by the user. So, whichever parameter name you planned to use in your URL, use the same name as the value for the `paramName` property in `LocaleChangeInterceptor`. And, one more thing to keep in mind is that the value you have given to the `language` request parameter in the link should match one of the suffixes of the translation message source file. For example, in our case, we created a Dutch translation message source file and named it `messages_nl.properties`. Here, the suffix is `nl`. If `messages.properties` was without any suffix, the default `en` suffix will be considered. That's why, in step 2, we gave `nl` and `en` as the values of the `language` parameters correspondingly for Dutch and English:

```
<a href="?language=en" >English</a>|<a href="?language=nl" >Dutch</a>
```

Finally, when we run our application and enter `http://localhost:8080/webstore/products/add`, we will be able to see our regular product add page with extra two links in the top-right corner for choosing the language.

Clicking on the **Dutch** link will change the request URL to `http://localhost:8080/webstore/products/add?language=nl`, which will bring `LocaleChangeInterceptor` to action and will read Dutch-based label messages from `messages_nl.properties`.

Note that if we didn't give any language parameter in our URL, Spring will use a normal message source file (`messages.properties`) for translation. If we gave a language parameter, Spring will use that parameter value as the suffix to identify the correct language message source file (`messages_nl.properties`).

Have a go hero – fully internationalize the product detail page

As already mentioned, I have internationalized a single web page (`addProducts.jsp`) for demonstration purposes. I encourage you to internationalize the product detail web page (`product.jsp`) in your project. You can use the Google Translate service (`https://translate.google.com/`) to find the Dutch translation of the labels. Along with that, try to add one more language support option of your choice.

Audit logging

Audit logging means maintaining a log record to show who had accessed a computer system and what operations they had performed. In our project, we have a web page to add products; we may need to maintain a record of who added which product on which date. We can create an interceptor to make such a log record.

Time for action – adding the data audit interceptor

Using a simple MVC interceptor, you can accomplish audit logging without making changes to your application code. Create an interceptor to record an audit log using the following steps:

1. Create a class called `AuditingInterceptor` under the package `com.packt. webstore.interceptor` in the source folder `src/main/java` and add the following code into it:

```
package com.packt.webstore.interceptor;

import java.text.DateFormat;
import java.text.SimpleDateFormat;
import java.util.Calendar;
import javax.servlet.http.HttpServletRequest;
import javax.servlet.http.HttpServletResponse;
import org.apache.log4j.Logger;
import org.springframework.web.servlet.handler.
HandlerInterceptorAdapter;

public class AuditingInterceptor extends HandlerInterceptorAdapter
{

  Logger logger = Logger.getLogger("auditLogger");
  private String user;
  private String productId;

  public boolean preHandle(HttpServletRequest request,
  HttpServletResponse arg1, Object handler) throws Exception {

    if(request.getRequestURI().endsWith("products/add") &&
    request.getMethod().equals("POST")){
      user = request.getRemoteUser();
      productId = request.getParameterValues("productId")[0];
    }
    return true;
  }


  public void afterCompletion(HttpServletRequest
  request,HttpServletResponse response, Object handler,
  Exception arg3) throws Exception {
    if(request.getRequestURI().endsWith("products/add") &&
    response.getStatus()==302){
```

```
        logger.info(String.format("A New product[%s] Added by %s
        on %s", productId, user, getCurrentTime()));
      }
    }

    private String getCurrentTime() {
    DateFormat formatter = new SimpleDateFormat("dd/MM/yyyy 'at'
    hh:mm:ss");
    Calendar calendar = Calendar.getInstance();
    calendar.setTimeInMillis(System.currentTimeMillis());
    return formatter.format(calendar.getTime());
    }

}
```

2. Now, configure one more interceptor in the web application context configuration file `DispatcherServlet-context.xml`; this means, add one more interceptor bean entry in the existing `<mvc:interceptors>` tag for `AuditingInterceptor` as follows:

```
<mvc:interceptors>
  <bean class=
"com.packt.webstore.interceptor.PerformanceMonitorInterceptor"/>
  <bean class= "org.springframework.web.servlet.i18n.
LocaleChangeInterceptor">
    <property name="paramName" value="language"/>
  </bean>

  <bean class= "com.packt.webstore.interceptor.
AuditingInterceptor"/>

</mvc:interceptors>
```

3. Open the property file called `log4j.properties` from the directory `src/main/resources` and add the following content at the end of the file and save it:

```
# Auditing Logger
log4j.logger.auditLogger=INFO, auditLogger
log4j.appender.auditLogger=org.apache.log4j.RollingFileAppender
log4j.appender.auditLogger.File= C:\\webstore\\webstore-Audit.log
log4j.appender.auditLogger.maxFileSize=1MB
log4j.appender.file.auditLogger.MaxBackupIndex=1
log4j.appender.auditLogger.layout=org.apache.log4j.PatternLayout
log4j.appender.auditLogger.layout.ConversionPattern=%d{yyyy-MM-dd
HH:mm:ss} %c : %m%n
```

4. Now, run the application and enter `http://localhost:8080/webstore/`
`products/add`. You will be able to see the regular product add page; just enter
some valid values and press the **Add** button.

5. Now, just open the audit logfile from `C:\\webstore\\webstore-Audit.log`.
You will be able to see the audit logs, which are somewhat similar to the following:

```
2013-12-17 12:11:54 auditLogger : A New product[P12345] Added by
Admin on 17/12/2013 at 12:11:54
```

What just happened?

In step 1, we just created the `AuditingInterceptor` class by extending the abstract class
`HandlerInterceptorAdapter`, and we only overrode two methods, namely, `preHandle`
and `afterCompletion`. Let's review each method in depth, one by one.

As we know, `preHandle` will be called before the controller method is executed. Inside
`preHandle`, we simply check whether the incoming request is of the type POST and whether
it tries to map the request to the add product page `products/add`. If it does, the remote
username and newly added product ID were stored in the corresponding member variables
of the `AuditingInterceptor` class:

```
public boolean preHandle(HttpServletRequest request,
HttpServletResponse arg1, Object handler) throws Exception {

    if(request.getRequestURI().endsWith("products/add") && request.
getMethod().equals("POST")){
        user = request.getRemoteUser();
        productId = request.getParameterValues("productId")[0];
    }
    return true;
}
```

In the `afterCompletion` method, we are simply logging the username and newly added
product ID after checking whether the response status is of the type `redirecting` (the
HTTP response status 302):

```
public void afterCompletion(HttpServletRequest
request,HttpServletResponse response, Object handler, Exception arg3)
throws Exception {
    if(request.getRequestURI().endsWith("products/add") &&
    response.getStatus()==302){
        logger.info(String.format("A New product[%s] Added by %s on %s",
        productId, user, getCurrentTime()));
    }
}
```

In step 2, we registered `AuditingInterceptor` with Spring MVC through Spring's special interceptor configuration tag. We want to record our related data auditing logs in a separate file. That's why, in step 3, we added a configuration related to data auditing in the `log4j.properties` file. You can see that we have configured the data auditing logfile location in `log4j.properties` as follows:

```
log4j.appender.auditLogger.File= C:\\webstore\\webstore-Audit.log
```

Finally, when we run our application and add some new products, we will be able to see the recorded data audit log entry in the `webstore-Audit.log` file.

Conditional redirecting

So far, we have seen many applications of the interceptor in Spring MVC, such as performance logging, internationalization, and audit logging. However, using interceptor, not only can we intercept the web request, but even bypass or redirect the original web request.

Time for action – intercepting offer page requests

For example, consider a situation where you want to show the special offer products page to only those users who have a valid promo code. The others trying to access the special offer products page with an invalid promo code should be redirected to an error page. Achieve this piece of functionality with the help of the interceptor by performing the following steps:

1. Create a class named `PromoCodeInterceptor` under the `com.packt.webstore.interceptor` package in the source folder `src/main/java` and add the following code into it:

```
package com.packt.webstore.interceptor;

import javax.servlet.http.HttpServletRequest;
import javax.servlet.http.HttpServletResponse;
import org.springframework.web.servlet.handler.
  HandlerInterceptorAdapter;

public class PromoCodeInterceptor extends
  HandlerInterceptorAdapter {

  private String promoCode;
  private String errorRedirect;
  private String offerRedirect;

  public boolean preHandle(HttpServletRequest request,
  HttpServletResponse response, Object handler) throws
  Exception {
```

```
      String givenPromoCode =
      request.getParameterValues("promo")==null ?
      "":request.getParameterValues("promo")[0];

      if(request.getRequestURI().endsWith
      ("products/specialOffer")){
        if(givenPromoCode.equals(promoCode)){
          response.sendRedirect
          (request.getContextPath()+"/"+offerRedirect);
        } else{
          response.sendRedirect(errorRedirect);
        }
        return false;
      }

      return true;
    }

    public String getPromoCode() {
      return promoCode;
    }

    public void setPromoCode(String promoCode) {
      this.promoCode = promoCode;
    }

    public String getErrorRedirect() {
      return errorRedirect;
    }

    public void setErrorRedirect(String errorRedirect) {
      this.errorRedirect = errorRedirect;
    }

    public String getOfferRedirect() {
      return offerRedirect;
    }

    public void setOfferRedirect(String offerRedirect) {
      this.offerRedirect = offerRedirect;
    }
}
```

2. Now, configure one more interceptor in the web application context
`DispatcherServlet-context.xml`; that means, add one more interceptor bean
entry in the existing `<mvc:interceptors>` tag for `PromoCodeInterceptor`,
as follows:

```
<mvc:interceptors>
  <bean class=
  "com.packt.webstore.interceptor.
  PerformanceMonitorInterceptor"/>
  <bean class=
  "org.springframework.web.servlet.
  i18n.LocaleChangeInterceptor">
  <property name="paramName" value="language"/>
  </bean>
  <bean class=
  "com.packt.webstore.interceptor.
  AuditingInterceptor"/>

  <bean class=
  "com.packt.webstore.interceptor.
  PromoCodeInterceptor">
  <property name="promoCode" value="OFF3R"/>
  <property name="errorRedirect" value="invalidPromoCode"/>
  <property name="offerRedirect" value="products"/>
  </bean>

</mvc:interceptors>
```

3. Open the `ProductController` class, and add one more request mapping method
to it as follows:

```
@RequestMapping("/invalidPromoCode")
public String invalidPromoCode() {
  return "invalidPromoCode";
}
```

4. Finally, add one more JSP view file called `invalidPromoCode.jsp` under the
directory `src/main/webapp/WEB-INF/views/`, and add the following code
snippet into it and save it:

```
<%@ taglib prefix="c" uri="http://java.sun.com/jsp/jstl/core"%>
<%@ taglib prefix="spring" uri="http://www.springframework.org/
tags" %>

<html>
  <head>
    <meta http-equiv="Content-Type" content="text/html;
    charset=ISO-8859-1">
    <link rel="stylesheet"
```

```
        href="//netdna.bootstrapcdn.com/bootstrap/
        3.0.0/css/bootstrap.min.css">
        <title>Invalid promo code</title>
    </head>
    <body>
        <section>
            <div class="jumbotron">
                <div class="container">
                    <h1 class="alert alert-danger">
                    Invalid promo code</h1>
                </div>
            </div>
        </section>

        <section>
            <div class="container">
                <p>
                    <a href="<spring:url value="/products" />"
                    class="btn btn-primary">
                        <span class="glyphicon-hand-left glyphicon"></span>
products
                    </a>
                </p>
            </div>

        </section>
    </body>
</html>
```

5. Now, run the application and enter `http://localhost:8080/webstore/ products/specialOffer?promo=offer`. You will see a page displaying an error message as follows:

6. Now, enter `http://localhost:8080/webstore/products/` `specialOffer?promo=OFF3R`. You will be redirected to a special offer product page.

What just happened?

The `PromoCodeInterceptor` class we created in step 1 is similar to `AuditingInterceptor`; the only difference is that we overrode only the `preHandle` method. In the `preHandle` method, we simply checked whether the incoming request was trying to access the special offer product page (`products/specialOffer`):

```
public boolean preHandle(HttpServletRequest request,
HttpServletResponse response, Object handler) throws Exception {
    String givenPromoCode = request.getParameterValues("promo")==null ?
    "":request.getParameterValues("promo")[0];

    if(request.getRequestURI().endsWith("products/specialOffer")){
        if(givenPromoCode.equals(promoCode)){
            response.sendRedirect
            (request.getContextPath()+"/"+offerRedirect);
        } else{
            response.sendRedirect(errorRedirect);
        }
        return false;
    }

    return true;
}
```

We check again whether the request contains the correct promo code as the HTTP parameter and redirect the request to the configured special offer page; otherwise, we redirect it to the configured error page.

Okay, we created the `PromoCodeInterceptor` class, but we have to configure this interceptor with our Spring MVC runtime, which is what we did in step 2, by adding the following bean definition within the Spring MVC special interceptor configuration tag:

```
<bean class= "com.packt.webstore.interceptor.PromoCodeInterceptor">
    <property name="promoCode" value="OFF3R"/>
    <property name="errorRedirect" value="invalidPromoCode"/>
    <property name="offerRedirect" value="products"/>
</bean>
```

The `PromoCodeInterceptor` class has three properties, namely, `promoCode`, `errorRedirect`, and `offerRedirect`. The `promoCode` property is used to configure the valid promo code; in our case, we assigned `OFF3R` as the valid promo code, so whoever is accessing the special offer page should provide `OFF3R` as the promo code in their HTTP parameter in order to access the page.

The next two attributes, `errorRedirect` and `offerRedirect`, are used in redirection. The `errorRedirect` property indicates the redirect URL mapping in the case of an invalid promo code, and the `offerRedirect` property indicates the redirect URL mapping for successful promo code redirection.

Note that I did not create any special offer product page. Just for demonstration purposes, I reused the same regular products page as the special offer products page; that's why, I assigned `products` as the value for the `offerRedirect` attribute, so in the case of a valid promo code, I will be redirected to the regular `products/` page. However, if I created any special offer product JSP page, I can assign that page's URL as the value for `offerRedirect`.

In step 3, we added one more request mapping method called `invalidPromoCode` to show an error page in the case of an invalid promo code. And in step 4, we added the corresponding error view file called `invalidPromoCode.jsp`.

Finally, in step 5, we purposely entered `http://localhost:8080/webstore/products/specialOffer?promo=offer` in our running application to demonstrate the `PromoCodeInterceptor` action; additonally, we saw the error page because the promo code we provided in the URL is `offer` (`?promo=offer`), which is incorrect. In step 6, we provided the correct promo code in the URL `http://localhost:8080/webstore/products/specialOffer?promo=OFF3R` so that we are able to see the configured special offer products page.

Summary

In this chapter, we understood the concept of the interceptor and learned how to configure the interceptor in Spring MVC. We learned how to do performance logging using the interceptor. We also learned how to use Spring's `LocaleChangeInterceptor` to support internationalization. Later, we learned how to do audit logging using the interceptor. Finally, we learned how to do conditional redirecting using the interceptor.

In the next chapter, I will introduce you to validation. You will learn how to do form validation and other types of custom validations.

7
Validate Your Products with a Validator

The most common expected behavior of any web application is that it should validate user data. Every time a user submits data into our web application, it needs to be validated. This is to prevent security attacks, wrong data, or simple user mistake errors. We don't have control over what users may type when submitting data into our web application. For example, they may type some text instead of a date, they may forget to fill mandatory fields, or suppose we used a length of 12 characters for a field in the database and the user entered data the length of 15 characters, then the data cannot be saved in the database. Similarly, there are lots of ways that a user can feed incorrect data into our web application. If we accept these values as valid, then it will create errors and bugs when we process such inputs. This chapter will explain the basics of setting up validation with Spring MVC.

After finishing this chapter, you will have a clear idea about the following:

- ◆ JSR-303 bean validation
- ◆ Custom validation
- ◆ Spring validation

Bean validation

Java bean validation (JSR-303) is a Java specification that allows us to express validation constraints on objects via annotations. It provides the APIs to validate and report violations. The hibernate validator is the reference implementation of the bean validation specification. We are going use the hibernate validator for validation. You can see the available bean validation annotation at the following URL:

```
http://docs.oracle.com/javaee/6/tutorial/doc/gircz.html
```

Time for action – adding bean validation support

In this section, you will learn how to validate a form submission in a Spring MVC application. In our project, we have the add products form already. Add some validation to this form by performing the following steps:

1. Open the `pom.xml` file—you can find `pom.xml` under the root directory of the project itself.

2. You will see some tabs at the bottom of the `pom.xml` file. Select the **Dependencies** tab and click on the **Add** button in the **Dependencies** section.

3. A **Select Dependency** window will appear; enter **Group Id** as `org.hibernate`, enter **Artifact Id** as `hibernate-validator`, enter **Version** as `4.3.1.Final`, select **Scope** as **compile**, and click on the **OK** button and save `pom.xml`.

4. Open the `Product` domain class and add the `@Pattern` annotation (`javax.validation.constraints.Pattern`) at the top of the `productId` field as follows:

```
@Pattern(regexp="P[0-9]+", message="{Pattern.Product.productId.
validation}")
private String productId;
```

5. Similarly, add the `@Size`, `@Min`, `@Digits`, and `@NotNull` annotations (`javax.validation.constraints.*`) at the top of the `name` and `unitPrice` fields, respectively, as follows:

```
@Size(min=4, max=50, message="{Size.Product.name.validation}")
private String name;

@Min(value=0, message="Min.Product.unitPrice.validation}")
@Digits(integer=8, fraction=2, message="{Digits.Product.unitPrice.
validation}")
@NotNull(message= "{NotNull.Product.unitPrice.validation}")
private BigDecimal unitPrice;
```

6. Open the message source file `messages.properties` from `/src/main/resources` in your project and add the following entries in it:

```
Pattern.Product.productId.validation = Invalid product ID. It
should start with character P followed by number.

Size.Product.name.validation = Invalid product name. It should be
minimum 4 characters to maximum 50 characters long.

Min.Product.unitPrice.validation = Unit price is Invalid. It
cannot have negative values.
```

```
Digits.Product.unitPrice.validation = Unit price is Invalid.It can
have maximum of 2 digit fraction and 8 digit integer.
NotNull.Product.unitPrice.validation = Unit price is Invalid. It
cannot be empty.
```

7. Open the `ProductController` class and change the
`processAddNewProductForm` request mapping method by adding an `@Valid`
annotation (`javax.validation.Valid`) in front of the `productToBeAdded`
parameter. After you are done with this, your `processAddNewProductForm`
method signature should look as follows:

```
public String processAddNewProductForm(
@ModelAttribute("newProduct") @Valid Product productToBeAdded,
BindingResult result, HttpServletRequest request) {
```

8. Now, within the body of the `processAddNewProductForm` method, add the
following condition as the first statement:

```
if(result.hasErrors()) {
  return "addProduct";
}
```

9. Open the `addProduct.jsp` page from `src/main/webapp/WEB-INF/views/`
in your project and add the `<form:errors>` tag for the `productId`, name, and
`unitPrice` input elements. For example, the product ID input tag will have the
`<form:errors>` tag beside it, as follows:

```
<form:input id="productId" path="productId" type="text"
class="form:input-large"/>
<form:errors path="productId" cssClass="text-danger"/>
```

Remember that the `path` attribute value should always be the same as the
corresponding `input` tag.

10. Now, add a global `<form:errors>` tag within the `<form:form>` tag as follows:

```
<form:errors path="*" cssClass="alert alert-danger"
element="div"/>
```

11. Add the bean configuration for `LocalValidatorFactoryBean` in your web
application context configuration file `DispatcherServlet-context.xml`
as follows:

```
<bean id="validator" class="org.springframework.validation.
beanvalidation.LocalValidatorFactoryBean">
  <property name="validationMessageSource" ref="messageSource"
    />
</bean>
```

12. Finally, assign the `validator` property value to the `<mvc:annotation-driven>` tag as follows:

```
<mvc:annotation-driven enable-matrix-variables="true"
validator="validator"/>
```

13. Now, run the application and enter `http://localhost:8080/webstore/products/add`. You will see a web page displaying a web form to add the product information; without filling any value in the form, simply click on the **Add** button. You will see validation messages at the top of the form as follows:

The Add new product web form displaying the validation message

What just happened?

Since we decided to use the bean validation (JSR-303) specification, we need an implementation of the bean validation specification. We decided to use the hibernate validator implementation in our project, so we need to add that JAR file to our project as a dependency. That's what we did in steps 1 to 3.

In steps 4 and 5, we added some `javax.validation.constraints` annotations, such as `@Pattern`, `@Size`, `@Min`, `@Digits`, and `@NotNull` to our domain class fields (`Product.java`). Using these annotations, we can define validation constraints on fields. There are more validation constraint annotations available under the `javax.validation.constraints` package. Just for demonstration purposes, I used a couple of annotations; you can check out the bean validation documentation for all the available lists of constraints.

For example, take the `@Pattern` annotation above the `productId` field; it will check whether the given value of the field matches the regular expression specified in the `regexp` attribute of the `@Pattern` annotation. In our example, we just enforce that the value given for the `productId` field should start with the character `P` and be followed by digits, as follows:

```
@Pattern(regexp="P[0-9]+", message="{Pattern.Product.productId.
validation}")
private String productId;
```

The `message` attribute of every validation annotation just acts as a key to the actual message from the message source file (`messages.properties`). In our case, we specified `Pattern.Product.productId.validation` as the key, so we need to define the actual validation message in the message source file. That's why, we added some message entries in step 6. If you noticed the corresponding value for the key `Pattern.Product.productId.validation` in the `messages.properties` file, you will notice the following value:

```
Pattern.Product.productId.validation = Invalid product ID. It should
start with character P followed by number.
```

> Note that you can even add localized error messages in the corresponding message source file if you want. For example, if you want to show error messages in Dutch, simply add error message entries in the `messages_nl.properties` file as well. During validation, this message source will be picked up automatically by Spring based on the chosen locale.

We defined the validation constraints in our domain object and also defined the validation error messages in our message source file; what else do we need to do? We need to tell our controller to validate the form submission request. We did this in steps 7 and 8 in the `processAddNewProductForm` method. Consider the following code snippet:

```
@RequestMapping(value = "/add", method = RequestMethod.POST)
public String processAddNewProductForm(@Valid
@ModelAttribute("newProduct") Product productToBeAdded, BindingResult
result) {
  if(result.hasErrors()) {
    return "addProduct";
  }

  if (result.getSuppressedFields().length > 0) {
    throw new IllegalAccessError("Attempting to bind disallowed
      fields");
  }

  productService.addProduct(productToBeAdded);
  return "redirect:/products";
}
```

We first annotated our method parameter `productToBeAdded` with the `@Valid` annotation (`javax.validation.Valid`). By doing so, we directed Spring MVC to use the bean validation framework to validate the `productToBeAdded` object—as you already know, the `productToBeAdded` object is our form-backed bean. After validating the incoming form bean (`productToBeAdded`), Spring will store the results in the `result` object, which again is another method parameter of the `processAddNewProductForm` method.

In step 8, we simply checked whether the `result` object contains any errors; if it does, we redirect to the same add product page. Otherwise, we proceed to add `productToBeAdded` to our repository.

So far, everything is fine. First, we defined the constraints on our domain object and the error messages in the message source file (`messages.properties`). Later, we validated and checked the validation result in the controller form processing method (`processAddNewProductForm`). However, we haven't mentioned how to display the error messages in the view file. We use Spring's special `<form:errors>` tag for this purpose.

We added this tag for the `productId`, `name`, and `unitPrice` input elements in step 9. If any of the input fields failed during validation, the corresponding error message will be picked up by this `<form:errors>` tag:

```
<form:errors path="productId" cssClass="text-danger"/>
```

The `path` attribute is used to identify the field in the form bean to look for errors, and the `cssClass` attribute is used to style the error message. I have used Bootstrap's style class, `text-danger`, but you can use any valid CSS style class that you prefer to apply on the error message.

Similarly, in step 10, we added a global `<form:errors>` tag to show all error messages as a consolidated view at the top of the form, as follows:

```
<form:errors path="*" cssClass="alert alert-danger" element="div"/>
```

Here, we used the `*` symbol for the `path` attribute; this means that we want to show all of the errors. And `element` attributes indicate which type of element Spring should use to list all of the errors.

So far, we have performed all of the coding-related exercises needed to enable validation, but we have to do one final configuration in our web application context to enable validation; that is, we need to introduce the bean validation framework to Spring MVC. In steps 11 and 12, we did just that; we created a bean configuration for `LocalValidatorFactoryBean` (`org.springframework.validation.beanvalidation.LocalValidatorFactoryBean`):

```
<bean id="validator" class="org.springframework.validation.
beanvalidation.LocalValidatorFactoryBean">
```

```
    <property name="validationMessageSource" ref="messageSource" />
</bean>
```

This `LocalValidatorFactoryBean` will initiate the hibernate validator when our application is being booted. The `validationMessageSource` property of `LocalValidatorFactoryBean` indicates which message source bean should look for error messages. Since we already configured a message source bean in our web application context as part of *Chapter 6, Intercept Your Store with Interceptor*, can make use of that `messageSource` bean as the value for the `validationMessageSource` property. We will already be able to see a bean definition with the name `messageSource` in our web application context.

Finally, we introduced our `validator` bean to Spring MVC through the `<mvc:annotation-driven>` tag by adding one extra property called `validator`, as follows:

```
<mvc:annotation-driven enable-matrix-variables="true"
validator="validator"/>
```

That is all we did to enable validation; now if we run our application and get the add product page using the URL `http://localhost:8080/webstore/products/add`, we will see the empty form ready to be submitted. If we submit this form without filling any information, we see error messages in red.

Have a go hero – adding more validation in the add products page

I just added validation for the first three fields in the product domain class; you can extend the validation for the remaining fields. Try to add localized error messages for the validation that you are defining.

The following are some hints that you can try out:

♦ Add a validation to show a validation message if the `category` filed is empty

♦ Try to add a validation to the `unitsInStock` field to validate that the minimum allowed number of units in stock is zero

Custom validation with JSR-303 / bean validation

In the previous *Time for action* section, we learned how to use standard JSR-303 bean validation annotations to validate the fields of our domain object. This works great for simple validations, but sometimes, we need to validate some custom rules that aren't available in standard annotations. For example, what if we need to validate that the newly added product ID is not the same as any of the existing product IDs? To accomplish such kinds of validations, we can use custom validation annotations.

Time for action – adding custom validation support

In this section, you will learn how to create custom validation annotations and use them. Add a custom product ID validation to your add product page to validate duplicate product IDs by performing the following steps:

1. Create an annotation interface called `ProductId` (`ProductId.java`) under the package `com.packt.webstore.validator` in the source folder `src/main/java`. Then, add the following code snippet in it:

```
package com.packt.webstore.validator;

import static java.lang.annotation.ElementType.ANNOTATION_TYPE;
import static java.lang.annotation.ElementType.FIELD;
import static java.lang.annotation.ElementType.METHOD;
import static java.lang.annotation.RetentionPolicy.RUNTIME;
import java.lang.annotation.Documented;
import java.lang.annotation.Retention;
import java.lang.annotation.Target;
import javax.validation.Constraint;
import javax.validation.Payload;

@Target( { METHOD, FIELD, ANNOTATION_TYPE })
@Retention(RUNTIME)
@Constraint(validatedBy = ProductIdValidator.class)
@Documented
public @interface ProductId {
  String message() default
    "{com.packt.webstore.validator.ProductId.message}";

  Class<?>[] groups() default {};

  public abstract Class<? extends Payload>[] payload() default
    {};
}
```

2. Now, create a class called `ProductIdValidator` under the package `com.packt.webstore.validator` in the source folder `src/main/java`. Then, add the following code into it:

```
package com.packt.webstore.validator;

import javax.validation.ConstraintValidator;
import javax.validation.ConstraintValidatorContext;
import org.springframework.beans.factory.annotation.Autowired;
```

```
import com.packt.webstore.domain.Product;
import com.packt.webstore.service.ProductService;

public class ProductIdValidator implements
ConstraintValidator<ProductId, String>{

  @Autowired
  private ProductService productService;

  public void initialize(ProductId constraintAnnotation) {
    //  intentionally left blank; this is the place to
       initialize the constraint annotation for any sensible
       default values.
  }

  public boolean isValid(String value,
     ConstraintValidatorContext context) {
     Product product;
     try {
       product = productService.getProductById(value);

     } catch (ProductNotFoundException e) {
       return true;
     }

     if(product != null) {
       return false;
     }

     return true;
  }
}
```

3. Open the message source file `messages.properties` from `/src/main/resources` in your project and add the following entry in it:

```
com.packt.webstore.validator.ProductId.message = A product already
exists with this product id.
```

4. Finally, open the `Product` domain class (`Product.java`) and annotate the `productId` field with the newly created `ProductId` annotation as follows:

```
@Pattern(regexp="P[0-9]+", message="{Pattern.Product.productId.
validation}")
@ProductId
private String productId;
```

5. Now, run the application and enter `http://localhost:8080/webstore/products/add`. You will see a web page displaying a web form to add the product information. Fill the complete value in the form; particularly, fill the product ID field with the value `P1234` and simply click on the **Add** button. You will see validation messages at the top of the form, as follows:

The Add new product web form displaying custom validation

What just happened?

In step 1, we just created our custom validation annotation called `ProductId`. Every custom validation annotation we create should need to be annotated with the `@Constraint` annotation (`javax.validation.Constraint`). The `@Constraint` annotation has an important property called `validatedBy`, which indicates the class that is performing the actual validation. In our case, we gave a value `ProductIdValidator.class` for the `validatedBy` property. So, our `ProductId` validation annotation will expect a class called `ProductIdValidator`. That's why, in step 2, we created the `ProductIdValidator` class by implementing the `ConstraintValidator` interface (`javax.validation.ConstraintValidator`).

We annotated the `ProductIdValidator` class with the `@Component` annotation (`org.springframework.stereotype.Component`); the `@Component` annotation is another stereotype annotation that is available in Spring. It is similar to the `@Repository` or `@Service` annotation. When our application is being booted, Spring creates and maintains an object for the `ProductIdValidator` class. So, `ProductIdValidator` becomes a managed bean in our web application context, which is the reason we are able to autowire the `productService` bean in `ProductIdValidator`.

Next, we autowired the `ProductService` object in the `ProductIdValidator` class; why did we do this? It is because inside the `isValid` method of the `ProductIdValidator` class, we used `productService` to check whether any product exists that has the given ID. Consider the following code snippet:

```
public boolean isValid(String value, ConstraintValidatorContext
context) {
  Product product;
  try {
    product = productService.getProductById(value);

  } catch (ProductNotFoundException e) {
    return true;
  }

  if(product!= null) {
    return false;
  }

  return true;
}
```

If any product exists that has the given product ID, we invalidate the validation by returning false; otherwise, we pass the validation by returning true.

In step 3, we just added our default error message for our custom validation annotation in the message source file (`messages.properties`). If you observed carefully, the key (`com.packt.webstore.validator.ProductId.message`) we used in our message source file is the same as the default key that we defined in the `ProductId` (`ProductId.java`) validation annotation:

```
String message() default
   "{com.packt.webstore.validator.ProductId.message}";
```

Finally, in step 4, we used the newly created `ProductId` validation annotation in our domain class (`Product.java`). It acts in a way similar to any other JSR-303 validation annotation.

Thus, you will be able to see the error message on the screen when you enter the existing product ID as the product ID for the newly added product.

Have a go hero – adding custom validation to a category

Create a custom validation annotation called `@Category` that will allow only some of the predefined configured categories to be entered. Consider the following things while implementing your custom annotation:

◆ Create an annotation interface called `CategoryValidator` under the `com.packt.webstore.validator` package

◆ Create a corresponding constraint validator called `CategoryValidator` under the package `com.packt.webstore.validator`

◆ Add the corresponding error message in the message source file

◆ Your `CategoryValidator` interface should maintain a list of allowed categories (`List<String> allowedCategories`) to check whether the given category exists under the list of allowed categories

◆ Don't forget to initialize the `allowedCategories` list in the constructor of the `CategoryValidator` class

◆ Annotate the `category` field of the `Product` domain class with the `@Category` annotation

After applying your custom validation annotation, `@category`, on the `category` field of the `Product` domain class, your add product page should reject the products of other categories that have not been configured in `CategoryValidator`.

Spring validation

We have seen how to incorporate the JSR-303 bean validation with Spring MVC. In addition to bean validation, Spring has its own classic mechanism to perform validation as well what is called Spring validation. The JSR-303 bean validation is much more elegant, expressive, and, in general, simpler to use compared to the classic Spring validation. However, the classic Spring validation is very flexible and extensible. For example, consider a cross-field validation where we want to compare two or more fields to see if their values can be considered as valid when combined. In such a case, we can use Spring validation.

In the last section, where we elaborated on the use of the JSR-303 bean validation, we validated some of the individual fields on our product domain object; we haven't done any validation that combines two or more fields. We don't know whether the combination of different fields makes sense.

Time for action – adding Spring validation

If you have a constraint that doesn't allow anyone to add more than 99 units of any product if the unit price is greater than 1000 USD for that product, add such a validation using Spring validation in the project. Perform the following steps:

1. Create a class called `UnitsInStockValidator` under the `com.packt.webstore.validator` package in the source folder `src/main/java`. Add the following code into it:

```
package com.packt.webstore.validator;

import java.math.BigDecimal;
import org.springframework.stereotype.Component;
import org.springframework.validation.Errors;
import org.springframework.validation.Validator;
import com.packt.webstore.domain.Product;

@Component
public class UnitsInStockValidator implements Validator{

  public boolean supports(Class<?> clazz) {
    return Product.class.isAssignableFrom(clazz);
  }

  public void validate(Object target, Errors errors) {
    Product product = (Product) target;

    if(product.getUnitPrice() != null && new
    BigDecimal(10000).compareTo(product.getUnitPrice())<=0 &&
    product.getUnitsInStock()>99) {
      errors.rejectValue("unitsInStock",
      "com.packt.webstore.validator.
      UnitsInStockValidator.message");
    }
  }

}
```

2. Open the message source file `messages.properties` from `/src/main/resources` in the project and add the following entry in it:

```
com.packt.webstore.validator.UnitsInStockValidator.message =
  You cannot add more than 99 units if the unit price is
  greater than 10000.
```

3. Open the `ProductController` class and autowire a reference to the `UnitsInStockValidator` class as follows:

```
@Autowired
private UnitsInStockValidator unitsInStockValidator;
```

4. Now, inside the `initialiseBinder` method in the `ProductController` class, add the following line:

```
binder.setValidator(unitsInStockValidator);
```

5. Now, run the application and enter `http://localhost:8080/webstore/products/add`. You will be able to see a web page showing a web form to add product information. Fill all the values in the form; in particular, fill the **Unit Price** field with the value `10000` and the **Units In Stock** field with the value `100`; now simply click on the **Add** button. You will see validation messages on the top of the form, shown as follows:

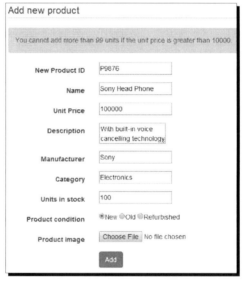

The Add new product web form displaying cross-field validation

What just happened?

In classic Spring validation, the main validation construct is the `Validator` interface (`org.springframework.validation.Validator`). The Spring `Validator` interface defines two methods for validation purposes, namely, `supports` and `validate`. The `supports` method indicates whether the validator can validate a specific class. If it can, the `validate` method can be called to validate an object of that class.

Every Spring-based validator we create should implement this interface. In step 1, we did just that; we simply created a class called `UnitsInStockValidator`, which implements the Spring `Validator` interface.

Inside the `validate` method of the `UnitsInStockValidator` class, we simply check whether the given `Product` object has a unit price greater than 1000 and the number of units in stock is more than 99; if it does, we reject that value with a corresponding error key to show the error message from the message source file, shown as follows:

```
@Override
public void validate(Object target, Errors errors) {
    Product product = (Product) target;

    if (product.getUnitPrice() != null && new
        BigDecimal(10000).compareTo(product.getUnitPrice())<=0 &&
        product.getUnitsInStock()>99) {
        errors.rejectValue("unitsInStock",
            "com.packt.webstore.validator.UnitsInStockValidator.message");
    }
}
```

In step 2, we simply added the actual error message for the error key `com.packt.webstore.validator.UnitsInStockValidator.message` in the message source file (`messages.properties`).

We created the validator, but to kick in the validation, we need to associate that validator with the controller. That's what we did in steps 3 and 4. In step 3, we simply added and autowired the reference to `UnitsInStockValidator` in the `ProductController` class. We also associated `unitsInStockValidator` with `WebDataBinder` in the `initialiseBinder` method as follows:

```
@InitBinder
public void initialiseBinder(WebDataBinder binder) {
    binder.setAllowedFields("productId","name","unitPrice",
    "description","manufacturer","category","unitsInStock",
    "productImage");
    binder.setValidator(unitsInStockValidator);
}
```

That's it! We created and configured our Spring-based validator to do the validation. Now, we run our application and enter `http://localhost:8080/webstore/products/add` to show the web form used for adding the product information. Fill the value in the form; in particular, fill the **Unit Price** field with the value `10000` and the **Units In Stock** field with the value `100`. Then, click on the **Add** button. You will see validation messages at the top of the form stating **You cannot add more than 99 units if the unit price is greater than 10000**.

It is good that we have added Spring-based validation into our application. However, since we configured our Spring-based validator (`unitsInStockValidator`) with `WebDataBinder`, the bean validation that we configured earlier will not take effect. Spring MVC simply ignores these JSR-303 bean validation annotations (`@Pattern`, `@Size`, `@Min`, `@Digits`, `@NotNull`, and so on).

Time for action – combining Spring and bean validations

You need to write the previous bean validations again in a classic Spring-based validation, which is not a good idea, but thanks to the flexibility and extensibility of Spring validation, you can combine both a Spring-based validation and bean validation together with a little extra code. Perform the following steps:

1. Create a class called `ProductValidator` under the `com.packt.webstore.validator` package in the source folder `src/main/java`. Then, add the following code into it:

```
package com.packt.webstore.validator;

import java.util.HashSet;
import java.util.Set;
import javax.validation.ConstraintViolation;
import org.springframework.beans.factory.annotation.Autowired;
import org.springframework.validation.Errors;
import org.springframework.validation.Validator;
import com.packt.webstore.domain.Product;

public class ProductValidator implements Validator{

    @Autowired
    private javax.validation.Validator beanValidator;

    private Set<Validator> springValidators;

    public ProductValidator() {
        springValidators = new HashSet<Validator>();
    }

    public void setSpringValidators(Set<Validator>
        springValidators) {
        this.springValidators = springValidators;
    }
```

```
public boolean supports(Class<?> clazz) {
  return Product.class.isAssignableFrom(clazz);
}

public void validate(Object target, Errors errors) {
  Set<ConstraintViolation<Object>> constraintViolations =
  beanValidator.validate(target);

  for (ConstraintViolation<Object> constraintViolation :
  constraintViolations) {
    String propertyPath =
    constraintViolation.getPropertyPath().toString();
    String message = constraintViolation.getMessage();
    errors.rejectValue(propertyPath, "", message);
  }

  for(Validator validator: springValidators) {
    validator.validate(target, errors);
  }
}
}
```

2. Now, open the web application context configuration file `DispatcherServlet-context.xml` and add the following bean definition to it:

```xml
<bean id="productValidator"
  class="com.packt.webstore.validator.ProductValidator">
  <property name = "springValidators">
    <set>
      <ref bean = "unitsInStockValidator"/>
    </set>
  </property>
</bean>
```

3. Create one more bean definition for the `UnitsInStockValidator` class, as follows, and save `DispatcherServlet-context.xml`:

```xml
<bean id="unitsInStockValidator"
  class="com.packt.webstore.validator.UnitsInStockValidator"/>
```

4. Open the `ProductController` class and replace the existing reference of the `UnitsInStockValidator` class with the newly created `ProductValidator` class, as follows:

```java
@Autowired
private ProductValidator productValidator;
```

5. Now, inside the `initialiseBinder` method of the `ProductController` class, replace the `binder.setValidator(unitsInStockValidator);` statement with the following statement:

```
binder.setValidator(productValidator);
```

6. Now, run the application and enter `http://localhost:8080/webstore/` `products/add` to check whether all the validations are working fine. Just click on the **Add** button without filling anything on the form; you will notice bean validation taking place. Similarly, fill the **Unit Price** field with the value `10000` and the **Units In Stock** field with the value `100` to see Spring validation. Consider the following screenshot:

The Add new product web form displaying bean validation and Spring validation together

What just happened?

Our aim was to combine bean validation and Spring-based validation (`unitsInStockValidator`) together. To achieve this, we created a common adapter validator called `ProductValidator` in step 1. If you'll look closely, the `ProductValidator` class is nothing but an implementation of a regular Spring validator.

We autowired our existing bean validator into the `ProductValidator` class through the following line:

```
@Autowired
private javax.validation.Validator beanValidator;
```

Later, we used this `beanValidator` reference inside the `validate` method of the `ProductValidator` class, as follows, to validate all of the bean validation annotations:

```
Set<ConstraintViolation<Object>> constraintViolations =
  beanValidator.validate(target);

for (ConstraintViolation<Object> constraintViolation :
  constraintViolations) {
```

```
String propertyPath =
    constraintViolation.getPropertyPath().toString();
String message = constraintViolation.getMessage();
errors.rejectValue(propertyPath, "", message);
}
```

The `beanValidator.validate(target);` statement returns all of the constraint violations. Then, using the `errors` object, we threw all of the invalid constraints as error messages. So, every bean validation annotation that we specified in the `Product` domain class will get handled within `for loop`.

Similarly, we have one more `for loop` to handle all of the Spring validations in the `validate` method of the `ProductValidator` class, as shown as follows:

```
for(Validator validator: springValidators) {
    validator.validate(target, errors);
}
```

This `for loop` iterates through the set of Spring validators and validates the entries one by one; however, if you notice, we haven't initiated the `springValidators` reference, so you may wonder where we have initiated the `springValidators` set. You can find the answer in step 2; we created a bean for the `ProductValidator` class in our web application context (`DispatcherServlet-context.xml`) and instantiated the `springValidators` set as follows:

```
<bean id="productValidtor"
    class="com.packt.webstore.validator.ProductValidator">
    <property name = "springValidators">
      <set>
        <ref bean = "unitsInStockValidator"/>
      </set>
    </property>
</bean>
```

We referred a bean called `unitsInStockValidator` within the `springValidators` set of the `productValidator` bean, so we have to create a bean for the `UnitsInStockValidator` class, which is what we did in step 3.

Then, we created a common adapter validator that can adopt bean validation and Spring validation and validates all Spring- and bean-based validations together. Now, we have to replace the `UnitsInStockValidator` reference with the `ProductValidator` reference in our `ProductController` class to kick in our new `ProductValidator` reference. We did that in steps 4 and 5. We simply replaced `UnitsInStockValidator` with `ProductValidator` in the binder, as follows:

```
@InitBinder
public void initialiseBinder(WebDataBinder binder) {
    binder.setAllowedFields("productId","name","unitPrice",
    "description","manufacturer","category","unitsInStock",
    "productImage", "language");
    binder.setValidator(productValidator);
}
```

We successfully configured our newly created `ProductValidator` with `ProductController`. To see it in action, we can just run our application and enter `http://localhost:8080/webstore/products/add`. Then, we enter some invalid values such as the existing product ID or fill the **Unit Price** field with the value `10000` and the **Units In Stock** field with the value `100`; you will notice the bean and Spring validation error messages on the screen.

Have a go hero – adding Spring validation to the product image

Create a Spring validation class called `ProductImageValidator` that will validate the size of the product image. It should only allow an image of a size that is less than or equal to the predefined configured size. Do the following when implementing `ProductImageValidator`:

◆ Create a validation class called `ProductImageValidator` under the `com.packt.webstore.validator` package by implementing the `org.springframework.validation.Validator` interface

◆ Add the corresponding error message in the message source file

◆ Your `ProductImageValidator` class should maintain a long variable called `allowedSize` to check whether the given image size is less than or equal it

◆ Create a bean for the `ProductImageValidator` class in the servlet context and add it under the `springValidators` set of the `productValidtor` bean

◆ Remember to set the `allowedSize` property in the `ProductImageValidator` bean

After applying your custom validation annotation `@category` on the `category` field of the `Product` domain class, your add product page should reject the products of other categories that have not been configured in `CategoryValidator`.

Summary

In this chapter, we learned the concept of validation and learned how to enable bean validation in Spring MVC to process forms. We also learned how to set up custom validation using the extension capability of the bean validation framework. After that, we learned how to do cross-field validation using Spring validation. Finally, we learned how to integrate bean validation and Spring validation together.

In the next chapter, we will learn how to develop an application using RESTful services. We will cover the basic concepts of HTTP verbs and try to understand how they are related to standard CRUD operations. We will also cover how to fire an Ajax request and how to handle it.

8

Give REST to Your Application with Ajax

REST *stands for* **Representational State Transfer** *and is a style of web application architecture. Everything in REST is considered as a resource, and every resource is identified by a URI. RESTful web services have been embraced by large service providers across the Web as an alternative to SOAP-based web services due to its simplicity.*

After finishing this chapter, you will have a clear idea about the following:

- ◆ REST web services
- ◆ Ajax

Introducing REST

As I already mentioned, in a REST-based application, everything, including static resources, data, and operations, are considered as resources and identified by a URI. For example, consider a piece of functionality that can help us add a new product to our store; we can represent this operation by a URI, something like `http://localhost:8080/webstore/products/add`, and we can pass the new product details in XML or JSON representation to that URL. So, in REST, URIs are used to connect clients and servers to exchange resources in the form of representations (HTML, XML, JSON, and so on). In order to exchange data, REST relies on basic HTTP protocol methods: `GET`, `POST`, `PUT`, and `DELETE`.

Spring provides extensive support to develop REST-based web services. In our previous chapters, we saw that whenever a web request was made, we returned a web page to serve that request; usually, such web pages will always contain some states (dynamic data). However, in REST-based applications, we only return the states, and it is up to the client to decide on how to render or present the data to the end user.

Normally, REST-based web services return data in two formats: XML and JSON. We are going to develop some REST-based web services that will return data in the JSON format. Once we get the JSON data, we'll then render it as an HTML page in the browser using a JavaScript library.

In our web store application, we have successfully listed some of the products; however, the store cannot make profit without facilitating the end user to pick up some products and place them in his/her shopping cart. So let's add a shopping cart facility to our store.

Time for action – implementing RESTful web services

We are going to add a shopping cart facility in two phases. Firstly, we will create a REST-style controller to handle all shopping-cart-related web requests. Secondly, we will add some JavaScript code to render the JSON data returned by the REST web service controller. First, let's implement some RESTful web services using Spring MVC controllers so that later we can add some JavaScript code to consume those web services.

1. Create a domain class named `CartItem` under the package `com.packt.webstore.domain` in the source folder `src/main/java`; then, add the following code to it:

```
package com.packt.webstore.domain;

import java.math.BigDecimal;

public class CartItem {

  private Product product;
  private int quantity;
  private BigDecimal totalPrice;

  public CartItem() {
    // TODO Auto-generated constructor stub
  }

  public CartItem(Product product) {
    super();
```

```
    this.product = product;
    this.quantity = 1;
    this.totalPrice = product.getUnitPrice();
}

public Product getProduct() {
  return product;
}

public void setProduct(Product product) {
  this.product = product;
  this.updateTotalPrice();
}

public int getQuantity() {
  return quantity;
}

public void setQuantity(int quantity) {
  this.quantity = quantity;
  this.updateTotalPrice();
}

public BigDecimal getTotalPrice() {
  return totalPrice;
}

public void updateTotalPrice() {
  totalPrice = this.product.getUnitPrice().multiply(new
    BigDecimal(this.quantity));
}

@Override
public int hashCode() {
  final int prime = 311;
  int result = 1;
  result = prime * result + ((product == null) ? 0 :
    product.hashCode());
  return result;
}
@Override
public boolean equals(Object obj) {
  if (this == obj)
  return true;
```

```
        if (obj == null)
        return false;
        if (getClass() != obj.getClass())
        return false;
        CartItem other = (CartItem) obj;
        if (product == null) {
          if (other.product != null)
          return false;
        } else if (!product.equals(other.product))
        return false;
        return true;
      }
    }
```

2. Similarly, add one more domain class named `Cart` to the same package, and add the following code to it:

```java
package com.packt.webstore.domain;

import java.math.BigDecimal;
import java.util.HashMap;
import java.util.Map;

public class Cart {

  private String cartId;
  private Map<String,CartItem> cartItems;
  private BigDecimal grandTotal;

  public Cart() {
    cartItems = new HashMap<String, CartItem>();
    grandTotal = new BigDecimal(0);
  }

  public Cart(String cartId) {
    this();
    this.cartId = cartId;
  }

  public String getCartId() {
    return cartId;
  }
```

```java
public void setCartId(String cartId) {
  this.cartId = cartId;
}

public Map<String, CartItem> getCartItems() {
  return cartItems;
}

public void setCartItems(Map<String, CartItem> cartItems) {
  this.cartItems = cartItems;
}

public BigDecimal getGrandTotal() {
  return grandTotal;
}

public void addCartItem(CartItem item) {
  String productId = item.getProduct().getProductId();

  if(cartItems.containsKey(productId)) {
    CartItem existingCartItem = cartItems.get(productId);
    existingCartItem.setQuantity(existingCartItem.getQuantity
      ()+ item.getQuantity());
    cartItems.put(productId, existingCartItem);
  } else {
    cartItems.put(productId, item);
  }
  updateGrandTotal();
}

public void removeCartItem(CartItem item) {
  String productId = item.getProduct().getProductId();
  cartItems.remove(productId);
  updateGrandTotal();
}

public void updateGrandTotal() {
  grandTotal= new BigDecimal(0);
  for(CartItem item : cartItems.values()){
    grandTotal = grandTotal.add(item.getTotalPrice());
  }
}
```

```
@Override
public int hashCode() {
  final int prime = 71;
  int result = 1;
  result = prime * result + ((cartId == null) ? 0 :
    cartId.hashCode());
  return result;
}

@Override
public boolean equals(Object obj) {
  if (this == obj)
  return true;
  if (obj == null)
  return false;
  if (getClass() != obj.getClass())
  return false;
  Cart other = (Cart) obj;
  if (cartId == null) {
    if (other.cartId != null)
    return false;
  } else if (!cartId.equals(other.cartId))
  return false;
  return true;
}
}
```

3. Create an interface named `CartRepository` under the package `com.packt.webstore.domain.repository` in the source folder `src/main/java`; then, add the following method declarations to it:

```
Cart create(Cart cart);

Cart read(String cartId);

void update(String cartId, Cart cart);

void delete(String cartId);
```

4. Create an implementation class named `InMemoryCartRepository` for the preceding interface under the package `com.packt.webstore.domain.repository.impl` in the source folder `src/main/java`; then, add the following code to it:

```
package com.packt.webstore.domain.repository.impl;

import java.util.HashMap;
import java.util.Map;
import org.springframework.stereotype.Repository;
import com.packt.webstore.domain.Cart;
import com.packt.webstore.domain.repository.CartRepository;

@Repository
public class InMemoryCartRepository implements CartRepository{

   private Map<String, Cart> listOfCarts;


   public InMemoryCartRepository() {
     listOfCarts = new HashMap<String,Cart>();

   }

   public Cart create(Cart cart) {
     if(listOfCarts.keySet().contains(cart.getCartId())) {
       throw new IllegalArgumentException(String.format("Can not
create a cart. A cart with the give id (%) aldrady exist",cart.
getCartId()));
     }

     listOfCarts.put(cart.getCartId(), cart);
     return cart;
   }

   public Cart read(String cartId) {
     return listOfCarts.get(cartId);
   }

   public void update(String cartId, Cart cart) {
     if(!listOfCarts.keySet().contains(cartId)) {
       throw new IllegalArgumentException(String.format("Can not
update cart. The cart with the give id (%) does not does not
exist",cartId));
     }
```

```
        listOfCarts.put(cartId, cart);
    }

    public void delete(String cartId) {
        if(!listOfCarts.keySet().contains(cartId)) {
            throw new IllegalArgumentException(String.format("Can not
delete cart. The cart with the give id (%) does not does not
exist",cartId));
        }

        listOfCarts.remove(cartId);
    }

}
```

5. Create an interface named `CartService` under the package `com.packt.webstore.service` in the source folder `src/main/java`; then, add the following method declarations to it:

```
package com.packt.webstore.service;

import com.packt.webstore.domain.Cart;

public interface CartService {

    Cart create(Cart cart);

    Cart read(String cartId);

    void update(String cartId, Cart cart);

    void delete(String cartId);

}
```

6. Create an implementation class named `CartServiceImpl` for the earlier interface under the package `com.packt.webstore.service.impl` in the source folder `src/main/java`; then, add the following code to it:

```
package com.packt.webstore.service.impl;

import org.springframework.beans.factory.annotation.Autowired;
import org.springframework.stereotype.Service;
import org.springframework.transaction.annotation.Transactional;
import com.packt.webstore.domain.Cart;
```

```
import com.packt.webstore.domain.repository.CartRepository;
import com.packt.webstore.service.CartService;

@Service
public class CartServiceImpl implements CartService{

  @Autowired
  private CartRepository cartRepository;

  public Cart create(Cart cart) {
    return cartRepository.create(cart);
  }

  public Cart read(String cartId) {
    return cartRepository.read(cartId);
  }

  public void update(String cartId, Cart cart) {
    cartRepository.update(cartId, cart);
  }

  public void delete(String cartId) {
    cartRepository.delete(cartId);

  }

}
```

7. Now, create a class named `CartRestController` under the package `com.packt.webstore.controller` in the source folder `src/main/java`; then, add the following code to it:

```
package com.packt.webstore.controller;

import javax.servlet.http.HttpServletRequest;

import org.springframework.beans.factory.annotation.Autowired;
import org.springframework.http.HttpStatus;
import org.springframework.stereotype.Controller;
import org.springframework.web.bind.annotation.ExceptionHandler;
import org.springframework.web.bind.annotation.PathVariable;
import org.springframework.web.bind.annotation.RequestBody;
import org.springframework.web.bind.annotation.RequestMapping;
import org.springframework.web.bind.annotation.RequestMethod;
import org.springframework.web.bind.annotation.ResponseBody;
```

```java
import org.springframework.web.bind.annotation.ResponseStatus;
import com.packt.webstore.domain.Cart;
import com.packt.webstore.domain.CartItem;
import com.packt.webstore.domain.Product;
import com.packt.webstore.exception.ProductNotFoundException;
import com.packt.webstore.service.CartService;
import com.packt.webstore.service.ProductService;

@Controller
@RequestMapping(value = "rest/cart")
public class CartRestController {

  @Autowired
  private CartService cartService;

  @Autowired
  private ProductService productService;

  @RequestMapping(method = RequestMethod.POST)
  public @ResponseBody Cart create(@RequestBody Cart cart) {
    return  cartService.create(cart);
  }

  @RequestMapping(value = "/{cartId}", method = RequestMethod.GET)
  public @ResponseBody Cart read(@PathVariable(value = "cartId")
String cartId) {
    return cartService.read(cartId);
  }

  @RequestMapping(value = "/{cartId}", method = RequestMethod.PUT)
  @ResponseStatus(value = HttpStatus.NO_CONTENT)
  public void update(@PathVariable(value = "cartId") String
cartId,  @RequestBody Cart cart) {
    cartService.update(cartId, cart);
  }

  @RequestMapping(value = "/{cartId}", method = RequestMethod.
DELETE)
  @ResponseStatus(value = HttpStatus.NO_CONTENT)
  public void delete(@PathVariable(value = "cartId") String
cartId) {
    cartService.delete(cartId);
  }
```

```java
  @RequestMapping(value = "/add/{productId}", method =
RequestMethod.PUT)
  @ResponseStatus(value = HttpStatus.NO_CONTENT)
  public void addItem(@PathVariable String productId,
HttpServletRequest request) {

    String sessionId = request.getSession(true).getId();
    Cart cart = cartService.read(sessionId);
    if(cart== null) {
      cart = cartService.create(new Cart(sessionId));
    }

    Product product = productService.getProductById(productId);
    if(product == null) {
      throw new IllegalArgumentException(new ProductNotFoundExcept
ion(productId));
    }

    cart.addCartItem(new CartItem(product));

    cartService.update(sessionId, cart);
  }

  @RequestMapping(value = "/remove/{productId}", method =
RequestMethod.PUT)
  @ResponseStatus(value = HttpStatus.NO_CONTENT)
  public void removeItem(@PathVariable String productId,
HttpServletRequest request) {

    String sessionId = request.getSession(true).getId();
    Cart cart = cartService.read(sessionId);
    if(cart== null) {
      cart = cartService.create(new Cart(sessionId));
    }

    Product product = productService.getProductById(productId);
    if(product == null) {
      throw new IllegalArgumentException(new ProductNotFoundExcept
ion(productId));
    }

    cart.removeCartItem(new CartItem(product));
```

```
        cartService.update(sessionId, cart);
    }

    @ExceptionHandler(IllegalArgumentException.class)
    @ResponseStatus(value = HttpStatus.BAD_REQUEST,  reason="Illegal
request, please verify your payload")
    public void handleClientErrors(Exception ex) { }

    @ExceptionHandler(Exception.class)
    @ResponseStatus(value = HttpStatus.INTERNAL_SERVER_ERROR,
reason="Internal server error")
    public void handleServerErrors(Exception ex) {   }
}
```

8. Now, run our webstore project from STS.

What just happened?

In step 1 and 2, we created two domain classes called `CartItem` and `Cart` to hold the information about the shopping cart. The `CartItem` class represents a single item in a shopping cart, and it holds information such as `product`, `quantity`, and `totalPrice`. Similarly, `Cart` represents the whole shopping cart itself, and `Cart` can have a collection of `cartItems` and `grandTotal`.

In steps 3 and 4, we created a repository layer to manage the `Cart` objects. In the `CartRepository` interface, we defined four methods to take care of CRUD operations (`create`, `read`, `update`, and `delete`) on the `Cart` objects. `InMemoryCartRepository` is just an implementation of `CartRepository`.

Similarly, in steps 5 and 6, we created the service layer for the `Cart` objects. The `CartService` interface has the same methods as that of the `CartRepository` and `CartServiceImpl` class; the only difference is that it internally uses `InMemoryCartRepository` to carry out all the CRUD operations.

Step 7 is very crucial in the whole sequence because in that step we created our REST-styled controller to handle all REST web services related to `Cart`. The `CartRestController` class mainly has four methods to handle web requests for CRUD operations on the `Cart` objects, namely `create`, `read`, `update`, and `delete`. Additionally, it has two methods, `addItem` and `removeItem`, to handle the adding and removing of `CartItem` from the `Cart` objects. We will have a deeper look at the first four CRUD methods.

If you see, on the surface, the `CartRestController` class is just like any other normal Spring MVC controller because it just has the same `@Controller` and `@RequestMapping` annotations. So what makes it so special to become a REST-styled controller is the `@ResponseBody` and `@RequestBody` annotations; see the following controller method:

```
@RequestMapping(method = RequestMethod.POST)
public @ResponseBody Cart create(@RequestBody Cart cart) {
   return  cartService.create(cart);
}
```

Usually, every controller method is used to return a view name so that the dispatcher servlet can find the appropriate view file and dispatch that view file to the client, but here we have returned the object (the `Cart` object). Instead of putting the object into the model, we have returned the object because we want to return the state of the object in JSON format. Remember that REST-based web services should return data in either JSON or XML format, and the client can use this data in their desired way; they may render it to an HTML page, or they may send it to some external system as is in the form of raw JSON/XML data.

Okay! Let's come to the point; the `create` controller method just returned a newly created `Cart` java object. How is it that this Java object got converted into JSON or XML format? Here, the `@ResponseBody` annotation steps into the picture. The `@ResponseBody` annotation will convert the given Java object into JSON/XML format and send it as a response in the body of an HTTP response. Similarly, when you send an HTTP request to a controller method with JSON/XML data in it, the `@RequestBody` annotation will convert it into the corresponding Java object. This is why the `create` method has the `cart` parameter annotated with the `@RequestBody` annotation and the return object annotated with the `@ResponseBody` annotation.

If you closely observe the `@RequestMapping` annotation of all those four CRUD methods, you will end up with the following table:

URL	HTTP method	Description
`http://localhost:8080/webstore/rest/cart`	POST	Creates a new cart
`http://localhost:8080/webstore/rest/cart/1234`	GET	Retrieves cart with the ID 1234
`http://localhost:8080/webstore/rest/cart/1234`	PUT	Updates cart with the ID 1234
`http://localhost:8080/webstore/rest/cart/1234`	DELETE	Deletes cart with the ID 1234

Though the request mapping URL is more or less the same, we can perform different operations based on the HTTP method; for example, if you send a GET request to the URL `http://localhost:8080/webstore/rest/cart/1234`, the `read` controller method will get executed and the `Cart` object with the ID `1234` will get returned in the JSON format. Similarly, if you send a PUT or DELETE request to the same URL, the `update` or `delete` controller method would get called correspondingly.

In addition to those four CRUD request-mapping methods, we have two more request-mapping methods that take care of adding and removing `CartItem` from the `Cart` object. These methods are considered as update methods; this is why both the `addItem` and `removeItem` methods have PUT as the request method type in their `@RequestMapping` annotation. For instance, if you send a PUT request to the URL `http://localhost:8080/webstore/rest/cart/add/P1236`, a product with the product ID `P1236` will be added to the `Cart` object. Similarly, if you send a PUT request to the URL `http://localhost:8080/webstore/rest/cart/remove/P1236`, a product with `P1236` will be removed from the `Cart` object.

Time for action – consuming REST web services

Okay! We have created our REST-style controller that can serve some REST-based web requests, but we have not seen our `CartRestController` class in action. Using a standard browser, we can only send GET or POST requests; in order to send a PUT or DELETE request, we need a special tool. There are plenty of HTTP client tools available to send such requests. Let's use one such tool called Postman to test our `CartRestController`. Postman is a Google Chrome browser extension, so you'd better install Google Chrome in your system before you download the Postman HTTP client. Perform the following steps:

1. Go to the Postman download page, `http://www.getpostman.com/`, from your Google Chrome browser and click on the **Download Postman** link. It will take you to the Chrome web store page; click on the **+ FREE** button to install the Postman tool in your browser. Consider the following screenshot:

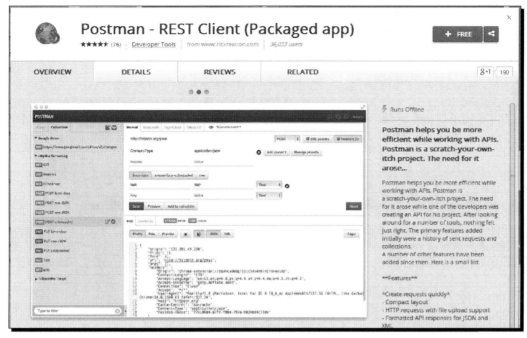

Postman—HTTP client app installation

2. Now, a Google login page will appear asking you to log in. Log in using your Google account.

3. A confirm dialog will be shown on your screen asking your permission to add the Postman extension to your browser; click on the **Add** button as shown in the following screenshot:

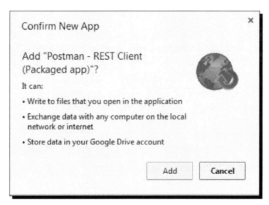

Postman—HTTP client app installation

4. Now open your Google Chrome browser and enter the URL, `chrome://apps/`. A web page will get loaded with all the available apps for your Chrome browser. Just click on the Postman icon to launch the Postman app. Before you launch Postman, ensure that your webstore project is running.

5. Now, in the Postman app, enter the request URL as `http://localhost:8080/webstore/rest/cart`, the request method as **POST**, then select the **raw** format, and finally the content type as **JSON(application/json)**. Consider the following screenshot:

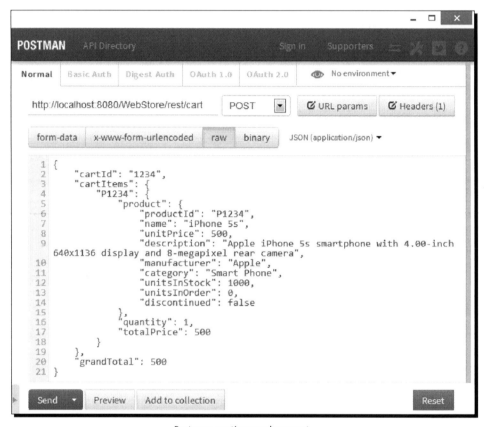

Postman–posting a web request

6. Now, enter the following JSON content in the content box and click on the **Send** button. You will get **HTTP respond status 200 OK**. Consider the following code snippet:

```
{
    "cartId": "1234",
    "cartItems": {
        "P1234": {
```

```
      "product": {
        "productId": "P1234",
        "name": "iPhone 5s",
        "unitPrice": 500,
        "description": "Apple iPhone 5s smartphone with 4.00-inch
  640x1136 display and 8-megapixel rear camera",
        "manufacturer": "Apple",
        "category": "Smart Phone",
        "unitsInStock": 1000,
        "unitsInOrder": 0,
        "discontinued": false,
        "condition": "NEW"
      },
      "quantity": 1,
      "totalPrice": 500
    }
  },
  "grandTotal": 500
}
```

7. Now, similarly in the Postman app, enter the target URL as
`http://localhost:8080/webstore/rest/cart/1234`, the request
method as **GET**, and click on the **Send** button. You will get the same JSON
cart data that you just posted in step 7 as the response.

8. To update the cart, in the Postman app, enter the target URL as
`http://localhost:8080/webstore/rest/cart/1234` and just change
the JSON data. For instance, in the content box, just change `quantity` to 3,
`totalPrice` to `1500` and `grandTotal` to `1500`, choose the request method as
PUT and the content type as **JSON(application/json)**, and send the request to the
same URL by clicking on the **Send** button. To verify whether your changes took
place, just repeat step 7. Consider the following code snippet:

```
{
  "cartId": "1234",
  "cartItems": {
    "P1234": {
      "product": {
        "productId": "P1234",
        "name": "iPhone 5s",
        "unitPrice": 500,
        "description": "Apple iPhone 5s smartphone with 4.00-inch
  640x1136 display and 8-megapixel rear camera",
        "manufacturer": "Apple",
        "category": "Smart Phone",
```

```
            "unitsInStock": 1000,
            "unitsInOrder": 0,
            "discontinued": false,
            "condition": "NEW"
        },
        "quantity": 3,
        "totalPrice": 1500
      }
    },
    "grandTotal": 1500
  }
```

9. Similarly, to delete the cart, just enter the `http://localhost:8080/webstore/`
`rest/cart/1234` URL. In the Postman app, enter the target URL and request
method as `DELETE` and click on the **Send** button. You will get an HTTP status **204 No
Content** as the response. To verify whether the cart got deleted, just repeat step 7;
you will get an empty response.

What just happened?

At the start of the chapter, we discussed that most of the REST-based web services are
designed to exchange data in JSON or XML format. This is because JSON and XML formats are
considered to be universal formats, and any system can easily understand, parse, and interpret
that data. In order to test REST-based web services that we have created, we need a tool that
can send different (`GET`, `PUT`, `POST`, or `DELETE`) types of HTTP requests with JSON data in its
request body. Postman is one such tool that is available as a Google Chrome extension.

From step 1 to 4, we installed the Postman app in our Google Chrome browser. In step 6
we sent our first REST-based web request to the target URL `http://localhost:8080/`
`webstore/rest/cart` to create a new cart in our webstore application. We did this by
sending a `POST` request with the whole cart information as JSON data to the target URL. If
you notice the following JSON data, it represents a cart with the cart ID as `1234`, and it has
just one product cart item (iPhone 5s) in it. Consider the following code snippet:

```
{
  "cartId": "1234",
  "cartItems": {
    "P1234": {
      "product": {
        "productId": "P1234",
        "name": "iPhone 5s",
        "unitPrice": 500,
        "description": "Apple iPhone 5s smartphone with 4.00-inch
640x1136 display and 8-megapixel rear camera",
```

```
            "manufacturer": "Apple",
            "category": "Smart Phone",
            "unitsInStock": 1000,
            "unitsInOrder": 0,
            "discontinued": false,
            "condition": "NEW"
        },
        "quantity": 1,
        "totalPrice": 500
      }
    },
    "grandTotal": 500
}
```

Now that we have posted our first cart, to verify whether that cart got stored in our system, we have sent another REST web request in step 7 to get the whole cart information in JSON format. Notice that this time the request type is GET and the target URL is http://localhost:8080/webstore/rest/cart/1234. Remember we learned that in a REST-based application, every resource is identifiable by a URI. Here, the URL http://localhost:8080/webstore/rest/cart/1234 represents a cart whose ID is 1234. If you send a GET request to the URL mentioned earlier, you will get the cart information in the form of JSON data; similarly, you can even update the whole cart by sending an updated JSON data as a PUT request to the same URL. This is what we did in step 8. In a similar fashion, we sent a DELETE request to the same URL to delete the cart whose ID is 1234.

Okay! We have tested or consumed our REST-based web services with the help of the Postman HTTP client tool, which is working quite well. However, in a real-world application, most of the time, these kinds of REST-based web services are consumed from the frontend with the help of a concept called Ajax. Using a JavaScript library, we can send an Ajax request to the backend. In the next section, we will see what Ajax requests are and how to consume a REST-based web service using JavaScript/Ajax libraries.

Handling a web service in Ajax

Asynchronous JavaScript and XML (Ajax) is a web development technique used on the client side to create asynchronous web applications. In a typical web application, every time a web request is fired as a response, we get a full web page loaded as a response; however, in an Ajax-based asynchronous web application, web pages are updated asynchronously by polling small data with the server behind the scenes. This means that using Ajax, it is possible to update parts of a web page without reloading the entire web page. With Ajax, web applications can send data to and retrieve data from a server asynchronously. The asynchronous aspect of Ajax allows us to write code that can send a request to a server and handle a server response without reloading the entire web page.

In an Ajax-based application, the XMLHttpRequest object is used to exchange data asynchronously with the server, where XML or JSON is often used as the format for transferring data. The "X" in AJAX stands for XML, but JSON is used instead of XML nowadays because of its simplicity; also, it uses fewer characters to represent the same data compared to XML. So, it can reduce the bandwidth requirements over the network to ensure data transfer is faster than normal.

Okay! We have implemented some REST-based web services that can manage the shopping cart in our application, but we need a frontend that can facilitate the end user to manage the shopping cart visually. So, let's consume those web services via Ajax in the frontend to manage the shopping cart.

Time for action – consuming REST web services via Ajax

In order to consume Rest web services via Ajax, perform the following steps:

1. Add a JavaScript file named controllers.js under the directory /src/main/ webapp/resources/js/; then, add the following code snippets to it and save it:

```
var cartApp = angular.module('cartApp', []);

cartApp.controller('cartCtrl', function ($scope, $http) {

  $scope.refreshCart = function(cartId) {
    $http.get('/webstore/rest/cart/'+$scope.cartId)
    .success(function(data) {
      $scope.cart = data;
    });
  };

  $scope.clearCart = function() {
    $http.delete('/webstore/rest/cart/'+$scope.cartId)
    .success($scope.refreshCart($scope.cartId));

  };

  $scope.initCartId = function(cartId) {
    $scope.cartId=cartId;
    $scope.refreshCart($scope.cartId);
  };

  $scope.addToCart = function(productId) {
    $http.put('/webstore/rest/cart/add/'+productId)
    .success(function(data) {
```

```
        $scope.refreshCart($http.get
('/webstore/rest/cart/get/cartId'));
        alert("Product Successfully added to the Cart!");
      });
    };
    $scope.removeFromCart = function(productId) {
      $http.put('/webstore/rest/cart/remove/'+productId)
      .success(function(data) {
        $scope.refreshCart($http.get
('/webstore/rest/cart/get/cartId'));
      });
    };
  });
```

2. Now, create a class named `CartController` under the package `com.packt.`
`webstore.controller` in the source folder `src/main/java`; then, add the
following code to it:

```java
package com.packt.webstore.controller;

import javax.servlet.http.HttpServletRequest;
import org.springframework.stereotype.Controller;
import org.springframework.ui.Model;
import org.springframework.web.bind.annotation.PathVariable;
import org.springframework.web.bind.annotation.RequestMapping;
import org.springframework.web.bind.annotation.RequestMethod;

@Controller
@RequestMapping(value = "/cart")
public class CartController {

  @RequestMapping
  public String get(HttpServletRequest request) {
    return "redirect:/cart/"+request.getSession(true).getId();
  }

  @RequestMapping(value = "/{cartId}", method = RequestMethod.GET)
  public String getCart(@PathVariable(value = "cartId") String
cartId, Model model) {
    model.addAttribute("cartId",cartId);
    return "cart";
  }
}
```

3. Add one more JSP view file named `cart.jsp` under the directory `src/main/webapp/WEB-INF/views/`; then, add the following code snippets to it and save it:

```
<%@ taglib prefix="c" uri="http://java.sun.com/jsp/jstl/core"%>
<%@ taglib prefix="spring" uri="http://www.springframework.org/
tags"%>

<html>
<head>
<meta http-equiv="Content-Type" content="text/html;
charset=ISO-8859-1">
<link rel="stylesheet"
  href="//netdna.bootstrapcdn.com/bootstrap/3.0.0/css/bootstrap.
min.css">

<script  src="https://ajax.googleapis.com/ajax/libs/
angularjs/1.0.1/angular.min.js"></script>
<script src="/webstore/resource/js/controllers.js"></script>

<title>Cart</title>
</head>
<body>
  <section>
    <div class="jumbotron">
      <div class="container">
        <h1>Cart</h1>
        <p>All the selected products in your cart</p>
      </div>
    </div>
  </section>

  <section class="container" ng-app="cartApp">
    <div ng-controller="cartCtrl" ng-
init="initCartId('${cartId}')">

      <div>
        <a class="btn btn-danger pull-left"
          ng-click="clearCart()"> <span
          class="glyphicon glyphicon-remove-sign"></span> Clear
Cart
        </a> <a href="#" class="btn btn-success pull-right"> <span
          class="glyphicon-shopping-cart glyphicon"></span> Check
out
        </a>
      </div>
```

```
<table class="table table-hover">
  <tr>
    <th>Product</th>
    <th>Unit price</th>
    <th>Qauntity</th>
    <th>Price</th>
    <th>Action</th>
  </tr>
  <tr ng-repeat="item in cart.cartItems">
    <td>{{item.product.productId}}-{{item.product.name}}</td>
    <td>{{item.product.unitPrice}}</td>
    <td>{{item.quantity}}</td>
    <td>{{item.totalPrice}}</td>
    <td><a href="#" class="label label-danger" ng-click="removeFromCart(item.product.productId)"> <span
        class="glyphicon glyphicon-remove" /></span> Remove
    </a></td>
  </tr>
  <tr>
    <th></th>
    <th></th>
    <th>Grand Total</th>
    <th>{{cart.grandTotal}}</th>
    <th></th>
  </tr>
</table>

<a href="<spring:url value="/products" />" class="btn btn-default">
    <span class="glyphicon-hand-left glyphicon"></span>
Continue shopping
  </a>
</div>
</section>
</body>
</html>
```

4. Open `product.jsp` from `src/main/webapp/WEB-INF/views/` and add the following AngularJS-related script links in the head section as follows:

```
<script src="https://ajax.googleapis.com/ajax/libs/
angularjs/1.0.1/angular.min.js">
</script>
```

5. Similarly, in the same head section add one more script links to our `controller.js` in the following manner:

```
<script src="/webstore/resource/js/controllers.js"></script>
```

6. Now, add the `ng-click` AngularJs directive to the Order Now `<a>` tag as follows:

```
<a href="#" class="btn btn-warning btn-large" ng-
click="addToCart('${product.productId}')">
    <span class="glyphicon-shopping-cart glyphicon"></span> Order
Now
</a>
```

7. Finally, add one more `<a>` tag as follows besides the Order Now `<a>` tag to show the **View Cart** button, then save the `product.jsp` page:

```
<a href="<spring:url value="/cart" />" class="btn btn-default">
    <span class="glyphicon-hand-right glyphicon"></span> View Cart
</a>
```

8. Now add the `ng-app` AngularJS directive to the Order Now `<section>` tag as follows:

```
<section class="container" ng-app="cartApp">
```

9. Then, add the `ng-controller` AngularJS directive to the surrounding `<p>` tag of the Order Now link as follows:

```
<p ng-controller="cartCtrl">
```

10. Now, run your application and enter the URL `http://localhost:8080/webstore/products/product?id=P1234`. You will be able to see the product details page of a product whose product ID is `P1234`.

11. Now click on the **Order Now** button; an alert message will be shown that says `Product successfully added to the cart!!`.

12. Now, click on the **View Cart** button; you will see a web page that shows a shopping cart page, as shown in the following screenshot:

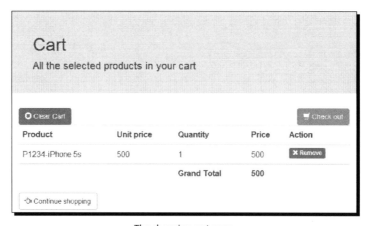

The shopping cart page

What just happened?

There are plenty of JavaScript frameworks available to send an Ajax request to the server; we decided to use AngularJs (http://angularjs.org/) as our frontend JavaScript library to send Ajax requests. It also has the concepts of Model, View, Controller, and so on, but the only difference is that it is designed to work in the frontend using JavaScript.

In step 1, we created our AngularJS-based controller called `controllers.js` in `/src/main/webapp/resources/js/`. Remember that we purposely put this file under the `resources` directory because from the client side, we want to access this file as a static resource; we don't want to go through Spring MVC controllers in order to get this file. If you remember correctly, we have already configured the location of the Spring MVC's resources in `DispatcherServlet-context.xml` in the previous chapters; it was done in the following manner:

```
<mvc:resources  location="/resources/"  mapping="/resource/**"/>
```

Okay! Let's get to the point; what have we written in `controllers.js`? We have written five frontend controller methods, namely `refreshCart`, `clearCart`, `initCartId`, `addToCart`, and `removeFromCart`. These methods are used to communicate with the server using Ajax calls. For example, consider the following controller method:

```
$scope.refreshCart = function(cartId) {
  $http.get('/webstore/rest/cart/'+$scope.cartId)
  .success(function(data) {
    $scope.cart = data;
  });
};
```

Within the `refreshCart` method, using AngularJS' `$http` object, we sent an HTTP GET request to the URI template `/webstore/rest/cart/'+$scope.cartId`. Based on the value stored in the `$scope.cartId` variable, the actual request is sent to the target REST URL. For instance, if `$scope.cartId` contains a value of `1234`, then a GET request will be sent to `http://localhost:8080/webstore/rest/cart/1234` to get a `cart` object as JSON data whose ID is `1234`. Once we got the `cart` object as JSON data, we stored it in the frontend Angular model using the `$scope` object as follows:

```
.success(function(data) {
  $scope.cart = data;
}
```

Similarly, all other AngularJS controller methods fire some Ajax web requests to the server, and retrieve or update `cart`. For example, the `addToCart` and `removeFromCart` methods just added `cartItem` and removed `cartItem` from the `cart` object.

We have just defined our AngularJS controller methods, but we have to invoke this method in order to do something useful. This is what we did in step 2; we just defined our regular Spring MVC controller named `CartController`, which has two request mapping methods, namely `get` and `getCart`. Whenever a usual web request comes to the URL `http://localhost:8080/webstore/cart`, the `get` method will be invoked, and inside the `get` method, we retrieved the session ID and used it as a cart ID to invoke the `getCart` method. Here we maintained the session ID as a cart ID. Consider the following code snippet:

```
@RequestMapping
public String get(HttpServletRequest request) {
  return "redirect:/cart/"+request.getSession(true).getId();
}
```

Within the `getCart` method, we simply stored `cartId` in the Spring MVC model and returned a view name as `cart`. We did this kind of setup because we want our application to redirect the request to the correct cart based on the session ID whenever a request comes to `http://localhost:8080/webstore/cart`. Since we have returned a view name as `cart`, our dispatcher servlet definitely would look for a view file called `cart.jsp`. This is why we created the `cart.jsp` file in step 3.

The `cart.jsp` file just acts as a template for our shopping cart page. The `cart.jsp` page internally uses the AngularJs controller's methods that we created in step 1 to communicate with the server. The `ng-repeat` directive of AngularJS would repeat the HTML table rows dynamically based on `cartItems` that are available in `cart`:

```
<tr ng-repeat="item in cart.cartItems">
  <td>{{item.product.productId}}-{{item.product.name}}</td>
  <td>{{item.product.unitPrice}}</td>
  <td>{{item.quantity}}</td>
  <td>{{item.totalPrice}}</td>
  <td><a href="#" class="label label-danger" ng-
click="removeFromCart(item.product.productId)">
    <span class="glyphicon glyphicon-remove" /></span> Remove
  </a></td>
</tr>
```

The `ng-click` directive from the remove `<a>` tag will call the `removeFromCart` controller method. Similarly, to add `cartItem` to the cart, in `product.jsp`, we added another `ng-click` directive in step 6 to invoke the `addToCart` method; we did this in the following manner:

```
<a href="#" class="btn btn-warning btn-large" ng-
click="addToCart('${product.productId}')"> <span
    class="glyphicon-shopping-cart glyphicon"></span> Order Now
</a>
```

So that's it! We have done everything to roll out our shopping cart in our application, After running our application, we can access our shopping cart under the URL `http://localhost:8080/webstore/cart` and we can even add products to the cart from each product details page as well.

Summary

In this chapter, we learned how to develop REST-based web services using Spring MVC, and we also learned how to test those web services using the Postman HTTP client tool. We also covered the basic concepts of HTTP verbs and understood how it is related to standard CRUD operations. Finally, we learned how to use the AngularJs JavaScript framework to send an Ajax request to our server.

In the next chapter, we will see how to integrate tiles and webflow frameworks.

9

Apache Tiles and
Spring Web Flow in Action

*When it comes to web application development, reusability and maintenance
are two important factors that need to be considered. Spring Web Flow is an
independent framework that facilitates you to develop highly configurable and
maintainable flow-based web applications. On the other hand, Apache Tiles is
another popular open source framework that encourages the use of reusable
template-based web application development.*

In this chapter, we are going to learn how to incorporate these two frameworks within a Spring
MVC application so that we can obtain maximum reusability of frontend templates with the
help of Apache Tiles and less maintenance in our application logic with the help of Spring
Web Flow. Again, remember that these two frameworks are totally independent; there is no
requirement that we should always use these frameworks together. Apache Tiles is mostly used
to reduce redundant code in the frontend by leveraging frontend templates, whereas Spring
Web Flow facilitates the development of a stateful web application with controlled navigation
flow. After finishing this chapter, you will have a clear idea about the following concepts:

◆   Developing flow-based applications using Spring Web Flow
◆   Decomposing pages using reusable Apache Tiles templates

Working with Spring Web Flow

Spring Web Flow facilitates us to develop a flow-based web application easily. A flow in a web application encapsulates a series of steps that guides a user through the execution of a business task, such as checking in to a hotel, applying for a job, and shopping cart checkout. Usually, a flow will have a clear start and end point. It includes multiple HTTP requests/responses, and the user must go through a set of screens in a specific order to complete the flow.

In all our previous chapters—the responsibility of defining the page (user interface) flow specifically lies on controllers—we weaved the page flows into individual controllers and views; for instance, we usually mapped a web request to a controller, and the controller was the one that decided which logical view needed to be returned as a response. This is simple to understand and sufficient for straightforward page flows, but when web applications get more and more complex in terms of user interface flows, maintaining a large and complex page flow becomes a nightmare.

If you are going to develop such a complex flow-based application, then **Spring Web Flow (SWF)** can be a good companion. Spring Web Flow allows you to define and execute **user interface (UI)** flows within your web application. Without further ado, let's dive straight into Spring Web Flow by defining some page flows in our project.

It is nice that we have implemented the shopping cart in our previous chapter; however, it is of no use if we do not provide a checkout facility to complete the processing of the order and then ship the products to the right customers. Let's do that in two phases. Firstly, let's create the required backend services, domain objects, and repository implementation in order to complete the order processing (here, strictly nothing related to Spring Web Flow is involved; it is just a supportive backend service that can be used later by the web flow definition in order to complete the checkout process). Secondly, we need to define the actual Spring Web Flow definition that can use our backend services in order to execute the flow definition. Here, we will set the configuration and definition of the actual web flow.

Time for action – implementing the order-processing service

We will start with implementing our order processing backend service first.
We proceed as follows:

1. Create a class named `Address` under the `com.packt.webstore.domain` package in the source folder `src/main/java` and add the following code into it. Note that I have skipped the getters, setters, equals, and hashcode methods in the following snippet. Please do add those when you create this class:

    ```
    package com.packt.webstore.domain;

    import java.io.Serializable;
    ```

```
public class Address implements Serializable{

  private static final long serialVersionUID =
-530086768384258062L;

  private String doorNo;
  private String streetName;
  private String areaName;
  private String state;
  private String country;
  private String zipCode;

  // add getters and setters for all the fields here.
  // Override equals and hashCode based on all the fields.
    // the code for the same is available in the code bundle which
can be downloaded from www.packtpub.com/support
  }
```

2. Create another class named `Customer` under the same package and add the following code into it:

```
package com.packt.webstore.domain;

import java.io.Serializable;

public class Customer implements Serializable{

  private static final long serialVersionUID =
2284040482222162898L;

  private String customerId;
  private String name;
  private Address billingAddress;
  private String phoneNumber;

  public Customer() {
    super();
    this.billingAddress = new Address();
  }

  public Customer(String customerId, String name) {
    this();
    this.customerId = customerId;
    this.name = name;
  }
```

```
    // add getters and setters for all the fields here.
    // Override equals and hashCode based on customerId field.
        // the code for the same is available in the code bundle which
    can be downloaded from www.packtpub.com/support


    }
```

3. Create one more domain class named `ShippingDetail` under the same package and add the following code into it:

```
package com.packt.webstore.domain;

import java.io.Serializable;
import java.util.Date;
import org.springframework.format.annotation.DateTimeFormat;

public class ShippingDetail implements Serializable{

    private static final long serialVersionUID =
6350930334140807514L;

    private String name;
    @DateTimeFormat(pattern = "dd/MM/yyyy")
    private Date shippingDate;
    private Address shippingAddress;


    public ShippingDetail() {
        this.shippingAddress = new Address();
    }

    // add getters and setters for all the fields here.
}
```

4. Similarly, create our final domain class named `Order` under the same package and add the following code into it:

```
package com.packt.webstore.domain;

import java.io.Serializable;

public class Order  implements Serializable{

    private static final long serialVersionUID =
-3560539622417210365L;
```

```
private Long orderId;
private Cart cart;
private Customer customer;
private ShippingDetail shippingDetail;

public Order() {
  this.customer = new Customer();
  this.shippingDetail = new ShippingDetail();
}

// add getters and setters for all the fields here.
// Override equals and hashCode based on orderId field.
  // the code for the same is available in the code bundle
which can be downloaded from www.packtpub.com/support
}
```

5. Now make the `Product, CartItem,` and `Cart` domain classes serializable by implementing the `Serializable` interface (`java.io.Serializable`) for all of these classes; we also need to add a `serialVersionUID` field to each of the earlier mentioned classes as well.

6. Next, create an interface named `OrderRepository` under the `com.packt.webstore.domain.repository` package in the source folder `src/main/java`, and add a single method declaration to it as follows:

```
Long saveOrder(Order order);
```

7. Create an implementation class called `InMemoryOrderRepositoryImpl` under the `com.packt.webstore.domain.repository.impl` package in the source folder `src/main/java` and add the following code into it:

```
package com.packt.webstore.domain.repository.impl;

import java.util.HashMap;
import java.util.Map;
import org.springframework.stereotype.Repository;
import com.packt.webstore.domain.Order;
import com.packt.webstore.domain.repository.OrderRepository;

@Repository
public class InMemoryOrderRepositoryImpl implements
OrderRepository{

  private Map<Long, Order> listOfOrders;
  private long nextOrderId;
```

```
public InMemoryOrderRepositoryImpl() {
  listOfOrders = new HashMap<Long, Order>();
  nextOrderId = 1000;
}

public Long saveOrder(Order order) {
  order.setOrderId(getNextOrderId());
  listOfOrders.put(order.getOrderId(), order);
  return order.getOrderId();
}

private synchronized long getNextOrderId() {
  return nextOrderId++;
}
}
```

8. Now, open the `OrderService` interface from the `com.packt.webstore.`
   `service` package in the source folder `src/main/java` and add single method
   declarations to it as follows:

```
package com.packt.webstore.domain.repository;

import com.packt.webstore.domain.Order;

public interface OrderRepository {
  Long saveOrder(Order order);
}
}
```

9. Next, open the implementation class `OrderServiceImpl` from the `com.packt.`
   `webstore.service.impl` package in the source folder `src/main/java` and add
   the following two autowired references to it:

```
@Autowired
private OrderRepository orderRepository;

@Autowired
private CartService cartService;
```

10. Now add a method implementation for the `saveOrder` method as follows in the
    `OrderServiceImpl` class:

```
public Long saveOrder(Order order) {
  Long orderId = orderRepository.saveOrder(order);
  cartService.delete(order.getCart().getCartId());
  return orderId;
}
```

11. Next, create an exception class called `InvalidCartException` under the `com.packt.webstore.exception` package in the source folder `src/main/java` and add the following code into it:

```
package com.packt.webstore.exception;

public class InvalidCartException extends RuntimeException {

  private static final long serialVersionUID =
-5192041563033358491L;
  private String cartId;

  public InvalidCartException(String cartId) {
    this.cartId = cartId;
  }

  public String getCartId() {
    return cartId;
  }
}
```

12. Now, open the `CartService` interface from the `com.packt.webstore.service` package in the source folder `src/main/java` and add one more method declaration to it as follows:

```
Cart validate(String cartId);
```

13. Next, open the implementation class `CartServiceImpl` from the package `com.packt.webstore.service.impl` in the source folder `src/main/java` and add a method implementation for the `validate` method as follows:

```
public Cart validate(String cartId) {
  Cart cart = cartRepository.read(cartId);
  if(cart==null || cart.getCartItems().size()==0) {
    throw new InvalidCartException(cartId);
  }

  return cart;
}
```

What just happened?

What we have done so far is familiar to you I guess; we created some domain classes (`Address`, `Customer`, `ShippingDetail`, and `Order`) as well as an `OrderRepository` interface and its implementation class `InMemoryOrderRepositoryImpl` to store the processed `Order` domain objects. Finally, we also created the corresponding `OrderService` interface and its implementation class, namely `OrderServiceImpl`.

On the surface, it looks as usual, but there are some minute details that need to be explained. If you notice, all the domain classes we created from steps 1 to 4 have just implemented the Serializable interface; not only that, we even implemented the Serializable interface for other existing domain classes as well, such as Product, CartItem, and Cart in step 5. This is because later we will use these domain objects in Spring Web Flow, and Spring Web Flow will store these domain objects in a session to manage the state between page flows. Session data could be saved into a disk or transferred to another web server during clustering. So, while bringing back the session object from the disk, Spring Web Flow will deserialize the domain object (form-backing bean) to maintain the state of the page. That's why it is a must to serialize the domain object / form backing bean. Spring Web Flow uses a term called Snapshot to mention these states within a session.

The remaining steps from step 6 to 13 are self-explanatory. We created the OrderRepository and OrderService interfaces and their corresponding InMemoryOrderRepositoryImpl and OrderServiceImpl implementations. The purpose of these classes is to save the Order domain object. The saveOrder method from OrderServiceImpl just deletes the corresponding Cart object from CartRepository after successfully saving the order domain object. Now, we have successfully created all the required backend services and domain objects in order to kick off the configuration and definition of our Spring Web Flow.

Time for action – implementing the checkout flow

We will now add Spring Web Flow support to our project and define the checkout flow for our shopping cart. Consider the following steps:

1. Open pom.xml; you will find pom.xml under the root directory of the project.

2. You will be able to see some tabs at the bottom of the pom.xml file. Select the **Dependencies** tab and click on the **Add** button in the **Dependencies** section.

3. A **Select Dependency** window will appear; enter **Group Id** as org.springframework.webflow, **Artifact Id** as spring-webflow, **Version** as 2.3.3.RELEASE, select **Scope** as **compile**, and click on the **OK** button and save pom.xml.

4. Create a directory structure, flows/checkout/, under the directory src/main/webapp/WEB-INF/ and create an XML file called checkout-flow.xml. Then, add the following content into it and save it:

```xml
<?xml version="1.0" encoding="UTF-8"?>
<flow xmlns="http://www.springframework.org/schema/webflow"
xmlns:xsi="http://www.w3.org/2001/XMLSchema-instance"
xsi:schemaLocation="http://www.springframework.org/schema/webflow
http://www.springframework.org/schema/webflow/spring-webflow.xsd">
```

```xml
  <var name="order" class="com.packt.webstore.domain.Order" />

  <action-state id="addCartToOrder">
    <evaluate expression="cartServiceImpl.
validate(requestParameters.cartId)"
      result="order.cart" />
    <transition to="InvalidCartWarning"
      on-exception="com.packt.webstore.exception.
InvalidCartException" />
    <transition to="collectCustomerInfo" />
  </action-state>

  <view-state id="collectCustomerInfo" view="collectCustomerInfo.
jsp" model="order">
    <transition on="customerInfoCollected"
to="collectShippingDetail" />
  </view-state>

  <view-state id="collectShippingDetail" model="order">
    <transition on="shippingDetailCollected"
to="orderConfirmation" />
    <transition on="backToCollectCustomerInfo"
to="collectCustomerInfo" />
  </view-state>

  <view-state id="orderConfirmation">
    <transition on="orderConfirmed" to="processOrder" />
    <transition on="backToCollectShippingDetail"
to="collectShippingDetail" />
  </view-state>

  <action-state id="processOrder">
    <evaluate expression="orderServiceImpl.saveOrder(order)"
result="order.orderId"/>
    <transition to="thankCustomer" />
  </action-state>

  <view-state id="InvalidCartWarning">
    <transition to="endState"/>
  </view-state>

  <view-state id="thankCustomer" model="order">
    <transition to="endState"/>
  </view-state>
```

```
<end-state id="endState"/>

<end-state id="cancelCheckout" view = "checkOutCancelled.jsp"/>

<global-transitions>
  <transition on = "cancel" to="endState" />
</global-transitions>

</flow>
```

5. Now open the web application context configuration file `DispatcherServlet-context.xml` and add the following web flow namespace attribute to the `<beans>` tag at the top:

```
xmlns:webflow-config="http://www.springframework.org/schema/
webflow-config"
```

6. Append the following schema location entry to the existing `xsi:schemaLocation` attribute of the `<beans>` tag:

```
http://www.springframework.org/schema/webflow-config http://www.
springframework.org/schema/webflow-config/spring-webflow-config-
2.3.xsd
```

7. Now add the following web flow configuration tags to the web application context configuration file (`DispatcherServlet-context.xml`):

```
<webflow-config:flow-executor id="flowExecutor"  flow-
registry="flowRegistry" />

<webflow-config:flow-registry id="flowRegistry"  base-path="/WEB-
INF/flows">
  <webflow-config:flow-location path="/checkout/checkout-flow.xml"
id="checkout"/>
</webflow-config:flow-registry>
```

8. Finally, define the beans for `FlowHandlerMapping` and `FlowHandlerAdapter` in `DispatcherServlet-context.xml` as follows and save the file:

```
<bean id="flowHandlerMapping" class="org.springframework.webflow.
mvc.servlet.FlowHandlerMapping">
    <property name="flowRegistry" ref="flowRegistry" />
  </bean>

<bean id="flowHandlerAdapter" class="org.springframework.webflow.
mvc.servlet.FlowHandlerAdapter">
    <property name="flowExecutor" ref="flowExecutor" />
</bean>
```

What just happened?

From steps 1 to 3, we just added the Spring Web Flow dependency to our project through a Maven configuration. It will download and configure all the required jars related to web flow in our project. In step 4, we created our first flow definition file called `checkout-flow.xml` under the directory `/src/main/webapp/WEB-INF/flows/checkout/`.

Spring Web Flow uses the flow definition file as a basis to execute the flow. In order to understand what has been written in this file, we need to get a clear idea about some of the basic concepts of Spring Web Flow. We will learn about those concepts a little bit and then we will come back to `checkout-flow.xml` to understand it.

Understanding the flow definition

A flow definition is composed of a set of states. Each state will have a unique ID in the flow definition. There are six types of states available in Spring Web Flow:

♦ `start-state`: Each flow must have a single start state that helps in the creation of the initial state of the flow. Note that if the start state is not specified, the very first defined state within the flow definition file becomes the start state.

♦ `action-state`: A flow can have many action states, and an action state executes a particular action. An action normally involves interaction with backend services, such as executing some methods in a Spring-managed bean; Spring Web Flow uses **Spring Expression Language** to interact with backend service beans.

♦ `view-state`: A view state defines a logical view and model to interact with the end user. A web flow can have multiple view states. If the `view` attribute is not specified, then the ID of the view state acts as the logical view name.

♦ `decision-state`: The decision state is used to branch the flow; based on the test condition, it routes the transition to the next possible state.

♦ `subflow-state`: A subflow is an independent flow that can be reused from inside another flow. When an application enters a subflow, the main flow is paused until the concerned subflow is completed.

♦ `end-state`: An end state denotes the end of a flow's execution. A web flow can have multiple end states, and through the `view` attribute of `end-state`, we can specify a view that will be rendered when the end state is reached.

We have just learned that a flow definition is composed of a set of states, but in order to make a move from one state to another, we need to define transitions in these states. Each state in a web flow (except for the start and end states) defines a number of transitions to move from one state to another. A transition can be triggered by an event that is signaled from the state.

Understanding the checkout flow

Okay! We just got the minimum required introduction for Spring Web Flow concepts. There are plenty of advanced concepts out there to master in Spring Web Flow; we are not going to look at all of those because that itself deserves a separate book. As of now, it is enough to understand the `checkout-flow.xml` flow definition file. However, before we do this, we will have a quick overview of our checkout flow. The following diagram will give you the overall idea of the checkout flow that we have just implemented:

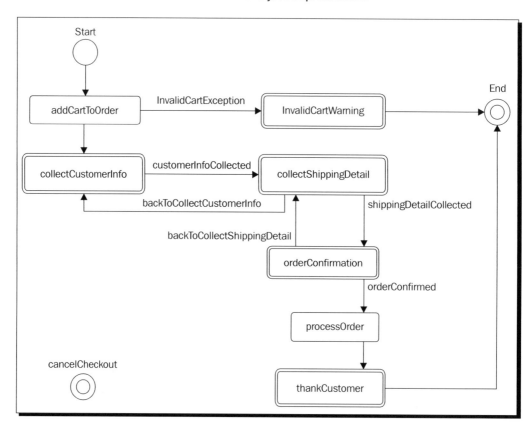

Our checkout flow diagram has a start state and an end state; each rounded rectangle in the diagram defines an action state, and each double-line-bordered rounded rectangle defines a view state. Similarly, each arrowed line defines a transition, and the name associated with it defines the event that causes that particular transition. The `checkout-flow.xml` file just contains the earlier mentioned flow in an XML representation.

If you open the `checkout-flow.xml` file, the first tag you will encounter within the `<flow>` tag is the `<var>` tag:

```
<var name="order" class="com.packt.webstore.domain.Order" />
```

The `<var>` tag creates a variable in a flow. This variable will be available to all the states in a flow, which means we can reference and use this variable inside any state within the flow. In the just mentioned `<var>` tag, we created a new instance of the `Order` class and stored it in a variable called `order`.

The next thing we defined within the `checkout-flow.xml` file was the `<action-state>` definition; as already learned, action states are normally used to invoke backend services. In the following `<action-state>` definition, we will invoke the `validate` method of the `cartServiceImpl` object and store the result in the `order.cart` object:

```
<action-state id="addCartToOrder">
  <evaluate expression =
  "cartServiceImpl.validate(requestParameters.cartId)"
  result="order.cart" />

  <transition to="InvalidCartWarning" on-exception =
  "com.packt.webstore.exception.InvalidCartException" />

  <transition to="collectCustomerInfo" />
</action-state>
```

As already defined, the `order` variable at the start of the flow will be available in every state of this flow. So, we have used that variable (`order.cart`) in the `<evaluate>` tag to store the result of the evaluated expression, namely `cartServiceImpl.validate(requestParameters.cartId)`.

The `validate` method of `cartServiceImpl` will try to read a `cart` object based on the given `cartId`. If it finds a valid `cart` object, then it will return it; otherwise, it will throw `InvalidCartException`. In such a case, we will route the transition to another state whose ID is `InvalidCartWarning`:

```
<transition to="InvalidCartWarning" on-exception = "com.packt.
webstore.exception.InvalidCartException" />
```

If such an exception is not thrown from the expression evaluation, we will naturally transit from the `addCartToOrder` state to the `collectCustomerInfo` state, as follows:

```
<transition to="collectCustomerInfo" />
```

If you notice the `collectCustomerInfo` state, it is nothing but a view state in `checkout-flow.xml`. We defined the view that needs to be rendered via the `view` attribute and the model that needs to be attached via the `model` attribute, as follows:

```
<view-state id="collectCustomerInfo" view="collectCustomerInfo.jsp"
model="order">
  <transition on="customerInfoCollected" to="collectShippingDetail" />
</view-state>
```

Upon reaching this view state, Spring Web Flow will render the `collectCustomerInfo` view and wait for the user to interact. Once the user enters the customer info details and presses the submit button, it will resume its transition to the `collectShippingDetail` view state. As already learned, a transition can be triggered via an event, so here the transition to the `collectShippingDetail` state would get triggered when the `customerInfoCollected` event is triggered. But how do you fire this event (`customerInfoCollected`) from the view? We will see this later in the chapter. Consider the following code snippet:

```
<transition on="customerInfoCollected" to="collectShippingDetail" />
```

The next state defined within the checkout flow is `collectShippingDetail`. Again, this is also a view state, and it has two transitions back and forth; one is to go back to the `collectCustomerInfo` state and the next is to go forward to the `orderConfirmation` state, as shown as follows:

```
<view-state id="collectShippingDetail" model="order">
  <transition on="shippingDetailCollected" to="orderConfirmation" />
  <transition on="backToCollectCustomerInfo" to="collectCustomerInfo"
/>
</view-state>
```

Note here that we haven't mentioned the `view` attribute in the `collectShippingDetail` state; in this case, Spring Web Flow would consider the ID of the view state as its view name.

The `orderConfirmation` state definition doesn't need much explanation; it is more like the `collectShippingDetail` view state where we furnish all the order-related details and then ask the user to confirm. Upon confirmation, we move to the next state, that is, `processOrder`:

```
<view-state id="orderConfirmation">
  <transition on="orderConfirmed" to="processOrder" />
  <transition on="backToCollectShippingDetail" to =
"collectShippingDetail" />
</view-state>
```

Next, the `processOrder` state is an action state that interacts with the `orderServiceImpl` object to save the `order` object. Upon successfully saving the `order` object, it stores the order ID in the flow variable (`order.orderId`) and transits it to the next state, which is `thankCustomer`:

```
<action-state id="processOrder">
  <evaluate expression="orderServiceImpl.saveOrder(order)"
result="order.orderId"/>
  <transition to="thankCustomer" />
</action-state>
```

The `thankCustomer` state is a view state that simply shows a thank you message with the confirmed order ID to the end user and transits it to the end state, as follows:

```
<view-state id="thankCustomer" model="order">
  <transition to="endState"/>
</view-state>
```

In our checkout flow, we have two end states: one is the normal end state where the flow execution arrives naturally after the flow ends, and the other one is the end state that is reached when the user presses the cancel button in any one of the views. Consider the following code snippet:

```
<end-state id="endState"/>
<end-state id="cancelCheckout" view="checkOutCancelled.jsp"/>
```

Note that in the `cancelCheckout` end state, we specified the name of the landing page via the `view` attribute, and the transition to the `cancelCheckout` end state happened through the `global-transitions` configuration:

```
<global-transitions>
  <transition on = "cancel" to="cancelCheckout" />
</global-transitions>
```

A global transition is for sharing some common transitions between states. Instead of repeating the transition definition every time within the state definition, we can define them within one global transition so that that transition will be available implicitly for every state in the flow. In our case, the end user may cancel the checkout process in any state; this is why we defined the transition to the `cancelCheckout` state in `global-transitions`.

We have totally understood the checkout flow definition (`checkout-flow.xml`). Now our Spring MVC should read this file during the boot up of our application so that it can be ready to dispatch any flow-related requests to the Spring Web Flow framework. We will be able to do this via some web flow configuration tags in the web application context (`DispatcherServlet-context.xml`) as mentioned in steps 5 to 8.

In steps 5 and 6, we added the required `webflow-config` namespace and schema location in `DispatcherServlet-context.xml`. In step 7, we created `flow-executor` and `flow-registry`. As the name implies, `flow-executor` executes a flow based on the given flow definition. The `flow-executor` configuration tag gets its flow definition from `flow-registry`. We can configure as many flow definitions as we want in `flow-registry`. A `flow-registry` configuration tag is a collection of flow definitions. When a user enters a flow, the flow executor creates and launches an exclusive flow instance for that user based on the flow definition:

```
<webflow-config:flow-executor id="flowExecutor" flow-
registry="flowRegistry" />


<webflow-config:flow-registry id="flowRegistry" base-path="/WEB-INF/
flows">
  <webflow-config:flow-location path="/checkout/checkout-flow.xml"
id="checkout"/>
</webflow-config:flow-registry>
```

In the preceding web flow configuration, we created `flow-registry` whose `base-path` is `/WEB-INF/flows`, so we need to put all our flow definitions under the `/WEB-INF/flows` directory in order to be picked up by `flow-registry`. That's why, in step 4, we created our `checkout-flow.xml` file under the directory `src/main/webapp/WEB-INF/flows/checkout/`. As already mentioned, `flow registry` can have many flow definitions, and each flow definition is identified by its ID within `flow-registry`. In our case, we added a single flow definition whose ID is `checkout` and whose relative location is `/checkout/checkout-flow.xml`. Remember that the `path` attribute of a `<webflow-config:flow-location>` tag is relative to the `base-path` attribute of the `<webflow-config:flow-registry>` tag.

One important thing to understand before we wind up the web flow configuration is that the ID of a flow definition forms the relative URL to invoke the flow. By this, what I mean is that in order to invoke the flow of our checkout via a web request, we need to fire a GET request to the URL `http://localhost:8080/webstore/checkout` because our flow ID is `checkout`. Moreover, in our flow definition (`checkout-flow.xml`), we haven't configured any start state, so the first state definition (the `addCartToOrder` action state) will become the start state; also, the `addCartToOrder` action state expecting `cartId` should be present in the request parameter of the invoking URL, which is shown as follows:

```
<action-state id="addCartToOrder">
  <evaluate expression = "cartServiceImpl.validate(requestParameters.
cartId)" result="order.cart" />

  <transition to="InvalidCartWarning"  on-exception="com.packt.
webstore.exception.InvalidCartException" />
  <transition to="collectCustomerInfo" />
</action-state>
```

So, the actual URL that can invoke this flow would be something similar to `http://localhost:8080/webstore/checkout?`**`cartId=55AD1472D4EC`**, where the part after the question mark (`cartId=55AD1472D4EC`) is considered as a request parameter.

It is good that we have defined our checkout flow and configured it with Spring Web Flow; however, we need to define two more beans in our web application context (`DispatcherServlet-context.xml`) to dispatch all flow-invoking requests to `flow-executor`. We did this in step 8:

```
<bean id="flowHandlerMapping" class= "org.springframework.webflow.mvc.
servlet.FlowHandlerMapping">
  <property name="flowRegistry" ref="flowRegistry" />
</bean>

<bean id="flowHandlerAdapter" class= "org.springframework.webflow.mvc.
servlet.FlowHandlerAdapter">
  <property name="flowExecutor" ref="flowExecutor" />
</bean>
```

The `flowHandlerMapping` parameter creates and configures a handler mapping based on the flow ID for each defined flow from `flowRegistry`. The `flowHandlerAdapter` acts as a bridge between the dispatcher servlet and Spring Web Flow in order to execute the instances of the flow.

Pop quiz – web flow

Q1. Consider the following web flow registry configuration; it has a single flow definition file. How will you form the URL to invoke the flow?

```
<webflow-config:flow-registry id="flowRegistry"  base-path="/WEB-INF/
flows">
  <webflow-config:flow-location path="/customer/validate.xml"
id="validateCustomer"/>
</webflow-config:flow-registry>
```

1. `http://localhost:8080/webstore/customer/validate`

2. `http://localhost:8080/webstore/validate`

3. `http://localhost:8080/webstore/validateCustomer`

Q2. Consider this flow-invoking URL: `http://localhost:8080/webstore/validate?customerId=C1234`. In a flow definition file, how will you retrieve the `customerId` HTTP request parameter?

1.  ```
    <evaluate expression = "requestParameters.customerId "
    result = "customerId" />
    ```
    ```

2. ```
   <evaluate expression = "requestParameters(customerId)"
   result = "customerId" />
   ```

3. ```
   <evaluate expression = "requestParameters[customerId]"
   result = "customerId" />
   ```

Time for action – creating views for every view state

We have done everything to roll out our checkout flow, but one last thing is pending, that is, creating all the views that need to be used in the view states of our checkout flow. In total, we have six view states in our flow definition (`collectCustomerInfo`, `collectShippingDetail`, `orderConfirmation`, `InvalidCartWarning`, `thankCustomer`, and `cancelCheckout`), so we need to create six JSP files. Let's create all of them:

1. Create a JSP view file called `collectCustomerInfo.jsp` under the directory `src/main/webapp/WEB-INF/flows/checkout/`, and add the following code snippet into it and save it. In the following code snippet, I have skipped the `<input>` tags for some of the fields of the `Customer` domain object. You can find the complete code for `collectCustomerInfo.jsp` in the code bundle of this book, which can be downloaded from `www.packtpub.com/support`. Consider the following code snippet:

   ```
   <%@ taglib prefix="c" uri="http://java.sun.com/jsp/jstl/core"%>
   <%@ taglib prefix="form" uri="http://www.springframework.org/tags/
   form"%>
   <%@ taglib prefix="spring" uri="http://www.springframework.org/
   tags"%>

   <html>
     <head>
       <meta http-equiv="Content-Type" content="text/html;
   charset="utf-8">
       <link rel="stylesheet"
   href="//netdna.bootstrapcdn.com/bootstrap/3.0.0/css/bootstrap.min.
   css">
       <title>Customer</title>
     </head>
     <body>
       <section>
         <div class="jumbotron">
           <div class="container">
             <h1>Customer</h1>
             <p>Customer details</p>
           </div>
         </div>
       </section>
       <section class="container">
   ```

```
      <form:form modelAttribute="order.customer" class="form-
horizontal">
        <fieldset>
          <legend>Customer Details</legend>

          <div class="form-group">
            <label class="control-label col-lg-2 col-lg-2"
for="customerId" />Customer Id</label>
            <div class="col-lg-10">
              <form:input id="customerId" path="customerId"
type="text" class="form:input-large" />
            </div>
          </div>

<!-- Similarly, add input tags for the remaining fields of the
customer domain object. I have skipped those tags here -->

          <input type="hidden" name="_flowExecutionKey"
value="${flowExecutionKey}"/>

          <div class="form-group">
            <div class="col-lg-offset-2 col-lg-10">
              <input type="submit" id="btnAdd" class="btn btn-
primary" value="Add" name="_eventId_customerInfoCollected" />
              <button id="btnCancel" class="btn btn-default"
name="_eventId_cancel">Cancel</button>
            </div>
          </div>

        </fieldset>
      </form:form>
    </section>
  </body>
</html>
```

2. Similarly, create one more JSP view file called `collectShippingDetail.jsp` under the same directory, and add the following code snippet into it and save it. In the following code snippet, I have skipped the `<input>` tags for some of the fields of the `Address` (`shippingAddress`) domain object. You can find the complete code for `collectShippingDetail.jsp` in the code bundle of this book, which can be downloaded from `www.packtpub.com/support`. Consider the following code snippet:

```
<%@ taglib prefix="c" uri="http://java.sun.com/jsp/jstl/core"%>
<%@ taglib prefix="form" uri="http://www.springframework.org/tags/
form"%>
<%@ taglib prefix="spring" uri="http://www.springframework.org/
tags"%>
```

```
<html>
  <head>
    <meta http-equiv="Content-Type" content="text/html;
charset="utf-8">
    <link rel="stylesheet"
href="//netdna.bootstrapcdn.com/bootstrap/3.0.0/css/bootstrap.min.
css">
    <title>Customer</title>
  </head>
  <body>
    <section>
      <div class="jumbotron">
        <div class="container">
          <h1>Shipping</h1>
          <p>Shipping details</p>
        </div>
      </div>
    </section>
    <section class="container">
      <form:form modelAttribute="order.shippingDetail"
class="form-horizontal">
        <fieldset>
          <legend>Shipping Details</legend>

          <div class="form-group">
            <label class="control-label col-lg-2 col-lg-2"
for="name" />Name</label>
            <div class="col-lg-10">
              <form:input id="name" path="name" type="text"
class="form:input-large" />
            </div>
          </div>

          <div class="form-group">
            <label class="control-label col-lg-2 col-lg-2"
for="shippingDate" />shipping Date (dd/mm/yyyy)</label>
            <div class="col-lg-10">
              <form:input id="shippingDate" path="shippingDate"
type="text" class="form:input-large" />
            </div>
          </div>

          <div class="form-group">
            <label class="control-label col-lg-2"
for="doorNo">Door No</label>
```

```
          <div class="col-lg-10">
             <form:input id="doorNo" path="shippingAddress.
doorNo" type="text"
                 class="form:input-large" />
          </div>
       </div>
<!-- Similarly, add input tags for the remaining fields of the
shippingAddress domain object. I have skipped those tags here -->

          <input type="hidden" name="_flowExecutionKey"
value="${flowExecutionKey}"/>

          <div class="form-group">
             <div class="col-lg-offset-2 col-lg-10">
                <button id="back" class="btn btn-default" name="_
eventId_backToCollectCustomerInfo">back</button>

                <input type="submit" id="btnAdd" class="btn btn-
primary"
                    value="Add"  name="_eventId_
shippingDetailCollected"/>
                <button id="btnCancel" class="btn btn-default"
name="_eventId_cancel">Cancel</button>
             </div>
          </div>

       </fieldset>
     </form:form>
   </section>
  </body>
</html>
```

3. Also, create one more JSP view file called `orderConfirmation.jsp` to confirm the order from the user under the same directory, and add the following code snippet into it and save it. In the following code snippet, I have skipped the `<input>` tags for some of the fields of the `Order` domain object. You can find the complete code for `orderConfirmation.jsp` in the code bundle of this book, which can be downloaded from `www.packtpub.com/support`. Consider the following code snippet:

```
<%@ taglib prefix="c" uri="http://java.sun.com/jsp/jstl/core"%>
<%@ taglib prefix="form" uri="http://www.springframework.org/tags/
form"%>
<%@ taglib prefix="spring" uri="http://www.springframework.org/
tags"%>
```

```
<%@ taglib prefix="fmt" uri="http://java.sun.com/jsp/jstl/fmt"%>

<html>
  <head>
    <meta http-equiv="Content-Type" content="text/html;
charset="utf-8">
    <link rel="stylesheet"
href="//netdna.bootstrapcdn.com/bootstrap/3.0.0/css/bootstrap.min.
css">
    <title>Order Confirmation</title>
  </head>

  <body>

    <section>
      <div class="jumbotron">
        <div class="container">
          <h1>Order</h1>
          <p>Order Confirmation</p>
        </div>
      </div>
    </section>
    <div class="container">
      <div class="row">
        <form:form modelAttribute="order" class="form-horizontal">
          <input type="hidden" name="_flowExecutionKey"
            value="${flowExecutionKey}" />

          <div class="well col-xs-10 col-sm-10 col-md-6 col-xs-
offset-1 col-sm-offset-1 col-md-offset-3">
            <div class="text-center">
              <h1>Receipt</h1>
            </div>
            <div class="row">
              <div class="col-xs-6 col-sm-6 col-md-6">
                <address>
                  <strong>Shipping Address</strong> <br>
                  ${order.shippingDetail.name}<br>

<!-- Similarly, furnish every field of the order object within an
html table using expression notation "${}". I have skipped those
tags here -->

              <button id="back" class="btn btn-default"
name="_eventId_backToCollectShippingDetail">back</button>
```

```
          <button type="submit" class="btn btn-success"
            name="_eventId_orderConfirmed">
            Confirm    <span class="glyphicon glyphicon-
chevron-right"></span>
          </button>
          <button id="btnCancel" class="btn btn-default"
            name="_eventId_cancel">Cancel</button>
        </div>
      </div>
    </form:form>
   </div>
  </div>
 </body>
</html>
```

4. Next, we need to create another JSP view file called `InvalidCartWarning.jsp` to show an error message in the case of an empty cart checkout; add the following code snippet to `InvalidCartWarning.jsp` and save it:

```
<%@ taglib prefix="c" uri="http://java.sun.com/jsp/jstl/core"%>
<%@ taglib prefix="spring" uri="http://www.springframework.org/
tags" %>

<html>
  <head>
    <meta http-equiv="Content-Type" content="text/html;
charset="utf-8">
    <link rel="stylesheet" href="//netdna.bootstrapcdn.com/
bootstrap/3.0.0/css/bootstrap.min.css">
    <title>Invalid cart </title>
  </head>
  <body>
    <section>
      <div class="jumbotron">
        <div class="container">
          <h1 class="alert alert-danger"> Invalid Cart</h1>
        </div>
      </div>
    </section>

    <section>
      <div class="container">
        <p>
          <a href="<spring:url value="/products" />" class="btn
btn-primary">
            <span class="glyphicon-hand-left glyphicon"></span>
products
```

```
            </a>
          </p>
        </div>

      </section>
    </body>
  </html>
```

5. To thank the customer after a successful checkout flow, we need to create one more JSP view file called `thankCustomer.jsp` as follows:

```
<%@ taglib prefix="c" uri="http://java.sun.com/jsp/jstl/core"%>
<%@ taglib prefix="spring" uri="http://www.springframework.org/
tags" %>
<%@ taglib prefix="fmt" uri="http://java.sun.com/jsp/jstl/fmt"%>


<html>
  <head>
    <meta http-equiv="Content-Type" content="text/html;
charset="utf-8">
    <link rel="stylesheet" href="//netdna.bootstrapcdn.com/
bootstrap/3.0.0/css/bootstrap.min.css">
    <title>Invalid cart </title>
  </head>
  <body>
    <section>
      <div class="jumbotron">
        <div class="container">
          <h1 class="alert alert-danger"> Thank you</h1>
          <p>Thanks for the order. your order will be delivered to
you on
          <fmt:formatDate type="date"  value="${order.
shippingDetail.shippingDate}" />!</p>
          <p>Your Order Number is ${order.orderId}</p>
        </div>
      </div>
    </section>

    <section>
      <div class="container">
        <p>
          <a href="<spring:url value="/products" />" class="btn
btn-primary">
            <span class="glyphicon-hand-left glyphicon"></span>
products
          </a>
        </p>
```

```
      </div>

    </section>
  </body>
</html>
```

6. If the user cancels the checkout in any of the views, we need to show the checkout cancelled message; for that, we need to have a JSP file called `checkOutCancelled.jsp` as follows:

```
<%@ taglib prefix="c" uri="http://java.sun.com/jsp/jstl/core"%>
<%@ taglib prefix="spring" uri="http://www.springframework.org/
tags" %>

<html>
  <head>
    <meta http-equiv="Content-Type" content="text/html;
charset="utf-8">
    <link rel="stylesheet" href="//netdna.bootstrapcdn.com/
bootstrap/3.0.0/css/bootstrap.min.css">
    <title>Invalid cart </title>
  </head>
  <body>
    <section>
      <div class="jumbotron">
        <div class="container">
          <h1 class="alert alert-danger">check out cancelled</h1>
          <p>Your Check out process cancelled! you may continue
shopping..</p>
        </div>
      </div>
    </section>

    <section>
      <div class="container">
        <p>
          <a href="<spring:url value="/products" />" class="btn
btn-primary">
            <span class="glyphicon-hand-left glyphicon"></span>
products
          </a>
        </p>
      </div>

    </section>
  </body>
</html>
```

7. As the last step, open `cart.jsp` from `src\main\webapp\WEB-INF\views\` and assign the `<spring:url value="/checkout?cartId=${cartId}"/>` value for the `href` attribute of the checkout link as follows:

```
<a href= "<spring:url value="/checkout?cartId=${cartId}"/>"
class="btn btn-success pull-right"> <span
class="glyphicon-shopping-cart glyphicon"></span> Check out
</a>
```

8. Now run the application and enter the `http://localhost:8080/webstore/products` URL. Next, click on the **Details** button of any of the products and click on the **Order Now** button on the product details page to add products to the shopping cart. Now go to the cart page by clicking on the **View Cart** button; you will be able to see the **Checkout** button on that page. Click on the **Checkout** button; you will be able to see a web page as follows for collecting customer info:

Customer details collection form

9. After furnishing all the customer details, if you click on the **Add** button, Spring Web Flow will take you to the next view state, which is collecting the shipping details and so on up to confirming the order. Upon confirming the order, Spring Web Flow will show you the thank you message view as the end state.

What just happened?

What we have done from step 1 to 6 is kind of similar, that is, creating the JSP view files for each view state. If you remember, we defined the `model` attribute for each view state in `checkout-flow.xml`. Consider the following code snippet:

```
<view-state id="collectCustomerInfo" view="collectCustomerInfo.jsp"
model="order">
  <transition on="customerInfoCollected" to="collectShippingDetail" />
</view-state>
```

This model object will get bound to the view via `modelAttribute` of the `<form:form>` tag as follows:

```
<form:form modelAttribute="order.customer" class="form-horizontal">
  <fieldset>
    <legend>Customer Details</legend>

    <div class="form-group">
       <label class="control-label col-lg-2 col-lg-2" for="customerId"
/>Customer Id</label>
       <div class="col-lg-10">
         <form:input id="customerId" path="customerId" type="text"
class="form:input-large" />
       </div>
    </div>
```

In the preceding snippet of `collectCustomerInfo.jsp`, you can notice that we bounded the `<form:input>` tag with the `customerId` field of the `customer` object, which comes from the model object (`order.customer`). Similarly, we bounded the `shippingDetail` and `order` objects with `collectShippingDetail.jsp` and `orderConfirmation.jsp` respectively.

It's good that we bounded the `Order`, `Customer`, and `ShippingDetail` objects with the views, but what will happen after we click on the submit button in each view, or say the the cancel or back buttons. To know the answer, we need to investigate the following code snippet from `collectCustomerInfo.jsp`:

```
<input type="submit" id="btnAdd" class="btn btn-primary" value="Add"
name="_eventId_customerInfoCollected" />
```

On the surface, the `<input>` tag we just mentioned acts as a submit button, but the real difference comes from the `name` attribute (`name="_eventId_customerInfoCollected"`). We have assigned the value `_eventId_customerInfoCollected` to the `name` attribute of the `<input>` tag with a purpose. The purpose is to instruct Spring Web Flow to raise an event once this form is submitted. When submitting this form, Spring Web Flow will raise an event based on the `name` attribute. Since we have assigned a value with the `_eventId_` prefix (`_eventId_customerInfoCollected`), Spring Web Flow could recognize it as an event name and raise an event with the name `customerInfoCollected`.

As already learned, transition from one state to another happens with the help of events. So, upon submitting the `collectCustomerInfo` form, Spring Web Flow will take us to the next view state, that is, `collectShippingDetail`:

```
<view-state id="collectCustomerInfo" view="collectCustomerInfo.jsp"
model="order">
  <transition on="customerInfoCollected" to="collectShippingDetail" />
</view-state>
```

Similarly, we can raise events while clicking on the cancel or back buttons; see the following code snippet from `collectShippingDetail.jsp`:

```
<button id="back" class="btn btn-default" name="_eventId_backToCollect
CustomerInfo">back</button>
```

```
<button id="btnCancel" class="btn btn-default" name="_eventId_
cancel">Cancel</button>
```

Okay! So we understand how to raise Spring Web Flow events from the view to direct the transition from one view state to another. However, we need to understand one more important concept regarding the Spring Web Flow execution, that is, each flow execution is identified by the flow execution key at runtime. During the flow execution, when a view state is entered, the flow execution pauses and waits for the user to perform an action (such as entering some data in the form). When the user submits the form or chooses to cancel it, the flow execution key is also sent along with the form data in order to resume the flow where it left off. This is done with the help of the hidden `<input>` tag as follows:

```
<input type="hidden" name="_flowExecutionKey"
value="${flowExecutionKey}"/>
```

If you look carefully, we have the earlier mentioned tag in every flow-related view file such as `collectCustomerInfo.jsp`, `collectShippingDetail.jsp`, and so on. Spring Web Flow will store a unique flow execution key under the model attribute name `flowExecutionKey` in every flow-related view; we need to store this value in the form of a variable called `_flowExecutionKey` in order to get identified by Spring Web Flow.

So that's all about view files that are associated with the definition of our checkout flow. However, we need to invoke the flow upon clicking the checkout button from the cart page. As we have already learned how to invoke our checkout flow, we need to fire a web request with the cart ID as a request parameter. In step 7, we changed the `href` attribute of the checkout link as follows to form a request URL that is something similar to `http://localhost:8080/webstore/checkout?cartId=55AD1472D4EC`.

So, now if you click on the checkout button after selecting some products into the shopping cart, you will be able to initiate the checkout flow. The following is the order confirmation page that will appear as the outcome of reaching the `orderConfirmation` state:

Order confirmation page

Have a go hero – adding a decision state

Although we have finished with our checkout flow, there is still some room to improve the flow. Every time the checkout flow starts, it collects the customer's details. What if a returning customer places an order? Probably, he/she may not like to provide customer details repeatedly every time. However, you can autofill details, thereby picking up customer details from existing records. Here are some of the improvements you can introduce to avoid collecting customer details in the case of regular customers:

♦ Create a customer repository and service layer to store, retrieve, and find customer objects. Probably, you can have methods such as the following in your `CustomerRepositoy` and `CustomerService` interfaces and in their corresponding implementation classes:

   ❑ `public void saveCustomer(Customer customer)`

   ❑ `public Customer getCustomer(String customerId)`

   ❑ `public Boolean isCustomerExist(String customerId)`

♦ Define a view state in `checkout-flow.xml` to collect the customer ID. Don't forget to create the corresponding JSP view file to collect the customer ID.

♦ Define a decision state in `checkout-flow.xml` to check whether a customer exists in `CustomerRepositoy` through `CustomerService`. Based on the retuning Boolean value, direct the transition to collect the customer details view state or prefill the `order.customer` object from `CustomerRepositoy`. The following is a sample decision state:

```
<decision-stateid="checkCustomerExist">
<if test="customerServiceImpl.isCustomerExist(order.customer.
customerId)"
then=" collectShippingDetail"
else=" collectCustomerInfo"/>
</decision-state>
```

♦ After collecting customer details, don't forget to store the information in `CustomerRepositoy` through an action state. Similarly, fill the `order.customer` object after the decision state.

Enhancing reusability through Apache Tiles

In the past, we developed a series of web pages (views), such as a page to show products, another page to add products, and so on, as part of our webstore application; though every view serves a different purpose, all of them share a common visual pattern, for example, each page has a header, content area, and so on. We have hardcoded and repeated those common elements in every JSP view page. This is not a good idea because in future, if we want to change the look and feel of any of these common elements, we will have to change every page in order to maintain a consistent look and feel across all the web pages.

To address this problem, modern web applications use template mechanisms; Apache Tiles is one such template composition framework. Tiles allow developers to define reusable page fragments (tiles) that can be assembled into a complete web page at runtime. These fragments can have parameters to allow dynamic content. This increases the reusability of templates and reduces code duplication.

Time for action – creating views for every view state

Enough of introduction; let's dive into Apache Tiles by defining a common layout for our web application and let the pages extend the layout:

1. Open `pom.xml`; you will find `pom.xml` under the project root directory.

2. You will be able to see some bottom tabs under `pom.xml`; select the **Dependencies** tab and click on the **Add** button of the **Dependencies** section.

3. A **Select Dependency** window will appear; enter **Group Id** as `org.apache.tiles`, **Artifact Id** as `tiles-extras`, and **Version** as `3.0.3`. Then, select **Scope** as **compile**, click on the **OK** button, and save `pom.xml`.

4. Similarly, add one more dependency with **Group Id** as `org.slf4j`, **Artifact Id** as `slf4j-api`, and **Version** as `1.7.5`. Then, select **Scope** as **compile**, click on the **OK** button, and save `pom.xml`.

5. Now create a directory structure, `tiles/definitions/`, under the directory `src/main/webapp/WEB-INF/`; then, create an XML file called `tile-definition.xml`, add the following content into it, and save it. In the following code snippet, I have skipped the `<definition>` tags for some of the fields of logical view names. You can find the complete code for `definition.xml` in the code bundle of this book, which can be downloaded from `www.packtpub.com/support`:

```
<?xml version="1.0" encoding="UTF-8" ?>
<!DOCTYPE tiles-definitions PUBLIC "-//Apache Software
Foundation//DTD Tiles Configuration 3.0//EN"
   "http://tiles.apache.org/dtds/tiles-config_3_0.dtd">
```

```
<tiles-definitions>

  <definition name="baseLayout" template="/WEB-INF/tiles/template/
baseLayout.jsp">
    <put-attribute name="title" value="Sample Title" />
    <put-attribute name="heading" value="" />
    <put-attribute name="tagline" value="" />
    <put-attribute name="navigation" value="/WEB-INF/tiles/
template/navigation.jsp" />
    <put-attribute name="content" value="" />
    <put-attribute name="footer" value="/WEB-INF/tiles/template/
footer.jsp" />
  </definition>

  <definition name="welcome" extends="baseLayout">
    <put-attribute name="title" value="Products" />
    <put-attribute name="heading" value="Products" />
    <put-attribute name="tagline" value="Available Products" />
    <put-attribute name="content" value="/WEB-INF/views/products.
jsp" />
  </definition>

  <definition name="products" extends="baseLayout">
    <put-attribute name="title" value="Products" />
    <put-attribute name="heading" value="Products" />
    <put-attribute name="tagline" value="Available Products" />
    <put-attribute name="content" value="/WEB-INF/views/products.
jsp" />
  </definition>

  <definition name="product" extends="baseLayout">
    <put-attribute name="title" value="Product" />
    <put-attribute name="heading" value="Products" />
    <put-attribute name="tagline" value="Product" />
    <put-attribute name="content" value="/WEB-INF/views/product.
jsp" />
  </definition>

  <!--similarly, add definition tags for every logical view name. I
have skipped this here, but you can find the full definition file
in the code bundle of this book.-->
</tiles-definitions>
```

6. Now create a directory called `template` under the directory `src/main/webapp/WEB-INF/tiles/`; then, create a JSP file called `baseLayout.jsp`, add the following content into it, and save it:

```jsp
<%@ taglib prefix="c" uri="http://java.sun.com/jsp/jstl/core"%>
<%@ taglib prefix="spring" uri="http://www.springframework.org/
tags"%>
<%@ taglib prefix="tiles" uri="http://tiles.apache.org/tags-
tiles"%>


<!DOCTYPE html>
<html lang="en">
  <head>
    <meta charset="utf-8">
    <meta http-equiv="X-UA-Compatible" content="IE=edge">
    <meta name="viewport" content="width=device-width, initial-
scale=1.0">

    <title><tiles:insertAttribute name="title" /></title>

    <link href="http://getbootstrap.com/dist/css/bootstrap.css"
rel="stylesheet">

    <link href="http://getbootstrap.com/examples/jumbotron/
jumbotron.css"  rel="stylesheet">

  </head>

  <body>

    <div class="container">
      <div class="header">
        <ul class="nav nav-pills pull-right">
          <tiles:insertAttribute name="navigation" />
        </ul>
        <h3 class="text-muted">Web Store</h3>
      </div>

      <div class="jumbotron">
        <h1>
          <tiles:insertAttribute name="heading" />
        </h1>
```

```
        <p>
          <tiles:insertAttribute name="tagline" />
        </p>
      </div>

      <div class="row">
        <tiles:insertAttribute name="content" />
      </div>

      <div class="footer">
        <tiles:insertAttribute name="footer" />
      </div>

    </div>
  </body>
</html>
```

7. Under the same directory (`template`), create another template JSP file called `navigation.jsp` and add the following content into it:

```
<%@ taglib prefix="spring" uri="http://www.springframework.org/
tags"%>

<li><a href="<spring:url value="/products"/>">Home</a></li>
<li><a href="<spring:URL value="/products/"/>">Products</a></li>
<li><a href="<spring:url value="/products/add"/>">Add Product</
a></li>
<li><a href="<spring:url value="/cart/"/>">Cart</a></li>
```

8. Similarly, create one last template JSP file called `footer.jsp` and add the following content to it:

```
<p>&copy; Company 2014</p>
```

9. We have created the common base layout template and the tile definition for all our pages. Now we need to remove the common page elements from all our JSP view files. For example, if you remove the `jumbotron` section from `products.jsp` and keep only the `container` section, it would look like the following. Note that you should not remove the `taglib` references and link references to JavaScript files:

```
<%@ taglib prefix="c" uri="http://java.sun.com/jsp/jstl/core"%>
<%@ taglib prefix="spring" uri="http://www.springframework.org/
tags"%>

<section class="container">
  <div class="row">
    <c:forEach var="product" items="${products}">
      <div class="col-sm-6 col-md-3" style="padding-bottom: 15px">
        <div class="thumbnail">
          <img
            src="<c:url value="/resource/images/${product.
```

```
productId}.png"></c:url>"
            alt="image" style="width: 100%" />
         <div class="caption">
           <h3>${product.name}</h3>
           <p>${product.description}</p>
           <p>${product.unitPrice} USD</p>
           <p>Available ${product.unitsInStock} units in
stock</p>
           <p>
             <a
               href=" <spring:url value="/products/
product?id=${product.productId}" /> "
               class="btn btn-primary"> <span
               class="glyphicon-info-sign glyphicon" /></span>
Details
             </a>
           </p>
         </div>
       </div>
     </div>
   </c:forEach>
  </div>
</section>
```

10. Similarly, remove the `jumbotron` section from every JSP view file that is under the `/src/main/webapp/WEB-INF/views` directory; do not remove the `taglib` references and link references to JavaScript files; for example, in `cart.jsp`, you should retain the following lines:

```
<%@ taglib prefix="c" uri="http://java.sun.com/jsp/jstl/core"%>
<%@ taglib prefix="spring" uri="http://www.springframework.org/
tags"%>

<script src="https://ajax.googleapis.com/ajax/libs/
angularjs/1.0.1/angular.min.js"></script>
<script src="/webstore/resource/js/controllers.js"></script>
```

11. Finally, for `TilesView`, add a `UrlBasedViewResolver` bean to our web application context configuration file (`DispatcherServlet-context.xml`), as follows:

```
<bean id="tilesViewResolver" class="org.springframework.web.
servlet.view.UrlBasedViewResolver">
  <property name="viewClass" value="org.springframework.web.
servlet.view.tiles3.TilesView" />
  <property name="order" value="-2" />
</bean>
```

12. In order to locate the tile definition file, we need to add a bean definition for
`TilesConfigurer` in `DispatcherServlet-context.xml`, as follows:

```
<bean id="tilesConfigurer" class="org.springframework.web.servlet.
view.tiles3.TilesConfigurer">
  <property name="definitions">
    <list>
      <value>/WEB-INF/tiles/definitions/tile-definition.xml</
value>
    </list>
  </property>
</bean>
```

13. Now run the application and enter the URL `http://localhost:8080/`
`webstore/products`; you will be able to see our regular product add page with an
extra navigation bar at the top and footer at the bottom. You can navigate to add the
products page by clicking on the **Add Product** link.

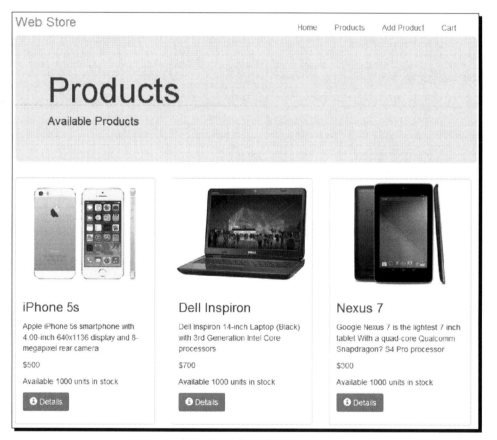

Products page with Apache Tiles view

What just happened?

To work with Apache Tiles, we need jars related to Apache Tiles; from steps 1 to 4, we added those jars via Maven dependencies. Step 5 is very important because we created our tiles definition file (`tile-definition.xml`) in this step. Understanding the tile definition file is crucial for developing applications based on Apache Tiles, so we will try to understand our tile definition file (`tile-definition.xml`).

A tile's definition file is a collection of definitions, and each definition can be associated with a template via the `template` attribute for the layout; refer to the following code to know how to do this:

```
<definition name="baseLayout" template = "/WEB-INF/tiles/template/
baseLayout.jsp" >
  <put-attribute name="title" value="Sample Title" />
  <put-attribute name="heading" value="Sample Header" />
  <put-attribute name="tagline" value="Sample Tagline" />
  <put-attribute name="navigation" value = "/WEB-INF/tiles/template/
navigation.jsp" />
  <put-attribute name="content" value="" />
  <put-attribute name="footer" value = "/WEB-INF/tiles/template/
footer.jsp" />
</definition>
```

Within each definition, we can define many attributes. These attributes can be a simple text value or a full-blown markup file. These attributes would be available in the template file via the `<tiles:insertAttribute>` tag. For example, if you open the base layout template (`baseLayout.jsp`), you will notice the following snippet under the `jumbotron <div>` tag:

```
<h1>
  <tiles:insertAttribute name="heading" />
</h1>
<p>
  <tiles:insertAttribute name="tagline" />
</p>
```

So, at runtime, Apache Tiles will replace the `<tiles:insertAttribute name="heading" />` tag with the value `Sample Header`; similarly, the `<tiles:insertAttribute name="tagline" />` tag will also be replaced with the `Sample Tagline` value.

So, `baseLayout` is associated with the template `/WEB-INF/tiles/template/baseLayout.jsp`, and we can insert the defined attributes such as `tile`, `heading`, and `tagline` in the template using the `<tiles:insertAttribute>` tag.

Apache Tiles allows us to extend a definition just like how we extend a Java class so that the defined attributes will be available for the derived definition, and we can even override these attribute values if we want. For example, look at the following definition from `tile-definition.xml`:

```
<definition name="products" extends="baseLayout">
  <put-attribute name="title" value="Products" />
  <put-attribute name="heading" value="Products" />
  <put-attribute name="tagline" value="Available Products" />
  <put-attribute name="content" value="/WEB-INF/views/products.jsp" />
</definition>
```

The mentioned definition is an extension of the `baseLayout` definition. We have only overridden the `title`, `heading`, `tagline`, and `content` attributes, and since we have not defined any template for this definition, it uses the same template that we configured for the `baseLayout` definition.

Similarly, we have defined the tile definition for every possible logical view name that can be returned from our controllers. Note that each definition name (except the `baseLayout` definition) is a logical view name.

From steps 6 to 8, we created the templates that can be used in the tile definition; first we created the base layout template (`baseLayout.jsp`), then the navigation template (`navigation.jsp`), and finally the footer template (`footer.jsp`).

Steps 9 and 10 explained how to remove the existing redundant content, such as the `jumbotron <div>` tag, from every JSP view page. Note that you have to be careful while doing things; don't accidently remove the `taglib` references and link references to JavaScript files.

In Step 11, we defined `UrlBasedViewResolver` for `TilesView` (org.`springframework.web.servlet.view.tiles3.TilesView`) in order to resolve logical view names into the tile's view. Finally, in step 12, we configured `TilesConfigurer` (org.`springframework.web.servlet.view.tiles3.TilesConfigurer`) to locate the tile's definition files by the Apache Tiles framework.

That's it! If you run the application and enter the URL `http://localhost:8080/webstore/products`, you will be able to see our regular products page with an extra navigation bar at the top and footer at the bottom as mentioned in step 13. You can navigate to add the products page by clicking on the **Add Product** link. Previously, every time a logical view name was returned by the controller method, the `InternalResourceViewResolver` came into action and found the corresponding `jsp` view for the given logical view name. Now, for every logical view name, `UrlBasedViewResolver` will come into action and compose the corresponding view based on the template's definition.

Pop quiz – Apache Tiles

Q1. Which of the following statements are true according to Apache Tiles?

1. A logical view name returned by the controller must be equal to the `<definition>` tag name

2. The `<tiles:insertAttribute>` tag acts as a placeholder in the template

3. A `<definition>` tag can extend another `<definition>` tag

Summary

Spring Web Flow and Apache Tiles are two separate frameworks. We only saw the minimum required concepts to get a quick overview of these frameworks in this chapter. In the beginning, we learned some of the basic concepts of the Spring Web Flow framework and then created the checkout flow for our webstore application. In the second part of this chapter, we saw how to use and leverage the Apache Tiles framework in order to bring maximum reusability in view files and maintain a consistent look and feel throughout all the web pages of our application.

In the next chapter, we will see how to test our web application using various APIs provided by Spring MVC.

10
Testing Your Application

For a web application developer, testing the web applications is always a challenging task, because getting a real-time test environment for web applications requires a lot of effort. Thanks to the Spring MVC Test framework, testing Spring MVC applications is simplified.

But why do we need to consider putting in efforts to test our application? Writing good test cases for our application is kind of like buying insurance for your application. Although it does not add any functional values to your application, it will definitely save your time and effort by detecting of functionality failures early. Consider that your application is growing bigger and bigger in terms of functionality; you need some mechanism to ensure that existing functionalities are not disturbed due to the introduction of new functionalities.

Testing frameworks provide you with this kind of mechanism to ensure that your application behavior is not altered due to refactoring or the addition of new code. It also ensures that the existing functionality works as expected.

In this chapter, we are going to see the following topics:

◆ Testing the domain object and validator

◆ Testing controllers

◆ Testing RESTful web services

Unit testing

In software development, unit testing is a software testing method in which the smallest testable parts of source code, called units, are individually and independently tested to determine whether they behave exactly as we expect. To unit test our source code, all we need is a test program that can run a bit of our source code (unit), provide some input to each unit, and check the results for the expected output. Most unit tests are written using some sort of test framework set of library code, designed to make writing and running tests easier. One such framework is called JUnit. It is a unit testing framework for the Java programming language.

Time for action – unit-testing domain objects

Let's see how to test one of our domain object using the JUnit framework to ensure it functions as expected. In an earlier chapter, we created a domain object to represent an item in a shopping cart, called `CartItem`. The `CartItem` class has a method called `getTotalPrice` to return the total price of that particular cart item based on the product and number of items it represents. Let's test whether the `getTotalPrice` method behaves properly. Follow these steps:

1. Open `pom.xml` and you will find `pom.xml` under the root directory of the project itself.

2. You will see some tabs at the bottom of the `pom.xml` file. Select the **Dependencies** tab and click on the **Add** button of the **Dependencies** section.

3. A **Select Dependency** window will appear; enter **Group Id** as `junit`, **Artifact Id** as `junit`, and **Version** as `4.11`; then select **test** as **Scope**, click on the **OK** button, and save `pom.xml`.

4. Now create a class called `CartItemTest` under the package `com.packt.webstore.domain` in the source folder, `src/test/java`. Add the following code into it and save the file:

    ```
    package com.packt.webstore.domain;
    import java.math.BigDecimal;
    import org.junit.Assert;
    import org.junit.Before;
    import org.junit.Test;

    public class CartItemTest {

        private CartItem cartItem;
    ```

```
@Before
public void setup() {
    cartItem = new CartItem();
}

@Test
public void cartItem_total_price_should_be_eaual_to_product_
unit_price_in_case_of_single_quantity() {
    //Arrange
    Product iphone = new Product("P1234","iPhone 5s", new
BigDecimal(500));
    cartItem.setProduct(iphone);

    //Act
    BigDecimal totalPrice = cartItem.getTotalPrice();

    //Assert
    Assert.assertEquals(iphone.getUnitPrice(), totalPrice);
}
}
```

5. Now right-click on `CartItemTest.java` and go to **Run As | JUnit Test**. You will see a failing test case in the JUnit window, as shown in the following screenshot:

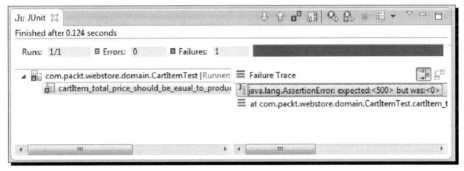

JUnit failing test case in CartItemTest

6. To make the test case pass, assign the value 1 to the `quantity` field of `CartItem` in the zero argument constructor of the `CartItem` class (as follows) and save the file:

```
public CartItem() {
    this.quantity = 1;
}
```

7. Now, right-click again on `CartItemTest.java` and go to **Run As | JUnit Test**. You will see that the test case has passed in the JUnit window, as shown in the following screenshot:

JUnit passed test case in CartItemTest

What just happened?

As I already mentioned, the `getTotalPrice` method of the `CartItem` class is designed to return the correct total price based on the product and the number of products it represents. But to ensure its proper behavior, we have written a test program called `CartItemTest` under the `com.packt.webstore.domain` package in the source folder, `src/test/java`, as mentioned in step 4.

In `CartItemTest`, we used some of the JUnit framework APIs, such as the `@Test` and `@Before` annotations. So, before we can use these annotations in our `CartItemTest` class, we need to add a JUnit jar as dependency in our project. That's what we did in steps 1 through 3.

Now, let's get to know the `CartItemTest` class thoroughly. The important method in the `CartItemTest` class is the one that is annotated with `@Test`, called `cartItem_total_price_should_be_eaual_to_product_unit_price_in_case_of_single_quantity`. The `@Test` annotation (`org.junit.Test`) marks a particular method as a test method. This is so that the JUnit framework can treat that method as a test method and execute it when we go to **Run As | JUnit Test**. Consider the following code snippet:

```
@Test
public void cartItem_total_price_should_be_eaual_to_product_unit_
price_in_case_of_single_quantity() {
    //Arrange
    Product iphone = new Product("P1234","iPhone 5s", new
BigDecimal(500));
    cartItem.setProduct(iphone);
```

```
//Act
BigDecimal totalPrice = cartItem.getTotalPrice();

//Assert
Assert.assertEquals(iphone.getUnitPrice(), totalPrice);
}
```

If you notice, the preceding method has been divided into three logical parts called Arrange, Act, and Assert:

- ◆ Arrange: This section arranges all the necessary preconditions and inputs to perform a test
- ◆ Act: This section acts on the object or method under test
- ◆ Assert: This section asserts that the expected results have occurred

In the Arrange part, we just instantiated a product domain object (iphone) with a unit price value of 500 and added that product object to the cartItem object by calling cartItem.setProduct(iphone);. We then added a single product to cartItem. We haven't altered the quantity aspect of the cartItem object. So, if we call the getTotalPrice method of cartItem. We must get 500 (in BigDecimal), because the unit price of the domain object (iphone) we have added in cartItem is 500.

In the Act part, we just called the method under test, which is the getTotalPrice method of the cartItem object, and stored the result in a BigDecimal variable called totalPrice. Later, in the Assert part, we used the JUnit API (Assert.assertEquals) to assert the equality between the unitPrice value of the product domain object and the calculated totalPrice of cartItem. Have a look at the following code:

```
Assert.assertEquals(iphone.getUnitPrice(), totalPrice);
```

The totalPrice parameter of cartItem must be equal to the unitPrice value of the product domain object we have added to cartItem. This is because we added the single-product domain object whose unitPrice and totalPrice value need to be the same.

When we run CartItemTest as mentioned in step 5, the JUnit framework tries to execute all the methods annotated with @Test in the CartItemTest class. So, based on the assertions' results, a test case may fail or pass. In our case, our test case failed. You can see that the failure trace shows an error message that says **expected <500> but was: <0>** in the screenshot immediately after step 5. This is because it didn't update the quantity field of the cartItem object when we added a product domain object to cartItem in the Arrange part. It is a bug. To fix this bug, we default the quantity field value to 1 whenever we instantiate cartItem, using the zero argument constructor as mentioned in the step 6. Now, if you run the test case again, it passes as expected.

Have a go hero – adding tests for cart

It is good that we have tested and verified the `getTotalPrice` method of the `CartItem` class. You can similarly write a test class for the `Cart` domain object class. In the `Cart` domain object class, there is a method to get the grand total (`getGrandTotal`) and write various test cases to check whether the `getGrandTotal` method works as expected.

Integration testing with the Spring Test Context framework

When individual program units are combined and tested as a group, it is known as integration testing. The Spring Test Context framework gives first class support for the integration testing of Spring-based applications. We have defined lots of Spring-managed beans in our web application context (`DispatcherServlet-context.xml`), such as services, repositories, and view resolvers, to run our application. These managed beans are instantiated during the startup of an application by the Spring framework. While performing integration testing, our test environment must also have those beans to test our application successfully. The Spring Test Context framework gives us the ability to define a test context, which is similar to the web application context (`DispatcherServlet-context.xml`). Let's see how to incorporate Spring Test Context to test our `ProductValidator` class.

Time for action – testing the product validator

Let's see how we can boot up our test context using the Spring Test Context framework to test our `ProductValidator` class:

1. Open `pom.xml` and you will find `pom.xml` under the root directory of the project itself.

2. You will be able to see some tabs at the bottom of the `pom.xml` file; select the **Dependencies** tab and click on the **Add** button of the **Dependencies** section.

3. A **Select Dependency** window will appear; enter **Group Id** as `org.springframework`, **Artifact Id** as `spring-test`, and **Version** as `4.0.3.RELEASE`; then select **Scope** as **test**, click on the **OK** button, and save `pom.xml`.

4. Now create an XML file called `test-DispatcherServlet-context.xml` under the `com.packt.webstore.validator` package in the source folder, `src/test/resources`. Add the following code into it and save it:

   ```
   <?xml version="1.0" encoding="UTF-8"?>
   <beans xmlns="http://www.springframework.org/schema/beans"
     xmlns:xsi="http://www.w3.org/2001/XMLSchema-instance"
   ```

```
  xmlns:context="http://www.springframework.org/schema/context"
  xmlns:mvc="http://www.springframework.org/schema/mvc"
  xmlns:webflow-config="http://www.springframework.org/schema/
webflow-config"

  xsi:schemaLocation="http://www.springframework.org/schema/beans
http://www.springframework.org/schema/beans/spring-beans.xsd
    http://www.springframework.org/schema/context http://www.
springframework.org/schema/context/spring-context-4.0.xsd
    http://www.springframework.org/schema/mvc http://www.
springframework.org/schema/mvc/spring-mvc-4.0.xsd
    http://www.springframework.org/schema/webflow-config http://
www.springframework.org/schema/webflow-config/spring-webflow-
config-2.3.xsd">



  <mvc:annotation-driven validator="validator"/>

  <context:component-scan base-package="com.packt.webstore" />

  <bean id= "messageSource" class="org.springframework.context.
support.ResourceBundleMessageSource">
    <property name="basename" value="messages"/>
  </bean>

  <bean id="validator" class="org.springframework.validation.
beanvalidation.LocalValidatorFactoryBean">
    <property name="validationMessageSource" ref="messageSource"
/>
  </bean>

  <bean id="productValidator" class="com.packt.webstore.validator.
ProductValidator">
    <property name = "springValidators">
      <set>
        <ref bean = "unitsInStockValidator"/>
      </set>
    </property>
  </bean>

  <bean id="unitsInStockValidator" class="com.packt.webstore.
validator.UnitsInStockValidator"/>

</beans>
```

5. Next, create a class called ProductValidatorTest under the com.packt.
webstore.validator package in the source folder, src/test/java. Add the
following code to it:

```
package com.packt.webstore.domain;

package com.packt.webstore.validator;

import java.math.BigDecimal;
import org.junit.Assert;
import org.junit.Test;
import org.junit.runner.RunWith;
import org.springframework.beans.factory.annotation.Autowired;
import org.springframework.test.context.ContextConfiguration;
import org.springframework.test.context.junit4.
SpringJUnit4ClassRunner;
import org.springframework.test.context.web.WebAppConfiguration;
import org.springframework.validation.BindException;
import org.springframework.validation.ValidationUtils;
import com.packt.webstore.domain.Product;
import com.packt.webstore.validator.ProductValidator;

@RunWith(SpringJUnit4ClassRunner.class)
@ContextConfiguration("test-DispatcherServlet-context.xml")
@WebAppConfiguration
public class ProductValidatorTest {

  @Autowired
  private ProductValidator productValidator;

  @Test
  public void product_without_UnitPrice_should_be_invalid() {
    //Arrange
    Product product = new Product();
    BindException bindException = new BindException(product,
"product");

    //Act
    ValidationUtils.invokeValidator(productValidator, product,
bindException);

    //Assert
    Assert.assertEquals(1, bindException.getErrorCount());
    Assert.assertTrue(bindException.getLocalizedMessage().
contains("Unit price is Invalid. It cannot be empty."));
```

```
  }

  @Test
  public void product_with_existing_productId_invalid() {
    //Arrange
    Product product = new Product("P1234","iPhone 5s", new
BigDecimal(500));
    product.setCategory("Tablet");

    BindException bindException = new BindException(product,
"product");

    //Act
    ValidationUtils.invokeValidator(productValidator, product,
bindException);

    //Assert
    Assert.assertEquals(1, bindException.getErrorCount());
    Assert.assertTrue(bindException.getLocalizedMessage().
contains("A product already exists with this product id."));
  }

  @Test
  public void a_valid_product_should_not_get_any_error_during_
validation() {
    //Arrange
    Product product = new Product("P9876","iPhone 5s", new
BigDecimal(500));
    product.setCategory("Tablet");

    BindException bindException = new BindException(product,
"product");

    //Act
    ValidationUtils.invokeValidator(productValidator, product,
bindException);

    //Assert
    Assert.assertEquals(0, bindException.getErrorCount());
  }

}
```

6. Now right-click on `ProductValidatorTest` and go to **Run As | JUnit Test**. You will be able to see the test cases that pass, as shown in the following screenshot:

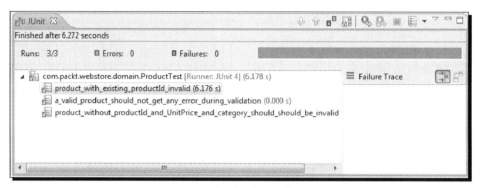

Customer details collection form

What just happened?

As I have already mentioned, Spring provides extensive support for integration testing. In order to develop a test case using the Spring Test Context framework, we need the `spring-test` jar. In step 3, we just added dependency to the `spring-test` jar. The Spring Test Context framework cannot run without the support of the `JUnit` jar. In step 4, we just created a test web application context configuration file called `test-DispatcherServlet-context.xml` that only defines the beans that are required for our test to execute. Later, in step 5, when we created our actual test case, the Spring Test Context framework used this file as base to create the test context.

Step 5 is very important because it represents the actual test class (`ProductValidatorTest`) to test the validity of our `Product` domain object. The goal of the test class is to check whether all the validations (including bean validation and Spring validation) that are specified in the `Product` domain class are working. I hope you remember that we specified some of the bean validation annotation, such as `@NotNull` and `@Pattern`, on the `Product` domain class in *Chapter 7, Validate Your Products with a Validator*.

One way to test whether those validations are taking place is by manually running our application and trying to enter invalid values. This approach is called manual testing. This is a very difficult job, whereas in automated testing, we can write some test classes to run test cases in a repeated fashion to test the functionality. Using JUnit, we can write such kinds of test classes.

The `ProductValidatorTest` class contains three test methods in total; we can identify a test method by the `@Test` annotation (`org.junit.Test`) of JUnit. Every test method can be logically separated into three parts, that is, Arrange, Act, and Assert. In the `Arrange` part, we instantiate and instrument the required objects for testing; in the `Act` part, we invoke the actual functionality that needs to be tested; and finally in the `Assert` part, we compare the expected result and the actual result that is the output of the invoked functionality. Have a look at the following code:

```
@Test
public void product_without_UnitPrice_should_be_invalid() {
  //Arrange
  Product product = new Product();
  BindException bindException = new BindException(product, "product");

  //Act
  ValidationUtils.invokeValidator(productValidator, product,
bindException);

  //Assert
  Assert.assertEquals(1, bindException.getErrorCount());
  Assert.assertTrue(bindException.getLocalizedMessage().contains("Unit
price is Invalid. It cannot be empty."));
}
```

In the `Arrange` part of this test method, we just instantiated a bare minimum `Product` domain object. We have not set any values for the `productId`, `unitPrice`, and `category` fields. We purposely set up such a bare minimum domain object in the `Arrange` part to check whether our `ProductValidator` class works properly in the `Act` part. According to the `ProductValidator` class logic, the present state of the `product` domain object is invalid. In the `Act` part, we invoke the `productValidator` object using the `ValidationUtils` class to check whether the validation works or not. During validation, `productValidator` will store the errors in a `BindException` object. In the `Assert` part, we simply checked whether the `bindException` object contained one error, using the JUnit `Assert` APIs, and checked whether the error message was as expected.

Another important thing we need to understand in our `ProductValidatorTest` class is that we used Spring's standard `@Autowired` annotation to get the instance of `ProductValidator`; the question here is who instantiated the `productValidator` object? The answer is in the `@ContextConfiguration` annotation. Note the `locations` attribute specified in the `@ContextConfiguration` annotation – it has the same name as our test context file (`test-DispatcherServlet-context.xml`).

As you might remember, we have learned that during the booting up of our application, Spring MVC will create a web application context (Spring container) with the necessary beans, as defined in the web application context configuration file. We need a similar kind of context even before running our test classes so that we can use those defined beans (objects) in our test class to test it properly. The Spring Test framework makes it possible via the `@ContextConfiguration` annotation.

Now we need a similar kind of running application environment with all the resource files. To achieve this, we used the `@WebAppConfiguration` annotation from the Spring Test framework. The `@WebAppConfiguration` annotation instructs the Spring Test framework to load the application context as `WebApplicationContext`.

Now we have seen almost all the important things related to executing a Spring integration test, but one final configuration we need to understand is how to integrate JUnit and the Spring Test Context framework in our test class. The `@RunWith(SpringJUnit4ClassRunner.class)` annotation does that job.

So, finally, when we run our test cases, we will see a green bar in the JUnit window, indicating that the tests were successful.

Time for action – testing the product controller

Let's see now how to test our controllers:

1. Create an XML file called `test-DispatcherServlet-context.xml` under the `com.packt.webstore.controller` package in the source folder, `src/test/resources`. Add the following code into it and save it:

```xml
<?xml version="1.0" encoding="UTF-8"?>
<beans xmlns="http://www.springframework.org/schema/beans"
  xmlns:xsi="http://www.w3.org/2001/XMLSchema-instance"
  xmlns:context="http://www.springframework.org/schema/context"
  xmlns:mvc="http://www.springframework.org/schema/mvc"
  xmlns:webflow-config="http://www.springframework.org/schema/
webflow-config"

  xsi:schemaLocation="http://www.springframework.org/schema/beans
http://www.springframework.org/schema/beans/spring-beans.xsd
    http://www.springframework.org/schema/context http://www.
springframework.org/schema/context/spring-context-4.0.xsd
    http://www.springframework.org/schema/mvc http://www.
springframework.org/schema/mvc/spring-mvc-4.0.xsd
    http://www.springframework.org/schema/webflow-config http://
www.springframework.org/schema/webflow-config/spring-webflow-
config-2.3.xsd">
```

```xml
    <mvc:annotation-driven validator="validator"/>

    <context:component-scan base-package="com.packt.webstore" />

    <bean class="org.springframework.web.servlet.view.
InternalResourceViewResolver">
        <property name="prefix" value="/WEB-INF/views/" />
        <property name="suffix" value=".jsp" />
    </bean>


    <bean id= "messageSource" class="org.springframework.context.
support.ResourceBundleMessageSource">
            <property name="basename" value="messages"/>
    </bean>

    <bean id="validator" class="org.springframework.validation.
beanvalidation.LocalValidatorFactoryBean">
        <property name="validationMessageSource" ref="messageSource"
/>
    </bean>

    <bean id="productValidator" class="com.packt.webstore.validator.
ProductValidator">
        <property name = "springValidators">
          <set>
            <ref bean = "unitsInStockValidator"/>
          </set>
        </property>
    </bean>

    <bean id="unitsInStockValidator" class="com.packt.webstore.
validator.UnitsInStockValidator"/>

</beans>
```

2. Create a class called `ProductControllerTest` under the `com.packt.
webstore.controller` package in the source folder, `src/test/java`,
and add the following code into it:

```java
package com.packt.webstore.controller;

import static org.springframework.test.web.servlet.request.
MockMvcRequestBuilders.get;
```

```
import static org.springframework.test.web.servlet.result.
MockMvcResultMatchers.model;
import java.math.BigDecimal;
import org.junit.Before;
import org.junit.Test;
import org.junit.runner.RunWith;
import org.springframework.beans.factory.annotation.Autowired;
import org.springframework.test.context.ContextConfiguration;
import org.springframework.test.context.junit4.
SpringJUnit4ClassRunner;
import org.springframework.test.context.web.WebAppConfiguration;
import org.springframework.test.web.servlet.MockMvc;
import org.springframework.test.web.servlet.setup.MockMvcBuilders;
import org.springframework.web.context.WebApplicationContext;
import com.packt.webstore.domain.Product;

@RunWith(SpringJUnit4ClassRunner.class)
@ContextConfiguration("test-DispatcherServlet-context.xml")
@WebAppConfiguration
public class ProductControllerTest {

  @Autowired
  private WebApplicationContext wac;

  private MockMvc mockMvc;

  @Before
  public void setup() {
    this.mockMvc = MockMvcBuilders.webAppContextSetup(this.wac).
build();
  }

  @Test
  public void testGetProducts() throws Exception {
    this.mockMvc.perform(get("/products"))
    .andExpect(model().attributeExists("products"));
  }

  @Test
  public void testGetProductById() throws Exception {
    //Arrange
    Product product = new Product("P1234","iPhone 5s", new
BigDecimal(500));
```

```
//Act & Assert
this.mockMvc.perform(get("/products/product")
.param("id", "P1234"))
.andExpect(model().attributeExists("product"))
.andExpect(model().attribute("product", product));
    }

}
```

3. Now right-click on the `ProductControllerTest` class and go to **Run As | JUnit Test**. You will be able to see that the test cases are being executed. You will be able to see the test results in the JUnit window.

What just happened?

Just like with the `ProductValidatorTest` class, we need to boot up the test context and run our `ProductControllerTest` class as the Spring integration test. So we used similar annotations on top of `ProductControllerTest`, as follows:

```
@RunWith(SpringJUnit4ClassRunner.class)
@ContextConfiguration("test-DispatcherServlet-context.xml")
@WebAppConfiguration
public class ProductControllerTest {
```

Apart from the two test methods that are available under `ProductControllerTest`, a single setup method is available as follows:

```
@Before
public void setup() {
   this.mockMvc = MockMvcBuilders.webAppContextSetup(this.wac).build();
}
```

The `@Before` annotation that is present on top of the preceding method indicates that this method should be executed before every test method. And within that method, we simply build our `MockMvc` object in order to use it in the following test methods. The `MockMvc` class is a special class provided by the Spring Test Context framework to simulate browser actions within a test case, such as firing HTTP requests. Have a look at the following code:

```
@Test
public void testGetProducts() throws Exception {
   this.mockMvc.perform(get("/products"))
   .andExpect(model().attributeExists("products"));
}
```

The preceding test method simply fires a GET HTTP request to our application using the mockMvc object, and as a result, we ensure that the returned model contains an attribute named products. Remember that the list method in the ProductController class is the one that handles the preceding web request, so it will fill the model with the available products under the attribute named products.

After running your test case, you will be able to see the green bar in the JUnit window that indicates the tests have passed.

Time for action – testing REST controllers

Similarly, we can test the REST-based controllers as well. Just perform the following steps:

1. Open pom.xml and you will find pom.xml under the root directory of the project itself.

2. You will be able to see some tabs at the bottom of the pom.xml file; select the **Dependencies** tab and click on the **Add** button of the **Dependencies** section.

3. A **Select Dependency** window will appear; enter **Group Id** as com.jayway.jsonpath, **Artifact Id** as json-path-assert, and **Version** as 0.8.1. Select **Scope** as test, click on the **OK** button, and save pom.xml.

4. Now create a class called CartRestControllerTest under the com.packt.webstore.controller package in the source folder, src/test/java. Now add the following code to it:

```
package com.packt.webstore.controller;

import static org.springframework.test.web.servlet.request.
MockMvcRequestBuilders.get;
import static org.springframework.test.web.servlet.request.
MockMvcRequestBuilders.put;
import static org.springframework.test.web.servlet.result.
MockMvcResultMatchers.jsonPath;
import static org.springframework.test.web.servlet.result.
MockMvcResultMatchers.status;
import org.junit.Before;
import org.junit.Test;
import org.junit.runner.RunWith;
import org.springframework.beans.factory.annotation.Autowired;
import org.springframework.mock.web.MockHttpSession;
import org.springframework.test.context.ContextConfiguration;
import org.springframework.test.context.junit4.
SpringJUnit4ClassRunner;
import org.springframework.test.context.web.WebAppConfiguration;
import org.springframework.test.web.servlet.MockMvc;
```

```
import org.springframework.test.web.servlet.setup.MockMvcBuilders;
import org.springframework.web.context.WebApplicationContext;

@RunWith(SpringJUnit4ClassRunner.class)
@ContextConfiguration("test-DispatcherServlet-context.xml")
@WebAppConfiguration
public class CartRestControllerTest {

  @Autowired
  private WebApplicationContext wac;

  @Autowired
  MockHttpSession session;

  private MockMvc mockMvc;

  @Before
  public void setup() {
    this.mockMvc = MockMvcBuilders.webAppContextSetup(this.wac).
build();
  }

  @Test
  public void read_method_should_return_correct_cart_Json_object()
throws Exception {
    //Arrange
    this.mockMvc.perform(put("/rest/cart/add/P1234").
session(session))
    .andExpect(status().is(204));

    //Act
    this.mockMvc.perform(get("/rest/cart/"+ session.getId()).
session(session))
    .andExpect(status().isOk())
    .andExpect(jsonPath("$.cartItems.P1234.product.productId").
value("P1234"));
  }

}
```

5. Now right-click on `CartRestControllerTest` and go to **Run As | JUnit Test**. You
will be able to see that test cases are being executed, and the test results will be
seen in the JUnit window.

What just happened?

While testing REST controllers, we need to ensure that the web response for the given web request contains the expected JSON object. To verify that, we need some specialized APIs to check the format of the JSON object. The json-path-assert jar provides these APIs. We added the Maven dependency to the json-path-assert jar from step 1 through 3.

In step 4, we created CartRestControllerTest to verify whether our CartRestController class works properly. The CartRestControllerTest class is very similar to ProductControllerTest; the only difference is the way we assert the result of a web request. In CartRestControllerTest, we have one test method to test the read method of the CartRestController class.

The read method of CartRestController is designed to return a cart object as a JSON object for the given cart ID. In CartRestControllerTest, we have tested this behavior through the read_method_should_return_correct_cart_Json_object test method. Have a look at the following code:

```
@Test
public void read_method_should_return_correct_cart_Json_object()
throws Exception {
  //Arrange
  this.mockMvc.perform(put("/rest/cart/add/P1234").session(session))
  .andExpect(status().is(204));

  //Act
  this.mockMvc.perform(get("/rest/cart/"+ session.getId()).
session(session))
  .andExpect(status().isOk())
  .andExpect(jsonPath("$.cartItems.P1234.product.productId").
value("P1234"));
}
```

In order to get a cart object for the given cart ID, we first need to store the cart object in our cart repository through a web request. That is what we did in the Arrange part of the preceding test method. The first web request we fired in the arrange part will add a product domain object in the cart whose ID is the same as the session ID.

In the `Act` part of the test case, we simply fired another REST-based web request to get the `cart` object as a JSON object. Remember that we used the session ID as our cart ID to store our cart object, so while retrieving, we need to give the same session ID in the request URL. For this, we can use the mock session object given by the Spring Test framework. You can see in the following code that we have autowired the session object in our `CartRestControllerTest` class:

```
this.mockMvc.perform(get("/rest/cart/"+ session.getId()).
session(session))
.andExpect(status().isOk())
.andExpect( jsonPath("$.cartItems.P1234.product.productId").
value("P1234"));
```

Once we get the `cart` domain object as a JSON object, we have to verify that it contains the correct product. We will be able to do that with the help of the `jsonPath` method of `MockMvcResultMatchers`, as specified in the preceding code snippets. After sending the REST web request go get the `cart` object, we verified that the response status is as expected and also checked whether the JSON object contains a product with the ID `P1234`.

Finally, when we run this test case, you will be able to see that the test cases are being executed and you will see the test results in the JUnit window.

Have a go hero – adding tests for the remaining REST methods

It is good that we have tested and verified the `read` method of `CartRestController`, but we have not tested the other methods of `CartRestController`. You can add tests for other methods of `CartRestController` in the `CartRestControllerTest` class to get familiar with the Spring Test framework.

Summary

In this final chapter, you learned the importance of testing a web application and saw how to unit test the domain object. Next we learned how to perform integration test on validator using the Spring Test framework. You also saw how to test a normal controller using the Spring Test Context framework. As the last exercise, you saw how to test REST-based controllers and how to use the mock session object from the Spring Test framework. In that exercise, you also learned how to verify the JSON path.

A
Using the Gradle Build Tool

Throughout this book, we have used Apache Maven as our build tool, but there are other popular build tools also used widely in the Java community. One such build tool is Gradle. Instead of XML, Gradle uses a Groovy-based Domain Specific Language (DSL) as the base for the build script, which provides more flexibility when defining complex build scripts. Compared to Maven, Gradle takes less time for incremental builds. So, Gradle builds are very fast and effective for large projects.

In this appendix, we will see how to install and use Gradle as the build tool in our project.

Installing Gradle

Perform the following steps to install Gradle:

1. Go to the Gradle download page by entering the URL `http://www.gradle.org/downloads` in your browser.

2. Click on the latest Gradle stable release download link; at the time of writing this, the stable release is `gradle-1.11-all.zip`.

3. Once the download is finished, go to the downloaded directory and extract the ZIP file into a convenient directory of your choice.

4. Create an environment variable called `GRADLE_HOME`. Enter the extracted Gradle ZIP directory path as the value for the `GRADLE_HOME` environment variable.

5. Finally, append the `GRADLE_HOME` variable to `PATH` by simply appending the text `;%GRADLE_HOME%\bin` to the `PATH` variable.

Now that you have installed Gradle on your Windows-based computer, to verify whether the installation was completed correctly, go to the command prompt, type `gradle -v`, and press *Enter*. The output shows the Gradle version and also the local environment configuration.

The Gradle build script for your project

To configure the Gradle build script for your project, perform the following steps:

1. Go to the root directory of your project from the filesystem, create a file called `build.gradle`, and add the following content into the file and save it:

```
apply plugin: 'war'
apply plugin: 'eclipse-wtp'

repositories {
  mavenCentral() //add central maven repo to your buildfile
}

dependencies {
    compile 'org.springframework:spring-webmvc:4.0.3.RELEASE',
    'javax.servlet:jstl:1.2',
    'org.springframework.security:spring-security-
web:3.1.4.RELEASE',
    'commons-fileupload:commons-fileupload:1.2.2',
    'org.apache.commons:commons-io:1.3.2',
    'org.springframework:spring-oxm:4.0.3.RELEASE',
    'org.codehaus.jackson:jackson-mapper-asl:1.9.10',
    'log4j:log4j:1.2.12',
    'org.hibernate:hibernate-validator:4.3.1.Final',
    'org.springframework.webflow:spring-webflow:2.3.3.RELEASE',
    'org.apache.tiles:tiles-extras:3.0.3',
    'org.slf4j:slf4j-api:1.7.5'

    compile('org.springframework.security:spring-security-
config:3.1.4.RELEASE') {
        //excluding a particular transitive dependency:
        exclude group: 'org.springframework', module: 'spring-asm'
    }

    providedCompile 'javax.servlet:javax.servlet-api:3.1.0'

    testCompile 'junit:junit:4.11',
    'org.springframework:spring-test:4.0.3.RELEASE',
    'com.jayway.jsonpath:json-path-assert:0.8.1'
}
```

2. Now go to the root directory of your project from the command prompt and issue the following command:

```
> gradle eclipse
```

3. Next, open a new workspace in your STS, go to **File | Import**, select the **Existing Projects into Workspace** option from the tree list (you can find this option under the **General** node), and then click on the **Next** button.

4. Click on the **Browse** button to select the root directory and locate your project directory. Click on **OK** and then on **Finish**.

Now, you will be able to see your project configured with the right dependencies in your STS.

Understanding the Gradle script

A task in Gradle is similar to a goal in Maven. The Gradle script supports many in-built plugins to execute build-related tasks. One such plugin is the `war` plugin, which provides many convenient tasks to help you build a web project. We can incorporate these tasks in our build script easily by applying a plugin in our Gradle script as follows:

```
apply plugin: 'war'
```

Similar to the `war` plugin, there is another plugin called `eclipse-wtp` to incorporate tasks related to converting a project into an eclipse project. The `eclipse` command we used in step 2 is actually provided by the `eclipse-wtp` plugin.

Inside the `repositories` section, we can define our remote binary repository location. When we build our Gradle project, we use this remote binary repository to download the required JARs. In our case, we defined our remote repository as the Maven central repository, as follows:

```
repositories {
  mavenCentral()
}
```

All of the project dependencies need to be defined inside of the `dependencies` section grouped under the scope declaration, such as `compile`, `providedCompile`, and `testCompile`. Consider the following code snippet:

```
dependencies {
  compile
  'org.springframework:spring-webmvc:4.0.3.RELEASE',
  'javax.servlet:jstl:1.2'.
}
```

If you look closely at the following dependency declaration line, the `compile` scope declaration, you see that each dependency declaration line is delimited with a : (colon) symbol, as follows:

```
'org.springframework:spring-webmvc:4.0.3.RELEASE'
```

The first part of the previous line is the group ID, the second part is the artifact ID, and the final part is the version information as provided in Maven.

So, it is more like a Maven build script but defined using a Gradle script, which is based on the Groovy language.

B
Pop Quiz Answers

Chapter 2, Spring MVC Architecture – Architecting Your Web Store

Pop quiz – request mapping

Q1	2

Pop quiz – the web application context

Q1	1
Q2	3

Pop quiz – web application context configuration

Q1	4

Chapter 3, Control Your Store with Controllers

Pop quiz – class-level request mapping

Q1	1
Q2	2

Pop quiz – request path variable

Q1	4
Q2	1 and 4

Pop quiz – the request parameter

Q1	2

Chapter 5, Working with View Resolver

Pop quiz – redirect view

Q1	3

Pop quiz – static view

Q1	2

Chapter 6, Intercept Your Store with Interceptor

Pop quiz – interceptor

Q1	2
Q2	2

Chapter 9, Apache Tiles and Spring Web Flow in Action

Pop quiz – web flow

Q1	3
Q2	1

Pop quiz – Apache Tiles

Q1	All three (1, 2, and 3)

Index

Thank you for buying
Spring MVC Beginner's Guide

About Packt Publishing

Packt, pronounced 'packed', published its first book "*Mastering phpMyAdmin for Effective MySQL Management*" in April 2004 and subsequently continued to specialize in publishing highly focused books on specific technologies and solutions.

Our books and publications share the experiences of your fellow IT professionals in adapting and customizing today's systems, applications, and frameworks. Our solution based books give you the knowledge and power to customize the software and technologies you're using to get the job done. Packt books are more specific and less general than the IT books you have seen in the past. Our unique business model allows us to bring you more focused information, giving you more of what you need to know, and less of what you don't.

Packt is a modern, yet unique publishing company, which focuses on producing quality, cutting-edge books for communities of developers, administrators, and newbies alike. For more information, please visit our website: www.packtpub.com.

About Packt Open Source

In 2010, Packt launched two new brands, Packt Open Source and Packt Enterprise, in order to continue its focus on specialization. This book is part of the Packt Open Source brand, home to books published on software built around Open Source licenses, and offering information to anybody from advanced developers to budding web designers. The Open Source brand also runs Packt's Open Source Royalty Scheme, by which Packt gives a royalty to each Open Source project about whose software a book is sold.

Writing for Packt

We welcome all inquiries from people who are interested in authoring. Book proposals should be sent to author@packtpub.com. If your book idea is still at an early stage and you would like to discuss it first before writing a formal book proposal, contact us; one of our commissioning editors will get in touch with you.

We're not just looking for published authors; if you have strong technical skills but no writing experience, our experienced editors can help you develop a writing career, or simply get some additional reward for your expertise.

open source
community experience distilled

Spring Security 3.x Cookbook
Over 60 recipes to help you successfully safeguard your
web applications with Spring Security

Anjana Mankale

Spring Security 3.x Cookbook

ISBN: 978-1-78216-752-5   Paperback: 300 pages

Over 60 recipes to help you successfully safeguard
your web applications with Spring Security

1. Learn about all the mandatory security measures
   for modern day applications using Spring Security.

2. Investigate different approaches to application level
   authentication and authorization.

3. Master how to mount security on applications used
   by developers and organizations.

Spring Web Services 2
Cookbook
Over 60 recipes providing comprehensive coverage of practical
real-life implementations of Spring-WS

Hamidreza Sattari
Shameer Kunjumohamed

Spring Web Services 2 Cookbook

ISBN: 978-1-84951-582-5   Paperback: 322 pages

Over 60 recipes providing comprehensive coverage
of practical real-life implementations of Spring-WS

1. Create contract-first web services.

2. Explore different frameworks of Object/XML
   mapping.

3. Secure web services by authentication, encryption/
   decryption, and using digital signature.

4. Learn contract-last web services using Spring
   Remoting and Apache CXF.

Please check **www.PacktPub.com** for information on our titles

Instant Spring Tool Suite

ISBN: 978-1-78216-414-2   Paperback: 76 pages

A practical guide for kick-starting your Spring projects using the Spring Tool Suite IDE

1. Learn something new in an Instant! A short, fast, focused guide delivering immediate results.

2. Learn how to use Spring Tool Suite to jump-start your Spring projects.

3. Develop, test, and deploy your applications, all within the IDE.

4. Simple, step-by-step instructions in an easy-to-follow format.

Spring Security 3.1

ISBN: 978-1-84951-826-0   Paperback: 456 pages

Secure your web applications from hackers with this step-by-step guide

1. Learn to leverage the power of Spring Security to keep intruders at bay through simple examples that illustrate real-world problems.

2. Each sample demonstrates key concepts allowing you to build your knowledge of the architecture in a practical and incremental way.

3. Filled with samples that clearly illustrate how to integrate with the technologies and frameworks of your choice.

Please check **www.PacktPub.com** for information on our titles

Made in the USA
Middletown, DE
19 January 2017